TANTRIC PSYCHOPHYSICS

"*Tantric Psychophysics* establishes a solid basis for comprehending consciousness and reality at the transcendental intersection between spirituality, philosophy, and science. Joye's skillful integration of key traditional teachings with mystical revelations and a modern transdisciplinary integrative approach beautifully illuminates points of common shared awareness and deepest truth. This book provides a trusty guide for those seeking to safely navigate the farthest expanses of self through meditation and contemplation."

CYNTHIA SUE LARSON, AUTHOR OF *QUANTUM JUMPS*

"*Tantric Psychophysics* is an atlas of the soul and the network of subtle pathways that connect it to, but can also release it from, the physical body and surrounding cosmos. Recalling her intellectual and actual circumnavigation of the globe in search of the wisdom of spiritual explorers and psychonauts, Joye threads their various insights into a practical handbook meant to guide the reader through mental and physical processes that induce liberating states of extrasensory consciousness."

TIMOTHY DESMOND, PH.D., AUTHOR OF
PSYCHE AND SINGULARITY

"Joye has written a remarkable book that presents a wide range of traditionally esoteric knowledge in the context of contemporary physics, physiology, and philosophy. Her integral, interdisciplinary approach to consciousness offers practical suggestions that can inform and inspire readers to experience new dimensions of awareness."

IRA RECHTSHAFFER, PH.D.,
PSYCHOTHERAPIST AND AUTHOR OF
WHAT WAS IN BUDDHA'S LEFT HAND?

"Drawing upon a deep wisdom gained from decades of practice and direct spiritual experience, Joye describes a wide range of contemplative practices from major traditions, clarifying and supporting these various techniques with insights from modern science and quantum physics. The resulting book offers a highly unique approach, free of culturally specific or scientific jargon, to explain clearly some of the most effective psychophysical tools that are available to the modern educated reader interested in the firsthand exploration of consciousness. *Tantric Psychophysics* is a one-of-a-kind approach to traditional mystical praxis. It is both pioneering and revelatory, an intellectual tour de force of exposition, and yet at the same time it offers a practical and easy-to-follow guide for integrating science and spirituality in the process of personal transformation."

James D. Ryan, Ph.D., professor emeritus of Asian philosophies and cultures at the California Institute of Integral Studies

"Entering altered states of consciousness is no longer the privilege of a select few. It is now at the doorstep of people in all walks of life with all kinds of worldviews and values. Joye's book provides a much-needed handbook for finding the path toward entering altered states and an important resource for meeting the challenge of living and thriving in today's world."

Ervin Laszlo, author of *The Immortal Mind*

"In an extraordinarily personal and deeply researched review of the embodied methods of achieving spiritual awareness, Joye provides us with a multicultural tour of the great souls in meditation and consciousness. People who have shared their methods and results are set side by side to provide a robust overview of the methods of inner awareness leading to enlightenment. Written in a style to be accessible to every reader, Joye provides deep insight into the inner workings of consciousness through different methods of meditation. A delightful and deeply insightful read."

John Alan Taylor, Ph.D., dean of library and learning support at Orange Coast College

"Shelli Joye is a consciousness cartographer whose works appeal to those with a courageous soul and an adventurous spirit. The well-researched and illustrated material collected in *Tantric Psychophysics* will be a great aid for anyone interested in the nature of consciousness. Highly recommend this fascinating work!"

Michael Pryzdia, Ph.D., senior lecturer at Arizona State University

"Shelli Joye is a master architect, bridging the gaps between our physics of today, consciousness, and spirituality, while revealing hidden secrets under her microscope of words and stories. Bravo!"

Lauren Palmateer, Ph.D., electrical engineer

TANTRIC PSYCHOPHYSICS

A Structural Map of Altered States and the Dynamics of Consciousness

SHELLI RENÉE JOYE, PH.D.

Inner Traditions
Rochester, Vermont

Inner Traditions
One Park Street
Rochester, Vermont 05767
www.InnerTraditions.com

SUSTAINABLE FORESTRY INITIATIVE Certified Sourcing
www.sfiprogram.org
SFI-00854

Text stock is SFI certified

Originally published in 2020 by the Viola Institute under the title *Tantric Psychophysics: The Exploration of Supersensible Dimensions*

Cataloging-in-Publication Data for this title is available from the Library of Congress

ISBN 978-1-64411-368-4 (print)
ISBN 978-1-64411-369-1 (ebook)

Printed and bound in the United States by Lake Book Manufacturing, Inc.
The text stock is SFI certified. The Sustainable Forestry Initiative® program promotes sustainable forest management.

10 9 8 7 6 5 4 3 2 1

Text design and layout by Virginia Scott Bowman
This book was typeset in Garamond Premier Pro and Gills Sans with Avenir Next Condensed and Amber Taste used as display typefaces

Because hyperlinks do not always remain viable, we are no longer including URLs in our resources, notes, or bibliographic entries. Instead, we are providing the name of the website where this information may be found.

To send correspondence to the author of this book, mail a first-class letter to the author c/o Inner Traditions • Bear & Company, One Park Street, Rochester, VT 05767, and we will forward the communication, or contact the author directly at **https://shellijoye.net**.

Dedicated to five teachers whom I met early in my life:
Dr. John Lilly, Alan Watts, Chögyam Trungpa Rinpoche,
Dr. Rammurti Mishra, and Fr. Bede Griffiths;
and to all my many other mentors and friends including
Dean Radin, Brian Swimme, Allan Combs,
Dmitri Andreyev, James Ryan, and Robert McDermott;
and to my amazing family,
Susanne, Alyssa, Jason, Teresa, Stella, and Nuggles.

Contents

PART ONE

INTRODUCTION TO TANTRIC PSYCHOPHYSICS

PART TWO

WESTERN TANTRIC PSYCHOPHYSICS

PART THREE

Hindu Tantric Psychophysics

PART FOUR

Tibetan Tantric Psychophysics

PART FIVE

Practical Advice for Modern Psychonauts

An Invitation to the Modern Psychonaut

As a product of over fifty years of my own introspective explorations and experiences, this book presents a wide variety of traditional and contemporary material to assist explorers of consciousness at any level to expand their ability to activate new psychophysical systems of awareness. It has been my experience that such an expansion of awareness can lead to the activation of traditionally "occult" or "hidden" powers of perception that have been formally described in traditional Tantric texts and taught by shamans and mystics in a great variety of cultures and ages.

Tantric Psychophysics should appeal to anyone seeking a cohesive map of human consciousness and practical guidance as to how to proceed at any stage in the development of new modes of perception for the exploration of new regions of awareness. The material offers a variety of integrated approaches useful not only to the contemplative practitioner but also to those seeking a deeper understanding of consciousness itself: what it is, and why it is, and what might be done with it. Congruent maps of consciousness developed in Tibet and India as well as those of the West are laid out in detail to provide a practical framework of understanding for scientists, philosophers, and the general reader, but should be of particular interest to those who are actively exploring these new regions of consciousness. In addition to reviewing Tibetan and Indian psychophysics, a part called "Western Tantric Psychophysics" presents the work of three prominent twentieth-century psychonauts: Rudolf Steiner, G. I. Gurdjieff, and Teilhard de Chardin, who called his work *hyperphysics*.*

Herein are a broad range of theories and techniques that will leave the reader with new approaches to explore the spirit world, the various Heavens, the implicate order, the Mind of God, Brahma, Ein Sof, and other rarified regions of awareness.† Such regions have been previously encountered, explored, and mapped in varying degrees by every global culture down through the millennia and have been the focus of exploration by generations of reclusive saints, mystics, shamans, and psychonauts. While much of this experiential knowledge was handed down in great secret from master to disciple, many of these pioneers did leave various written records of their experiments in consciousness, records of which are now accessible via modern technology.

For over half a century I have consistently studied, practiced, experienced, and pondered the results of the many techniques described in this book. I have included additional material that I have found useful during my own lifetime of exploring consciousness, a journey that began for me in the summer of 1967 with my first psychonautic experience catalyzed by LSD-25 on a California beach during a star-filled moonless night. The past half century has brought an explosion of revelations to the forefront in printed material, lectures, and a plethora of new schools exploring esoteric methods for the enhancement of consciousness. Practical information that was formerly concealed within the arcana of mystical traditions and studied by only a very small number of explorers has now become widely available for those who seek to awaken these possibilities.

Since first meeting Chögyam Trungpa Rinpoche as a young engineer I have continued formal contemplative practices daily and have gradually been able to integrate my experiences with what I know of

---

**Hyperphysics* is a term used by the scientist/priest Pierre Teilhard de Chardin for the physics of consciousness which he developed in numerous essays over his lifetime, a subject that is explored in chapter 5 and is found to be congruent with the principles of Tantric psychophysics.

†These are a few among innumerable words that different cultures and languages have used to point to the whole of Being that is the ontological reality of the universe.

physics, engineering, and philosophy. Included in this book is a wide range of essential information, much of it distilled from traditional Tantric texts and my own earlier publications. It is my hope that this material will be of practical use to those with a passion for exploring consciousness through direct effort and firsthand experience.

May you and yours stay well, and may this book help you to grow and thrive in the new worlds open to us all through psychonautic exploration!

Shelli Renée Joye, Ph.D.
Lassen Forest, California

PREFACE

How I Became a Psychonaut and Discovered Tantra

Throughout history there have been many individuals who have discovered that their human brain-mind systems can be reprogrammed in various ways to act as powerful tools for the direct entrance into vast new dimensions of conscious experience. Depending upon the culture and language, such rarified dimensions have been referred to with such terminology as "Higher Worlds," "the Akasha," "Heaven," "Eternity," or "the Void." The practices associated with meditation can lead directly to experiences of "non-dual awareness," (e.g., "*samādhi,*" "cosmic consciousness," "trance," "satori," or "enlightenment," dependent on the traditions of the practitioner). However, efforts to sit down and actually practice these techniques on a regular basis require a certain threshold of motivation and knowledge that can be, at the outset, difficult to obtain without some clear understanding of the objectives sought and a map of the territory to be explored. At the very least, repeated studies have shown that these psychophysical exercises work to strengthen one's ability to maintain a calm, tranquil, centered state of being in the midst of a world filled with anxiety, change, chaos, and confusion.

The idea that we can modify our own consciousness through developing and activating our own instruments of supersensible perception (i.e., repurposing regions of our brain-mind to function as cosmic transceivers), has been supported by the recent neurophysiological confirmation of what is called *neuroplasticity,* the ability of the human brain to grow, change, and repurpose systems within itself during the lifetime of each individual. It was my own luck to have been introduced to this concept early in my life, while attending a lecture given by John Lilly in which he introduced his new book, *Programming and Metaprogramming in the Human Biocomputer.* Lilly's hypothesis was that we are all capable of reprogramming our "biocomputer" to adapt and evolve new ways of operating, responding, and neurally fabricating (through neuroplasticity) new modes of perception.

To my surprise, Lilly expressed a conviction that the future of contemplative practice in the West held great promise, evidenced by the highly technical training undergone by large numbers of young scientists, engineers, mathematicians, and other academics.

Lilly explained that the current generation of adolescent students and young adults, during their school years of regular sustained attention upon abstract intellectual material, were inadvertently metaprogramming their brain-minds to develop and maintain new skills for the focusing of consciousness through the phenomenon of neuroplastic imprinting. These very same skills are also required for success in traditional practices of advanced meditation and contemplation. Clearly, said Lilly, college students, particularly in the areas of math, science, and engineering, were reprogramming their brain, creating (growing) new subsystems capable of sustaining one-pointed focus of awareness for prolonged periods, with the ability to ignore extended distractions.

Individuals completing advanced technical programs are likely to have developed the skills for making quick progress in the attainment of deep states and stages of meditation. Lilly believed that the many hours of practice in holding attention focused on a single point of abstract material would be of great use in the future, should they ever become interested in exploring consciousness through introspection; accordingly, there would be a great resurgence of skilled contemplatives in the future.[1]

What then *is* consciousness? While most people assume that they know what it is, consciousness continues to puzzle the scientific community. Until recently, consciousness was not even regarded as being a "thing" worthy of study and had been mostly ignored, much in the same way as fish ignore the water in which they swim. Many people assume that psychologists and psychiatrists *do* understand consciousness, and yet they would be wrong. Consciousness continues to be one of the greatest remaining mysteries among the sciences. Psychologists observe and record human behavior, but no psychologist claims to even begin to understand the physics or biology of consciousness, the actual *phenomenon of consciousness* itself. The situation has been quite different in most Asian cultures, where generations of individuals have sought to understand consciousness through direct exploration and experimentation using every means available. Unfortunately, these efforts and their documented results have been labeled "mysticism" or "shamanism" by the scientific community and categorically dismissed without any concerted effort to examine the voluminous accounts of experiential data that might be worthy of consideration in the efforts to understand the nature and dynamics of the phenomenon called consciousness.

While significant research projects are currently underway to explore consciousness, often staffed with highly trained medical doctors, neurophysiologists, engineers, chemists, and even quantum physicists, several underlying preconceptions work to limit any truly broad, open-minded approach to the study of consciousness. Common to all of these efforts is the underlying assumption that consciousness is a phenomenon that only recently emerged in biological creatures, due to some as yet unidentified biophysical process involving neurons, generating collective holographic patterns generated by the firing of neurons, that can eventually be identified in laboratory experiments. Brain scientists assume that it is this electrical activity of billions of neurons that gives rise to consciousness, and many go further by asserting that consciousness is a rare phenomenon that is likely to be found nowhere else in the universe. Nevertheless, funding sources for "consciousness studies" continue to remain low compared to projects that are seen to further information technology, energy production, robotics, and even the entertainment industries, possibly because investors see no feasible financial gain in understanding consciousness.

In contrast, modern professional philosophers tend to view the phenomenon of consciousness as more than simply a biological phenomenon generated by neurons. Many philosophers see consciousness as more fundamental than a biological construct. Many adhere to the philosophical stance of *panpsychism*—the view that consciousness is a phenomenon that pervades the universe and should be seen as *the fundamental reality* out of which everything else has emerged. Philosophers see consciousness less as something arising from recent biological activity but more as a substrate, the underlying ground of the entire cosmos of space-time phenomena. Yet neither the current scientific nor the philosophic approaches have yielded satisfactory results in their efforts to understand the phenomenon of consciousness.

But while the study of pure consciousness is relatively new to material scientists and professional philosophers alike, exploring the mysteries of consciousness has been at the heart of shamanic inquiry throughout history, although in religious writing and discourse we seldom find the word *consciousness.* Instead, the words most frequently encountered throughout the world in discussions and written records dealing with the exploration of consciousness are terms such as *spirit, soul, anima, prāṇa,* or *chi.*

Perhaps it is this wide-ranging difference in terminology, or the fact that the subject matter is found deeply embedded within specific religious and cultural traditions (and often "dead" languages) that prevents modern-day academics from investigating the maps of consciousness laid down by contemplative saints, mystics, and shamans over the many centuries through direct experiential, first-person observation and experience. Yet throughout history psychonauts* have availed themselves of this rich cultural-specific ancestral knowledge.

Yet now in the early twenty-first century we find a growing community of psychonauts—unencumbered by the self-imposed limitations of established religious dogma, the myopia of materialist sciences, or the widespread consensual restrictions of social norms—daring to experience and explore new realms of consciousness outside of the purview of the scientific and religious establishments. Modern psychonauts are able to venture beyond the bounds of everyday human awareness using a wide range of means currently available, including the use of

*The term *psychonaut,* from the Greek words ψυχή *psychē* ("soul, spirit, or mind") and ναύτης *naútēs* ("sailor, navigator"), denotes an individual who intentionally explores wide ranging states and stages of non-ordinary consciousness through a variety of means, including the skillful application of traditional religious or shamanistic contemplative techniques, extreme physical exercise, fasting, and through the ingestion of entheogens (e.g., LSD, mescaline, psilocybin, ayahuasca, and cannabis).

entheogenic drugs, physical exercises, and a variety of contemplative techniques.

Such intrepid noninstitutional explorers, experimenting with what have previously been considered esoteric and often secret practices found in the more arcane and mystical areas of religious traditions, have, in a relatively short period of time, begun to develop new ways of tuning and directing consciousness to reach extraordinary modes of being and increasingly intense levels of lucid awareness that are requisite for the direct exploration of the vast supersensible dimensions that make up the cosmos within which we exist. These psychophysical exercises, often accompanied with the aid of psychotropic substances (particularly cannabis) open up dimensions of supersensible experience normally only attainable during dream states.

The big surprise for many readers may be that traditional practices, which often go by the names mindfulness, contemplation, or meditation, are not simply approaches to clearing one's mind or achieving states of serene tranquility amid a world gone awry. They are also keys to approaching, unlocking, and activating a number of latent yet extremely powerful perceptual modes that are currently at the extreme frontiers of human sensory evolution. Such abilities emerge at the growth tip of an ascending arc of human sensory development and are operationally activated at the cutting edge of human conscious awareness. In Tibet and India the numerous techniques that have been discovered and developed to reach such higher stages of perceptual awareness are encapsulated in the word *tantra,* which literally means "a loom, a weaving" but can now be interpreted more accurately as an interweaving of traditions and teachings, threads of practical techniques that have been found extremely effective for reaching higher states of awareness.

My own introduction to rarified states of conscious perception (which are the objectives of all Tantric practices) began at age twenty-one. During the summer of my final year in my electronics engineering program, I left Texas to work as a software programmer at the Point Mugu Missile Base in southern California, just north of Los Angeles. It was during that summer of 1967 that I experienced my first encounter with an entheogen in the form of "Owsley acid," an exceptionally pure form of LSD, at night on a beach where the Little Sur Creek flowed out into the Pacific, just south of Big Sur. This experience radically changed the course of my life from my early fascination for electronic communications toward a new, much stronger, and lifelong quest to explore the nature of consciousness both experientially and in terms of what I had learned in my study of physics, engineering, and cybernetics. It also led, upon my return to my engineering program in Texas that fall, to further exploration of these newly discovered realms of consciousness.

My mind was opening to amazing new dimensions. On weekends I spent long evenings in the hill country near Austin exploring the psychedelic worlds through LSD, peyote, and psilocybe mushrooms. Nevertheless, I managed to graduate with my engineering degree and relocate from Texas to New York City, where I was able to find numerous teachers and books to help satisfy my ravenous appetite for material on contemplative practices and altered states of consciousness.

In New York I had the good fortune to develop and cultivate a consistent daily effort to explore consciousness through a wide variety of contemplative practices as taught not only by mainstream religions but also those found in the more esoteric approaches of the Buddhist Vajrayāna and Hindu Tantras, particularly in the theories of sound and consciousness elaborated in Kashmir Shaivism.

While employed as an engineer in the World Trade Center in New York I had become increasingly interested in consciousness, hatha yoga, and psychotropic experiences. My first serious relationship with a spiritual teacher (outside of my own childhood experience in Roman Catholicism) was with Chögyam Trungpa Rinpoche (1939–1987), a Nyingma *tulku** whom I first met at a lecture in New York. Trungpa (fig. 0.1) is known to have been the first *tulku* to introduce the esoteric practices of Vajrayāna to Western students of meditation.

For several years I was able to study with Chögyam Trungpa in New York city and go on retreats he conducted at Tail of the Tiger, his monastic center in Barnet, Vermont. I continued to study with a wide range of teachers in New York until, encouraged during a workshop in

---

*In Tibet and Mongolia, *tulkus* are recognized incarnations of a departed spiritual masters, individuals so far advanced in the contemplative arts that they are able to choose the circumstances of their next incarnation.

Fig. 0.1. Chögyam Trungpa at age fourteen.

1974 given by the contemplative writer Alan Watts, I applied to a graduate program to study Sanskrit and Asian philosophy at the California Institute of Integral Studies* in San Francisco. In 1978, I completed my master's thesis on "The History, Philosophy, and Practice of Tantra in South India." Twenty years later, while living in Saudi Arabia, I had the good fortune to travel to South India to spend time on retreat in a small ashram, Shantivanam ("Forest of Peace"), established in 1938 by French Benedictine priest Father Jules Monchanin (1895–1957). There I was able to go deeper in my explorations while meditating on the nearby banks of the Cauvery River, reputed to be the holy river of South India. Upon returning from Saudi Arabia, I entered a doctoral program in philosophy, cosmology, and consciousness studies in San Francisco, where I completed my doctoral studies and successfully defended my dissertation at the California Institute of Integral Studies.*

Over this time period the cumulative growth of experiential practice allowed me to develop my own particular "contemplative technologies" based upon those practices that I found worked particularly well for me on a regular basis. It is my belief that each individual can discover and

*Known at the time (prior to 1980) as the California Institute of Asian Studies.

develop his or her own uniquely appropriate combination of psycho-spiritual technique and practice to optimize explorative entries into the oceans of consciousness.

After completing all course work I relocated to a cabin in the lower Cascade Range in northeastern California where I was able to explore consciousness in the silence of the Lassen Forest, where I continued my research and completed writing my dissertation.

Since then, in the shadowy silence of Mount Lassen Volcano, I have been able to go even deeper into contemplative practice, reading and integrating more of my many books. I now feel the time ripe to share what I have learned and experienced with you in the book you now hold in your hands.

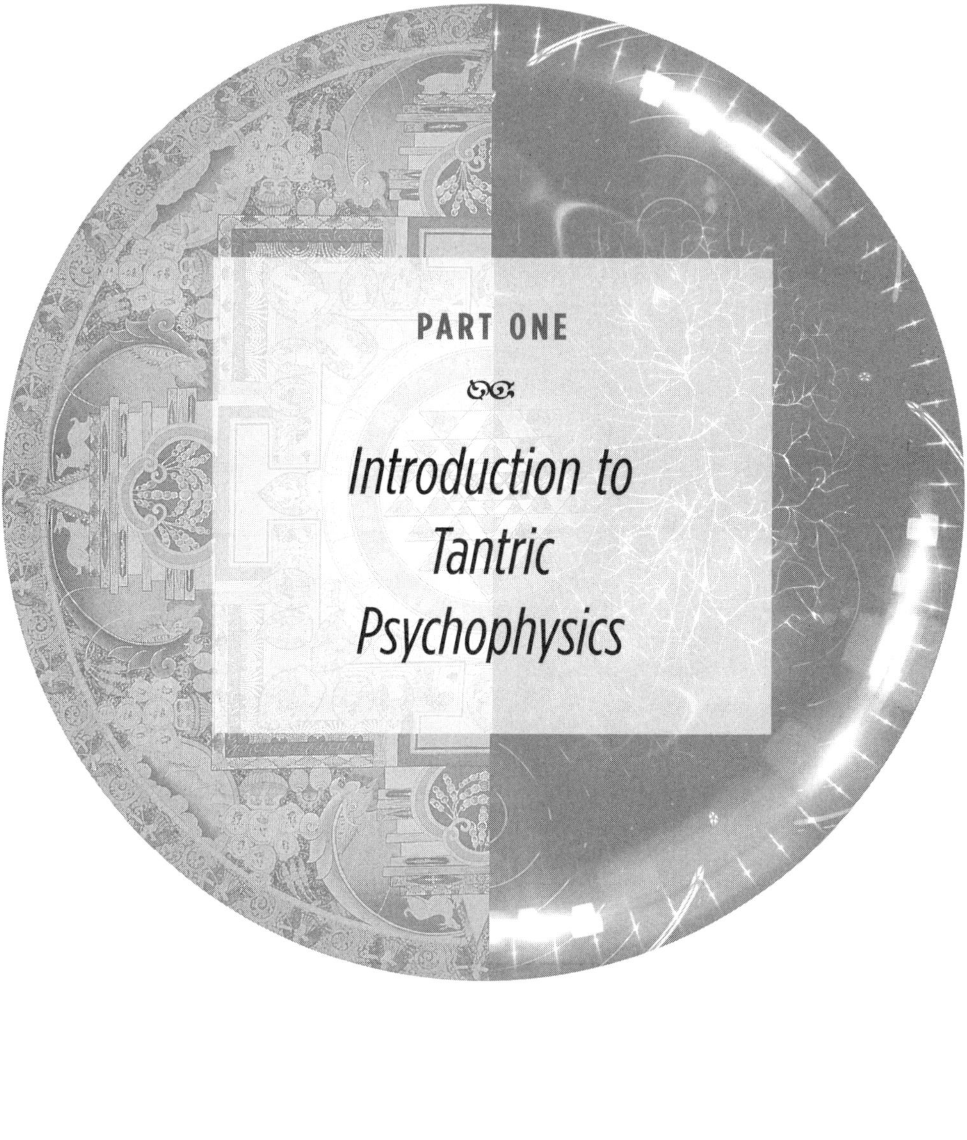

PART ONE

Introduction to Tantric Psychophysics

1

TANTRA

An Integral Approach to Esoteric Practices

The word *Tantra* is a Sanskrit word that can be translated as "a loom, a weaving, an instrument, or a system." It denotes an inclusive domain of knowledge derived from direct human experience of nonordinary regions of consciousness. The word has been found on clay texts inscribed as early as 1500 BCE near the Indus River in northwestern India. The word *psychophysics* is an approach to a physics of consciousness first articulated in 1860 by Gustav Theodor Fechner (1801–1887), who pioneered the application of scientific principles and mathematics to the understanding of human consciousness and perception.

The phrase "Tantric psychophysics," then, encapsulates the specific approaches explored here to integrate modern science and traditional esoteric wisdom in the effort to describe and to understand the geometry and the dynamics of consciousness within each individual human nexus of consciousness (i.e., brain-mind, soul, spirit, *puruṣa,* etc.). It is my belief that a clearly expressed articulation of this knowledge can be of great use by individuals seeking to modulate, to expand, and to explore consciousness directly through the use of consciousness itself as the primary instrument. Serious but independent and often isolated "psychonauts" have discovered that it is definitely possible for an individual to develop, master, and utilize consciousness itself as the vehicle to explore the vast dynamic energies of a universe manifesting consciousness and awareness at a multiplicity of levels and dimensions.

Since its inception in 1860, the science of psychophysics has been developed primarily to study human sensory systems. Modern psychophysics draws upon concepts from physics and mathematics to map the relationships between subjective conscious experience and the stimuli that activate the various human senses. Psychophysics has become the primary scientific tool for research psychologists in the study of sensations brought into the field of awareness through the primary external sensory systems of touch, sight, hearing, taste, and smell. In a similar way, it is the objective of this book to apply modern concepts from physics and physiology to the study of the more rarified sensory modes of awareness that are often described and discussed by Tantric contemplatives. Such supersensory modes of awareness, typically experienced by mystics in darkness, silence, and during dream states, are categorically different from those sensations coming into awareness from one's external sensory systems.

Many key translations of Sanskrit and/or Tibetan terms into English are misleading through overreliance upon words normally associated only with one's external senses. For example, in reading Tantric texts, one often encounters such descriptive translations as "the clear light," or "the voice of silence," or even more subjective phrases describing sensations such as "all-encompassing unity," "feelings of love," and "peace of mind." While these are all directly sensed qualia (experienced sensations), it is not at all clear to modern research where such sensory systems are to be found in human physiology nor how to begin to detect or to measure them.

This book offers a new branch of psychophysics, a focus upon the many numinous internal sensory experiences that are the subject of traditional sources of mystical insight. It does this by using the tools of twenty-first-century science: quantum physics, psychology, electronics, software engineering, and one of the newest fields, consciousness studies. A psychophysics of Tantra offers a modern integrated approach to describing and understanding Tantric experiences that arise as awareness moves into higher domains and new internal sensory systems are activated.

Using an integral, transdisciplinary approach, the classical teachings of esoteric Tantra, yoga, mysticism, and the occult are presented here within the context of an expanded psychophysics. These multiple approaches provide a more coherent context than that encountered by trying to absorb the concepts solely from within the isolation of the particular cultural trappings (and languages) from which they sprang. To acquire a practical understanding of Tantric techniques, one should not be required to master Sanskrit, Tibetan, or Latin or need to assimilate innumerable esoteric terms. While much of the material presented here is based upon the recorded experiences of individuals (and subsequent "disciples") that have become a part of specific cultural traditions (Hinduism, Buddhism, Christianity, Taoism, and so on), I have made every effort to extract the experiential knowledge itself out from the specific religio-cultural traditions in which it is embedded, somewhat like extracting gold ore from sedimentary rock. Where possible I have re-expressed the information in more technical, science-based, nontheological terms using contemporary language and concepts.

This book offers a wide range of esoteric knowledge presented in the context of contemporary physics, physiology, and philosophy. This broad approach supports the exploration of non-ordinary states of conscious awareness that may be glimpsed through the ingestion of psychotropic substances and traditional psychophysical practices. Presented in contemporary language and supported with numerous diagrams, this discussion of practical psychophysics maps the numerous supersensible regions of consciousness that may be attained by the intrepid explorer of the psyche, and will be of great use to those who set sail in the oceans of consciousness through the aid of entheogens, religious ritual, or any combination of innumerable contemplative techniques described here. This approach should be of great utility for serious students in their efforts to acquire some practical working knowledge leading to the direct activation of supersensible* perception, a new mode of perception for most contemporary humans and one that opens wide the portal to lucid psychonautic exploration of dimensions beyond space-time.

While the non-ordinary regions of consciousness explored here are

*"Supersensible"—Beyond the range of the external sensory systems; numinous inner awareness as experienced internally as visions, dreams, and so on. See the author's book *Developing Supersensible Perception: Knowledge of the Higher Worlds through Entheogens, Prayer, and Nondual Awareness* (2019).

seldom accessed during normal human waking hours, the maps provided in these chapters offer cognitive landmarks to guide those who may initially find themselves lost within unfamiliar states and stages of esoteric regions in this vast ocean of cosmic consciousness. The acquisition of such knowledge and its practical applications present powerful tools that can even be used profitably during regular nightly excursions into dreamtime dimensions.

The detailed descriptions of stages and states of consciousness set forth in this book emerge from generations of experimental, experiential knowledge handed down by practicing psychonauts in numerous cultures. While we shall focus upon the philosophies and practices of Tantra that have emerged from within Indian and Tibetan cultures, we shall also examine Western metaphysical approaches to mapping consciousness. We conclude the book with a chapter, "Practical Advice for Modern Psychonauts," that lays out an integral map of consciousness in a weaving of principles of cosmology, brain physiology, quantum mechanics, and holography that results in a synthesis that should be of significant utility for those who may be active in, or interested in beginning, psychonautic exploration.

For the vast majority of contemporary physicists, psychologists, and engineers the subject of Tantric mysticism is likely to be of no interest at all. Tantric subject matter has been widely ignored in the halls of science due to the mistaken Western assumption that Tantra is merely a "yoga of sex" or a superstitious "cult of ecstasy." Nothing could be farther from the truth. As the Cambridge-trained Tibetan scholar John Blofeld writes:

> Mysticism, or the search for divine truth within the mind, has always existed among small groups everywhere; but the Tantric mystical techniques have few parallels in other religions or in other schools of Buddhism; many of them are virtually unique. . . . What is unique about the Tantric method is its wealth of techniques for utilizing all things good and evil to that end. It makes elaborate use of rites because the power generated by emotion and by aesthetic satisfaction is a force too valuable to waste.[1]

It is my contention that the modern scientific community may be missing a great opportunity to make progress in understanding the nature of consciousness through neglecting to consider the maps of consciousness that have been developed and successfully used by Tantric psychonauts in their exploration of the inner cosmos. Science has long neglected the wealth of available data that can be found in the recorded experiences of generations of psychonauts bequeathed to us from myriad cultural groups on the planet. While the scientific community has used objective consciousness as a tool to develop maps of the external space-time material world, the Tantric "metaphysical scientists" have focused upon the use of subjective consciousness to explore and map the nonmaterial worlds that can be opened up through skillful manipulation of consciousness itself.

But there have been a rare few scientists who have made it their life work to pioneer the physics of consciousness in an integrated way through considering material normally ignored within the scientific community. Among these are Gustav Fechner (1801–1887), who, in founding what is now known as the science of psychophysics with his ground-breaking publication of *Elements of Psychophysics,* in 1860 laid the claim that "Psychophysics is an exact doctrine of the relation of function or dependence between body and soul."[2] Another of these rare few is Rudolf Steiner (1861–1925), the Austrian scientist and philosopher who lectured and published extensively* in the early part of the twentieth century to lay the foundations for a new subject that he termed *esoteric science.*†

Based upon his own experience of the paranormal, Steiner believed that the modern scientific establishment should not ignore the numerous accounts of supernormal modes of perception that have come down to us through written records left by generations of psychics,

*Rudolf Steiner produced over 400 volumes of written material, which include his books and writings (about forty volumes), and over 6,000 published transcriptions from his lectures.

†In 1909 in his *Outline of Esoteric Science,* Steiner wrote, "Esoteric Science is the science of what takes place esoterically in the sense that it is perceived, not outside in nature but where one's soul turns when it directs its inner being to the spirit."

saints, and mystics. Throughout his years of lecturing and his numerous publications Steiner described ways in which newly activated sensory systems have been able to offer access to higher regions of consciousness and direct entry into what Steiner termed "the Higher Worlds."[3]

Comprehensive maps and models of consciousness can be of great use to those who are either interested in, beginning to explore, or actively making progress in developing advanced capabilities for navigating supersensible regions through the application of new modes of inner awareness. Such practical models of consciousness are largely missing from modern-day educational institutions and contemporary religious teachings. Nor has there yet arisen within the scientific establishment any truly comprehensive map or model of consciousness that can be clearly grasped by the twenty-first-century psychonaut.

Yet in India and Tibet, we find still find "traditional" maps drawn up over generations by ancestors of those living today, though often distorted by censorship such as that of Victorian missionaries in their extensive efforts to "cleanse" Hindu and Muslim arts and literature throughout the Christian British Empire. In Christian cultures a similar filter of self-censorship has ravaged and expunged the works of mystics that might have been passed down to us directly. Those engaged in serious psychonautics in earlier centuries lived with the possibility of being condemned for witchcraft.

Those trying to grasp a model or map of consciousness today have many threads to explore, yet in order to find enough pieces of the puzzle to begin to construct a clear, overarching picture of consciousness, their journey is best approached with an initially wide interdisciplinary search for information while looking to discover connecting threads and areas of congruence which might validate the claims and teachings found in various schools of traditional mysticism such as Tibetan Vajrayāna or Indian Vedanta.

Traditionally, a "map of consciousness" (a "religion," or a "way," or a "teaching") is usually described using specific terms that are conventional only to a specific culture or field of study. For example, a priest will describe consciousness using the theological and social terms that are familiar to a particular religious culture and community, while a physicist will describe consciousness in the language that other physicists will be able to understand. The technical terms used in all of these specialities include many acronyms and principles that the writer assumes the audience will implicitly understand.

Accordingly, rather than trying to approach consciousness from a perspective within a single discipline in the usual linear, rather narrow self-referential fashion, we will develop a practical psychophysics of consciousness from multiple perspectives, weaving together supporting elements from philosophy, physics, physiology, Tibetan and Indian religious traditions, and most importantly, elements from direct experiential observation or introspection—the approach valued by the "father of American psychology," William James (1842–1910). Above all, we seek to validate these principles of psychophysics by seeking congruent patterns among numerous strands of wisdom embedded in different perspectives, and in so doing to detect mutually supporting elements among these diverse disciplines. In this way a reader is more able to grasp the subject panoramically and can find early "hooks" into material that corresponds with the individual's particular educational depth and experiential background.

THE INTEGRAL INTERDISCIPLINARY APPROACH

The integral, interdisciplinary approach to consciousness presented here not only examines theoretical material from numerous perspectives, but also offers practical suggestions and techniques that can catalyze new experiences and activate enhanced capabilities of the human psyche (the *siddhi** or "accomplishments, magical powers, attainment, perfections, or success" discussed in Patañjali's *Yoga Sūtras*). By acquiring sufficient theory in support of the practical techniques as they are described, the reader is better prepared for exploring alternate dimensions of awareness in a contemporary context.

It is my contention that if we approach Tantra as an object (or field) of Indological study, even an academically interesting subtopic of Asian culture and history, we would be missing the point of Tantra itself.

*Note that throughout this book italicized words will indicate transliteration of the Sanskrit; translations of Patañjali's *Sūtras* in this book are my own except where noted.

Rather, we should approach Tantra as a living stream of Gaia herself, as the Great Tantric Mother of Indian seers, or as Pachamama ("World Mother") of the Incas, or perhaps as the feminine force of Nature who wants us to learn and experience and grow, both as individuals and as a species. To do this we must use every means available that might be suitable considering our own unique experience, stage of psychic evolution, and particular social and physical environment. In short, one might say that the goal is to discover one's own uniquely appropriate methods to "roll one's own" psychonautic map and medicine bag of techniques.

In this spirit of Tantra, we will approach Tantric psychophysics integrally—that is, we will not take a purely philosophical, anthropological, or scientific approach, or even a comparative approach, but will bring into focus multiple approaches that can be seen to weave a tapestry with threads of understanding from what may at first seem to be disparate disciplines and wide-ranging sources, both ancient and contemporary. In exploring Tantra, we use an *integral methodology*[4] taught by Haridas Chaudhuri (1913–1975), with whom I was fortunate enough to study the various schools of Indian philosophy as a graduate student. His discussion of the "integral" approach was my first encounter with the use of the word outside of calculus, where "integral" is used to identify a specifically powerful mathematical technique first developed by Newton.

Chaudhuri spoke of the need for a less academic, more "integral" approach to knowledge. He urged a multidisciplinary technique that can be applied to any object of study, where one begins from several starting points to focus upon a single object of study, often from seemingly unconnected, disparate specialties. Rather than simply analyzing or elaborating upon a subject from within the subject's own field—for example, philosophical discussion of topics in philosophy—the integral approach seeks to gain multiple perspectives from which to ascertain unexpected correlations, or in contemporary terms, "to connect the dots" between diverse disciplines in order to view previously unperceived patterns. And finally, Chaudhuri insisted, the most important tool must be the element of introspection, an "experiential dimension" of inquiry inclusive of the observer within the observation.

Accordingly, I use Chaudhuri's integral approach to develop a new model of consciousness from seemingly disparate disciplines that includes ideas, models, and experiences not only from traditional Hindu and Tibetan Buddhist Tantric sources, but also from such diverse fields as physiology, electrical engineering, Indian philosophy, and Western Theosophy. The remainder of this chapter explores examples general concepts of consciousness and contemplation before diving into the more specific knowledge sources of Western metaphysics, Indian Tantra, and Tibetan Vajrayāna.

TANTRIC PSYCHONAUTICS: CONSCIOUSNESS AND CONTEMPLATION

The words *consciousness* and *contemplation* have both undergone significant changes over the past centuries, and particularly during the past few decades. In the Christian West during the Middle Ages *contemplation* was defined as "gazing with love upon God," or "the experience of union with God," falling under the exclusive domain of relational prayer.

Today with the convergence of East-West thought and culture, due in part to globalization, contemplation is understood less as a religious practice and more as an introspective approach to a higher evolutionary and participatory experience of "non-dual consciousness"—loosely defined as a sharing of consciousness with all that is, including the source or substrate of consciousness that panpsychists believe to be the source and foundation of the universe of space and time. However, this has led to an even wider variation in the meaning of "consciousness." Some use the word to refer exclusively to human consciousness, and among this group there are many who do not believe that consciousness exists among plants and even animals. Others believe that consciousness is everywhere, even in nonbiological entities such as rocks and planets. Yet another group, often termed psychonauts—having experienced the effects of psychedelics (also termed entheogens)—believe that we are swimming in an ocean of consciousness that we are just beginning to perceive, a vast region that needs to be explored.

Today, contemplation has come to be seen not only as a religious practice, but one adopted by secular psychonauts interested in exploring an ocean of consciousness by a wide variety of means, including psychotropic drugs.

PSYCHONAUTS OF CONSCIOUSNESS

Descriptions of mystical and religious experiences have been handed down in every culture by spiritual-religious explorers of consciousness. Religious texts and tradition provide strong evidence that there exist modes of consciousness that *can* and *have been* explored beyond the ranges of conventional daily waking awareness; all traditions offer deep prayer and contemplation as doorways to experience *beyond* space and time. In the twenty-first century, secular-associated explorers of these non-ordinary realms have come to be known as psychonauts, a term which means "sailor of the soul." The ocean upon which the psychonaut sets sail is the ocean of consciousness.

We do not have to be shamans to have psychonautic adventures. Additional evidence is close at hand—our universal nightly human experience of dream states, which seem *not* to be a product of normal time, space, or mental cognition. But in the modern age, we find rich descriptions of psychonautic exploration in the writings (and public notoriety) of such widely diverse figures as the poet Allen Ginsberg, the psychologist Timothy Leary, and the neuroscientist John C. Lilly (fig. 1.1, p. 12).

Psychonautics can be best understood as a research paradigm in which the researcher is voluntarily immersed within an altered mental state induced by meditation, special exercises, or mind-altering chemicals in order to explore non-ordinary states of consciousness and, where possible, to subsequently record descriptions of the experienced states. Allen Ginsberg, the poet, traveled to the Peruvian jungles to experience ayahuasca. Timothy Leary, in turn, is notorious for his introduction of LSD experiments while serving as a Harvard psychology professor, and John Lilly, the M.D. and electrical engineer, spent a lifetime experimenting with psychotropics and interspecies communication.

Highly educated and exceptionally intelligent, these psychonauts of the late twentieth century were, at the outset, widely regarded in their respective fields as pioneers of consciousness, yet generally ignored or dismissed "in the halls of science." Even those with degrees in the hard sciences, such as Lilly, have too often been cast into a limbo of disregard, notoriety, or disrepute by their more conservative establishment

Fig. 1.1. *From left to right,* Allen Ginsberg, Timothy Leary, and John Lilly. Polaroid photograph taken Easter Sunday 1991, at the home of Dr. Oscar Janiger. Photo by Philip H. Bailey.

peers. Particularly in the late 1960s, the stigma of working directly with drugs fell heavily upon those who experimented with psychotropic substances such as LSD, peyote, mushrooms, and cannabis.

Of these early explorers of consciousness, Lilly (fig. 1.2) was clearly the most highly trained in the hard-science technical subjects of physics, mathematics, and electronics, with a bachelor of science from Stanford and an M.D. from Dartmouth. Early in his career Lilly developed a passion for exploring modes of communication:

> It is only rarely that we have experiences that allow us to say that there are possibilities of communication other than those currently

> represented by the visual image, by the vocal expression, or by the written word.[5]

In the late 1950s, influenced by his early fascination with communications and electronics (Lilly had built and licensed an early HAM radio station), he obtained funding from the National Science Foundation and set up Dolphin Point Laboratory on the island of St. Thomas in the Virgin Islands to conduct pioneering research in the field of "inter-species communication."[6]

Fig. 1.2. John Cunningham Lilly (1915–2001).

The research protocol involved recording both audio and electromagnetic dolphin/human interaction in a darkened indoor pool, among pairs of human-dolphin bonded subjects. Some of the experiments included sessions in which the human subject ingested measured doses of LSD-25. Lilly subsequently applied the mathematical technique of Fourier domain analysis to the recordings in each frequency band in an attempt to identify common patterns associated with different categories of information exchange.[7] Eventually research funding ran dry, the US Navy requisitioned Lilly's dolphins to work on a classified military project in California, and the research was discontinued.

Following his decade of dolphin research Lilly began to focus more explicitly on exploring the effects of LSD–25 and ketamine (categorized as a "dissociative anesthetic") on both himself and colleagues. Experimental procedure consisted of extended sessions of immersion in isolation tanks of his own design during which subjects would float in warm saline water in silent, ventilated, lightproof enclosures:

> I set up experiments using LSD in the solitude, isolation, and confinement tank, floating in the darkness, and silence, freed of all inputs to my body from the external reality. In these experiments, I discovered other spaces, found other maps, and discovered a relatively safe means of going into these places.[8]

When LSD-25 became impossible to obtain, Lilly substituted ketamine, a legal drug with reported effects of causing "the mind to separate from the body," an effect which Lilly found of great use in his isolation tank research. Lilly would self-inject ketamine, then spend several hours immersed in an isolation tank. Upon emerging from the tank, Lilly would immediately record recollections of his experiences in a log. The following is a typical entry.

> Everything was happening on such a vast scale that I was merely an observer of microscopic size, and yet I was more than this. I was part of some vast network of similar beings all connected, somehow or other responsible for what was going on. I was given an individuality for temporary purposes only. I would be reabsorbed into the network when the time came.[9]

In 1969, Lilly put forth a view of human consciousness as multiple levels of software operating simultaneously. This software (possibly associated with hard-coded DNA) is programmable and reprogrammable at the lowest levels, which he calls meta-programs. Humans, both individually and in various grouped subnetworks, have the ability to meta-program their own internal software once they begin to grasp a basic understanding of the software architecture. This ability to change oneself—to reprogram one's consciousness, to change through understanding, through *theoria* and *praxis*—is one of the topics handed down in all cultural traditions and religions, abstracted in many different symbolic languages.

It is evident that serious efforts have indeed been made by Lilly and others to explore consciousness in order to examine the outlines of an architecture of consciousness firsthand. A careful consideration of their work reveals the outlines of a noetic science that, for psychonauts, may prove to be the equivalent of the indispensable fourteenth-century *rutters*. Rutters were written compilations of sailing experiences used by Portuguese navigators in the same way that the following chapters may provide a reasonable, practical map of the vast ocean of consciousness revealed to those who have undergone religious, psychotropic, or near-death experiences.

Having examined the importance of an integral approach to understanding contemplation, we can now begin to incorporate specific traditional approaches to contemplation from within Asian and Western cultures.

2

What Tantra Is and Is Not

At first glance "Tantric Psychophysics" conjures up images of various erotic sexual poses that were immediately condemned and censored by early British missionaries to India. But the term itself has little to do with sex, other than in the eyes of the general public where a simple internet search on "Tantra" yields the misleading view that Tantra is primarily about sex. Likewise, the reaction of British colonials in India was one of shock and condemnation when confronted with innumerable carvings depicting explicit Tantric themes of ritual intercourse (fig. 2.1, p. 18) highlighting the union of universal male and female principles.

Yet *tantra* as a Sanskrit word can be translated rather innocuously as "a loom, a weaving, an instrument or a system." The connotation is that the subject is an inclusive source of knowledge derived from *direct human experience.* Tantra is a methodology developed as an instrument to retrieve an integrated knowledge that culminates in deep wisdom; a knowledge more immediate and comprehensive than that which might be obtained through mastering individual subjects, such as philosophy, religion, physiology, or physics. Tantra is more accurately understood as an approach to the exploration of consciousness that adopts anything "that works" for the attainment of a wider and more intense range of direct awareness and understanding of conscious realities and regions that are seldom experienced in normal everyday life.

The earliest use of the word *tantra* is found in the *Rig Veda,* the oldest of the Vedic Sanskrit texts, composed around 1500 BCE in northern India. In this Vedic symbolism, *tantra* appears to indicate the *warp* of a loom, the vertical series of threads that are transformed by intersections with the horizontal threads (often called the *woof*) into solid cloth. As such, the word *tantra* implies an "interweaving of traditions and teachings as threads" that create a solid, practical, useful set of techniques or practices that lead to knowledge of higher worlds.[1]

While the roots of the word *tantra* might indicate "threads of technique on a loom of experience," the term has also been interpreted as an "extending" or "continuing." It is in such a sense that ancient cultures in India applied the term to multiple systems that evolved largely from the Vedic philosophy and religion, and were later adopted by a broader, more inclusive spectrum of practitioners.[2] Whereas Brahmanical Vedic religious practice was open exclusively only to males of a highly specific social caste, the Tantra practices offered a lowering of such barriers and came to incorporate not only women and members of societies prohibited from Vedic worship, but also those elements of non-Vedic culture that were experienced to be of particular value and efficacy.

Tantra is a methodology, a system synthesizing innumerable practical applications through which human consciousness may reach that experiential knowledge of the non-dual Absolute, called Brahman in the Upanishads. The Tantric practitioner seeks to realize the union of opposites, to acquire knowledge by experience—to experimentally "know" that state of non-duality expressed so paradoxically in the Upanishads—and works to contact, connect with, and fuse the dualities in the microcosm of the human body into an experience of macrocosmic unity, one that both transcends and includes the manifest cosmic universe. The web of knowledge that is called Tantra gives particular credence to "what works," and thus myriad practices that have been found efficacious have been handed down through the ages and have been incorporated into its broad spectrum of liturgical and psychophysical practices.

The material presented here is not an attempt to approach comprehensivity in its treatment of the forest that is Hindu or Tibetan Buddhist (or American) Tantra. Rather it is a general survey, an effort to give some general form to the terrain and to describe a sufficient number of prominent landmarks and relate them to contemporary maps of science to serve as a general (however incomplete) map to the territory of Tantra. The intent is to increase the efficacy of the reader's own efforts to explore consciousness directly, and in order to

Fig. 2.1. Erotic sculpture from Temple of Khajuraho,
Madhya Pradesh, India.
Photo by Sankara Subramanian.

facilitate an understanding of Tantric maps and methods for the modern educated reader, the material in the following chapters has been grounded as far as possible in scientific principles, terminology, and numerous diagrams.

Tantra is, above all, a practical approach to the exploration of what has been called mystical experience. Tantric experiential practices weave together innumerable techniques that have been found effective for catalyzing states of supersensory perception. Here the British traveler and scholar John Blofeld describes the goal:

> It should be remembered that the prime concern is practice. If something is conducive to spiritual advancement, it is good; whether the theory behind it is properly understood or not matters much or little according to the extent to which that understanding affects the quality and direction of the practice.[3]

Nothing has been wasted in Tantric efforts to practice "what works" to attain non-ordinary states of consciousness, and sexual union or *maithuna* (fig. 2.2) has been among the most notorious practices attributed to Tantric practitioners.

Fig. 2.2. Indian and Tibetan ritual intercourse. Left image by Jeff Hart and adapted by Fowler and Fowler. Right image by Joe Mabel.

However, the actual effort involves having the practitioners visualize their relationship as being that between Shiva and Shakti, the divine male and divine female principles, and a primary instruction was that the individuals were to stop short of actually exchanging bodily fluids. The scriptures warn that unless this spiritual transformation occurs the union is incomplete.[4]

Orthodox proponents of traditional religions in India have often scorned and condemned those who were attracted to Tantric practices, many of which were known to have been conducted by women "Tantrikas" and even "untouchables," those at the very bottom of the caste system's social hierarchy. It is understandable that many of these criticisms should have arisen from members of the Brahman caste.

However, it is likely that these rituals, which so shocked the British occupiers, were not regularly performed except by small groups of highly trained adepts; the usual Tantric ceremony was purely symbolic and even more fastidious than the ceremonial *pujas* in Hindu temples.[5] Yet Tantric knowledge was disseminated widely in the subcontinent over the centuries, and has been practiced and developed further in Tibet and India over millennia of psychic experimentation by generations of seekers in their passion to explore the more esoteric realms of the psyche. Unfortunately, it is also a category of knowledge that modern science has largely ignored, and when it has been acknowledged at all, this metaphysical, "esoteric science" has been dismissed outright as being of dubious worth, likely dangerous, and not worth investigating.

By contrast, modern science has rigorously confined its focus almost exclusively upon repeatable experiments involving measurements in space and time. The assumption that the "real world" of space-time is all that is worth studying has become almost a religious tenet of its own for the material scientist, and the subject areas of metaphysics (religion, mysticism, art, and philosophical speculation) have been, perhaps until very recently, categorically excluded from scientific journals. How did this come about?

One plausible antecedent to the split can be seen in an incident that occurred over two thousand years ago, attributed to a Greek librarian in the attempt to organize the thousands of document scrolls being stored within the first public library. To differentiate the subjects of physics (geometry and physical sciences) from all others, this early Greek public servant coined the word *metaphysics*; *μετά* or *meta* meaning "beyond," "upon," or "after," which simply means to separate any material other than geometry of physical science to a location "after physics" on the library shelves.

Modern science seems to jealously guard this ancient Greek librarian's delineation. But this split between physics and metaphysics has grown so deep and so sharp in its mutual exclusion that opportunities for better understanding (and operating within) the cosmos have been obscured through this artificial, often tacit, segregation. It is time to seek correspondences between modern physics and metaphysics to effect a reconciliation and bring them together to work in synergy.

Tantra as a widespread Indian metaphysical science originated almost four thousand years ago during the Vedic period (c. 1750–500 BCE) and reached prominence in Kashmir in the ninth century CE. Shortly thereafter it spread north into Tibet with Buddhism. Solidly established in both Hindu and Buddhist lineages, Tantra can be examined within a deep historical stream of evolving Indian cultural-religious exploration, and yet, taken out of the religio-cultural context, it can also be viewed as a body of complex, pragmatically effective psychophysical exercises for modifying and expanding consciousness and, as such, it is still quite relevant in the twenty-first century.

It is to this end that this book focuses. We will not attempt to outline a history of Tantra, nor explore the deepest intricacies of the various school of Tantric metaphysics, but instead will show how a psychophysics of Tantra can be established through the interweaving of physics, quantum physics, and metaphysics. In particular we shall, in the spirit of Tantra, weave a web, a tapestry of understanding interlaced with the threads of these radically contrasting fields of study. In so doing we will contrast and combine the current electromagnetic field theory of consciousness with the Tantric theories of vibration—expressed both in traditional Indian and Tibetan teachings—as well as with Western science and metaphysical conjectures. The overriding theme that pervades this book is that all of these disciplines explore the same phenomenon, but from different cultural and academic perspectives. They all offer models and paradigms emerging from widely different historical, cultural, and intellectual perspectives. In our modern world of increasingly interconnected information we might call this methodology Tantric data mining, a methodology from which we may build a new psychophysics from analysis and correlation in metaphysical observations over a broad spectrum of time, culture, and experience.

Before we begin our deeper exploration of Tantric psychophysics, it is useful to begin with the basic conceptual framework of a geometry of consciousness as presented in the following chapter. This framework provides the structure upon which pieces of the puzzle can be attached as we proceed and establishes a context within which new ideas from multiple traditions can more readily be viewed and understood. To do this we diagram and discuss the basic geometry and cosmology of a universe of consciousness that has been developed by the physicist David Bohm and the philosopher and systems theorist Ervin Laszlo. The model here presented integrates concepts from both physics and consciousness and provides a conceptual model of the reality that will be used as a framework upon which to understand Tantric psychophysics and the dynamics of consciousness. More importantly, this model will help readers to understand how contemplatives are able to develop and utilize their own brain-mind systems to explore these rarified dimensions of awareness.

3

The Psychophysics of the Cosmos

To begin traveling into the heart of Indian Yoga, Tibetan Tantra, metaphysics, and psychophysics, it is important to visualize a unifying contemporary model of consciousness as it manifests in the universe. This map will aid the reader by offering a common framework to visualize and contextualize all of the other psychonautical maps presented in the following chapters. A somewhat abbreviated* visual cosmological map of consciousness in the universe is presented in figure 3.1 on the next page.

The figure presents an ontological model of consciousness based upon the life work of the physicist David Bohm (1916–1992) and the neuroscientist Karl Pribram (1919–2015). Working in tandem for over twenty years, they developed a holoflux[1] theory of consciousness in which the entire universe can be seen to exist as a process of holonomic folding and unfolding of energy-information between two separate regions or domains that together contain all of the dimensions of reality predicted by modern quantum theory.

*See author's *Sub-Quantum Consciousness; The Electromagnetic Brain;* and *Developing Supersensible Perception* for a deeper technical discussion and fuller development of a psychophysics of consciousness as sketched in this chapter.

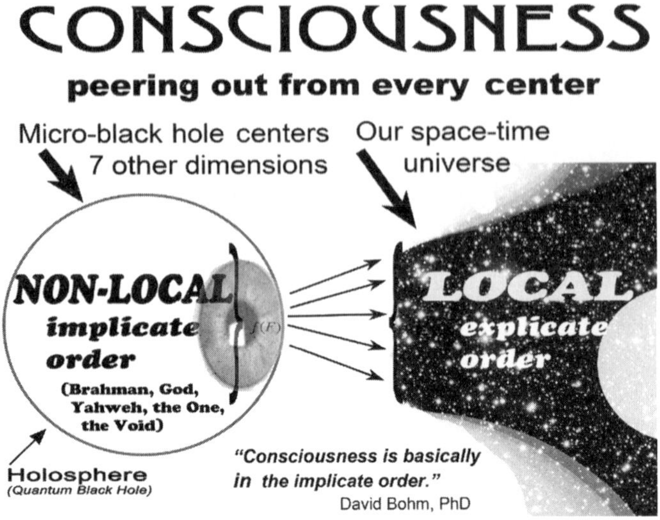

Fig. 3.1. Cosmological map of consciousness projecting the universe.

DAVID BOHM'S TWO DOMAINS: HOW PIXELATED SPACE PROJECTS THE UNIVERSE

David Bohm gave names to the two domains that his mathematics revealed: the *implicate order* and the *explicate order.* These two domains are everywhere—interpenetrating, folding into and out from one another in one continuous cycle. It should be noted that while the region on the left side of fig. 3.1 shows the non-local implicate order to be the locus of what has been termed by various cultures God, Brahman, Yahweh, the One, and the Void, these concepts were never discussed by Bohm or Pribram in their scientific publications. In keeping with the modern scientific paradigm they developed their model using principles of modern physics and neurophysiology while avoiding any philosophical or metaphysical speculation.

This same relationship can be seen mirrored in the Chinese Taoist yin-yang symbol (fig. 3.2), discussed as early as 3,500 years ago in the *I Ching* or *Book of Changes.* The yin-yang symbol represents the universe as consisting of two distinct yet interpenetrating domains (*yin* being the creative dark, passive, female domain, and *yang* the light, active, male domain). The symbol shows the two domains cyclically

Fig. 3.2. Yin-yang symbol showing cyclical enfoldment/unfoldment.

folding into and out from one another, and yet the dots within the heart of each region imply that at they are also the source and origin of one another.

In developing his model of the implicate and explicate orders, Bohm's overriding motive was to visualize his conception of the ontological reality of a universe that had recently been mapped by Albert Einstein's application of advanced mathematics. Bohm's work of thirty years led up to the 1980 publication of his book, *Wholeness and the Implicate Order,* which presented his perceptive model of the cosmological reality/ontology of the universe as existing in two interpenetrating domains of continually transforming energy-consciousness.

Thus, the space-time explicate order returns (the Latin *implicare* means "to fold inward") information from our observable space-time universe into the implicate order. Having entered the implicate order, none of the information is lost. It is stored within the timeless, spaceless eternity of the implicate order.

Another feature of Bohm's hypothesis is that the implicate order manifests throughout space-time as a plenum (fig. 3.3, p. 26). This plenum, an expanding sphere of close-packed micro black holes, forms the bedrock of the space-time cosmos. This three-dimensional array of tiny "points" acts much like pixels on our digital display screens, but instead of projecting a flat colorful image, the universe uses these "3D pixels" to project the entire universe into space and time.

This pixelated conception of the universe is not completely new.

Fig. 3.3. The plenum consists of an expanding sphere.
Copyright J. R. Bale, Balefire Communications.

As early as the fifth century BCE, the concept of the plenum had been discussed among Greek philosophers, and extensively written about by Democritus in the fourth century BCE. In the seventeenth century CE, the concept of the plenum* was revived once again by the French philosopher, mathematician, and scientist René Descartes (1596–1650). Descartes believed that there are no spaces that are empty, but that there exists a plenum at the bottom of space upon which the rest of the universe rests.

David Bohm posited the existence of an implicate order outside of, yet distributed throughout, the space-time dimensions as a plenum at

*From the Latin, meaning "full space," from a root that means "full," "greatly crowded."

the very smallest dimensions possible, according to quantum mechanics and the speed of light. The most widely accepted theory among quantum physicists is that there is a limit to the dimension we call space. Bohm used such quantum theoretical considerations to point out a fallacy still held by many, the classical Cartesian assumption that space is continuous:

> What of the order between two points in space? The Cartesian order holds that space is continuous. Between any two points, no matter how close they lie, occur an infinity of other points. Between any two neighboring points in this infinity lies another infinity and so on. This notion of continuity is not compatible with the order of quantum theory. . . . Thus the physicist John Wheeler has suggested that, at very short distances, continuous space begins to break up into a foam-like structure. Thus the "order between" two points moves from the order of continuity to an order of a discontinuous foam.[2]

According to Bohm, at the ultimate bottom level of these subdivided infinities, between two points in space, like an end-of-stop bumper terminating a railroad track, will be found a cosmologically fixed boundary at the Planck length of 10^{-33} cm, beyond which no further subdivision is meaningfully possible. It is here, at this smallest of possible spatial coordinates, that we encounter the origin of the dimension of space that finds its maximum in the diameter of the currently expanding universe (the bandwidth continually increases, at the speed of light).

Viewed another way, to use the depths of the ocean as an analog or metaphor, Bohm's sub-quantum mechanics can be viewed as being at the bottom of a dimensional ocean with a floor significantly below the depths of the region mapped and explored by the mathematics of quantum mechanics (fig. 3.4, p. 28). In the diagram, the scalar region above this "ocean floor" lies within the explicate order of space-time, while the region below the Planck length of 10^{-33} cm lies within the mysterious implicate order.

The Pribram-Bohm holoflux theory of consciousness goes further, telling us that at the bottom of space, at the smallest possible scalar dimensions possible, there exists a plenum of micro black holes.[3] These

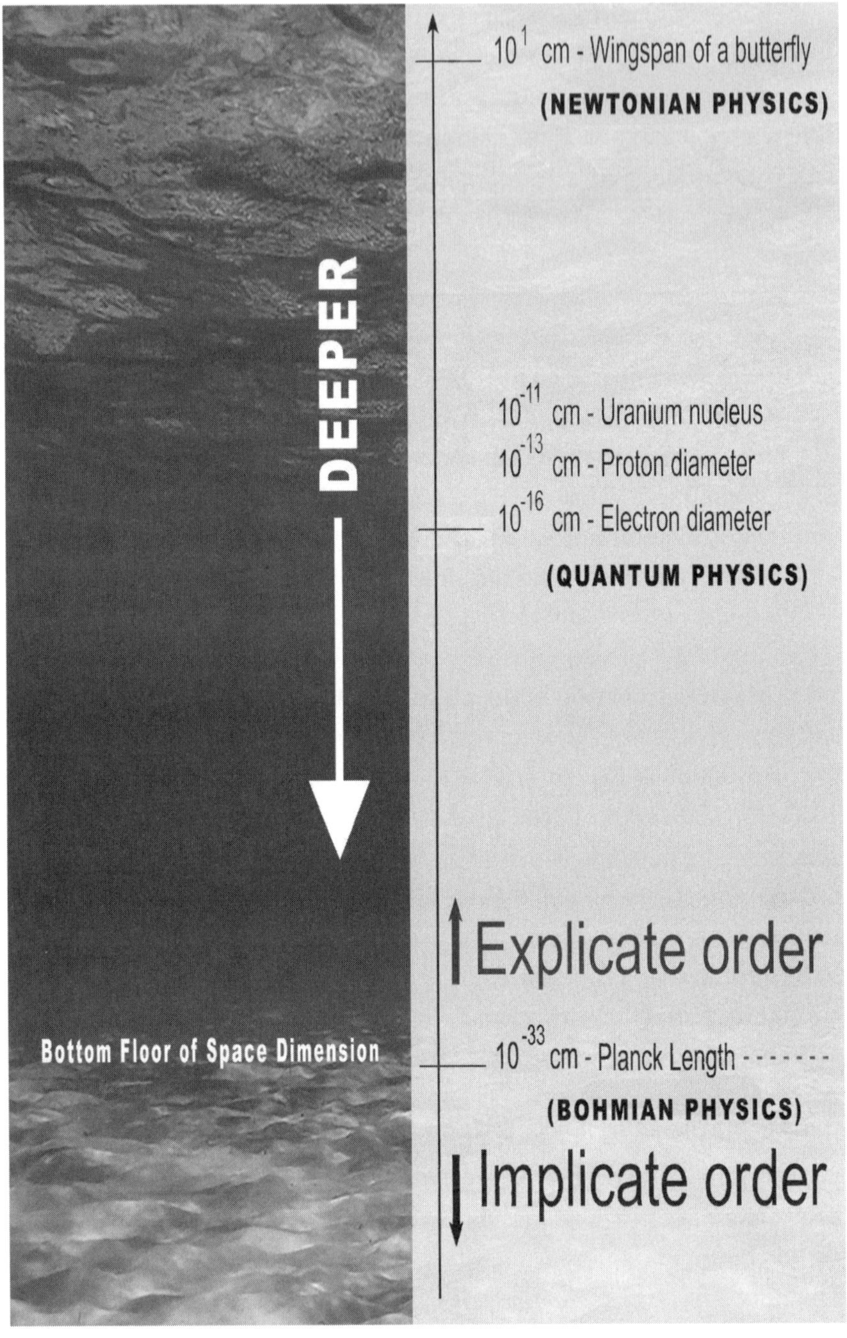

Fig. 3.4. Sub-quantum ocean-floor metaphor.

micro black holes, or holospheres, are bounded by spherical shells, each having diameters of 10^{-33} cm, the Planck length, a length below which, according to Einstein's mathematics, space has no meaning. Below this spherical boundary and "within" these micro black holes is Bohm's implicate order, the region where there is no space or time as we know them (and, as will be discussed in later chapters, the objective of advanced contemplative psychonautic exploration).

However, according to Bohm, "consciousness *is in* the implicate order," (emphasis added), and thus each one of these innumerable close-packed holospheres can be viewed as a somewhat separate conscious entity—perhaps identical with the fundamental entities of consciousness or "actual entities" discussed by the mathematician and philosopher Alfred North Whitehead (1861–1947)—looking out from a plenum of actual-entity holospheres existing at the very bedrock bottom of three-dimensional space.

In this cosmology the universe is spherical, and this particular phase of space-time (perhaps there are myriad others?) began from a point of singularity: a single Planck diameter holosphere or micro black hole, breaking out from what Bohm calls the "implicate order," and thus dividing the totality of the universe into two domains.

This breakout into space-time enlarges quantumly (by leaps of one Planck length between shells) in a continuing expansion of shell formation moving outward at the speed of light. Thus, the most extreme bound of this universe can be considered the outermost shell. This can be visualized as myriad shells much like those of nested Russian dolls, with each shell separated by exactly one Planck length. The moment a shell begins to manifest in space-time, it immediately ceases expanding due to the fact that nothing in space can exist smaller than a single Planck length. Accordingly, these infinitely thin shells of energy become individual event horizons sandwiched between the implicate order and the space-time universe. The "turbulence" on the surface of each shell can manifest encoded information as predicted by the Bekenstein Bound.* Thus these shells contain a summary of all information within their bounded regions.

---

*Jacob Bekenstein calculated the maximum amount of information that can be stored in a finite region of space and found that it could be encoded on the surface of a sphere bounding the spatial region.

The key here is that the centers of new micro black holes are generated on each shell surface, and so new "centers of the universe" are continually spawned at the boundary of each shell. Thus, a virtually infinite plethora of shells are being generated, and all of these shells' centers can be considered "the center of the universe," as well as "centers of consciousness," absolute entities looking outward into space-time. So it is not simply "one big bang" that created the universe at some mythological beginning, but a continuous big bang of innumerable tiny holospheres that project their own system of concentric shells out into the space-time universe.

Each of these shells intersect with one another to project the holographic displays of what we call "objects" that are seen by us with our space-time sensory systems. Thus we do not directly see the holographic patterns that are unfolding, but we do see them as "things" such as butterflies and zebras! In this Pribram-Bohm model of the universe we see a dynamic process. Information flows *out* of space-time and *into* the implicate order, while simultaneously energy in shells of information are projected *out from within* the implicate order to create what we see as images and objects with our space-time eyes.

AKASHA AND THE HOLOFIELD THEORY OF ERVIN LASZLO

In full support of David Bohm's implicate/explicate schema is the holofield theory of Ervin Laszlo, who, like Bohm, describes the universe as consisting of two domains. Laszlo, using different terms, divides the universe into an "M-dimension" ("M" for "Material") and a nonspatial, nontemporal information field he calls the "A-dimension" or "Akasha."[4] A graduate of the Sorbonne and a professor of philosophy, systems sciences, and future studies, Laszlo had been twice nominated for the Nobel Peace Prize; he writes of the universe, including human beings, appearing to be "nonlocally" coherent, part of a unified field of consciousness.[5]

In agreement with John Archibald Wheeler, who held that information is even more fundamental to the universe than energy, Laszlo describes the "information field," which he also calls the "A-field," as lying outside of space-time and yet interacting dynamically with material manifesting in space and time.[6] In reference to this A-field, or A-dimension, Laszlo frequently uses the term *Akasha,* referencing the Sanskrit word *ākāśa,* described in Vedic texts in India as early as 5,000 BCE, in which Akasha is closely associated with vibration.[7] In the Vedas its function is identified with *shabda,* the first vibration, the first ripple beginning our universe, and also with *spanda,* which has been described as "vibration/movement of consciousness."[8] The Akasha has been visualized by the Indian professor of inorganic chemistry I. K. Taimni as a sort of space out of which integrated energy vibrations emanate (much as Bohm's holoflux emanates from out of the implicate order and projects holographic "objects" as the holoflux modulates the pixelated plenum in space-time). Taimni writes:

> There is . . . a mysterious integrated state of vibration from which all possible kinds of vibrations can be derived by a process of differentiation. That is called *Nāda* in Sanskrit. It is a vibration in a medium called Ākāśa which may be translated as "space" in English. But the conception of Ākāśa . . . is quite different from that of Science. It is not mere empty space but space which, though apparently empty, contains within itself an infinite amount of potential energy. . . . This infinite potentiality for producing vibrations of different kinds in any intensity or amount is due to the fact that at the back of Ākāśa or hidden within it, is consciousness.[9]

In Laszlo's cosmology, the universe is the interaction of two dimensions, an "A-dimension" and an "M-dimension." The M-dimension contains that which manifests (i.e., the cosmos, the galaxies in space-time), and is that upon which material science has been primarily focused. The M-dimension can be seen as congruent with David Bohm's explicate order. Laszlo's other dimension is the A-dimension, his Akashic dimension outside of space-time, which can be identified with Bohm's implicate, enfolded order.[10] According to Laszlo, there is continual two-way interaction between the A-dimension and the M-dimension. In a cybernetic cycle, the A-dimension provides the blueprint for manifesting changes occurring in the timespace M-dimension, while information recording these changes flows back to and are recorded in the nontemporal vibrations of the A-dimension.[11]

Laszlo also puts forth in his theory that the A-field is the quantum vacuum itself, that the field is the fundamental energy and information-carrying field, interconnecting all things in and between all dimensions, nonlocally, in a multiverse. And Laszlo further describes the A-field, which he says is currently unknown to physics, as being a "vacuum-based holofield."[12] But Laszlo again declares, as did Bohm, that any such posited field must be firmly rooted in what science already knows about the nature of physical reality:

> The concept of such a field cannot be an ad hoc postulate, nor can it be an extra-scientific hypothesis. It must be rooted in what science already knows about the nature of physical reality. . . . We assume that the interaction of such a field with quanta and quanta-based systems—atoms, molecules, cells, organisms, ecologies, and systems even of cosmological dimension—produces nonlocal interaction within and among them.[13]

Unfortunately, while Laszlo states clearly that his concept must be rooted in science, he provides no clear connection between the A-field and the tenets of modern science, neither through mathematics nor physics, and this leaves his theory incomplete.

Nevertheless, Laszlo's intuited metaphor of the A-field being some sort of "blueprint" can be used to explain why evolution is not a random process. If we assume that through some mechanism the arc of the creating cosmos is guided by information stored in the A-field, then all of the "fine-tuned constants" discovered in our universe, and marveled at by cosmologists, might be more readily explained. If we assume that the A-field contains (and shares) information from billions upon billions of experimental attempts, in previously evolving space-time universes, to create new forms (new forms of particles, new forms of galaxies, new forms of matter, life, and consciousness), then it is the influx of this information collapsing from the A-field into the M-field that produces the exquisitely tuned constants that are enjoyed in the structure of our particular universe. Such a viewpoint accords well with the recent ideas of the theoretical physicist Lee Smolin, that "for cosmology to progress, physics must abandon the idea that laws are timeless and eternal and embrace instead the idea that even they evolve in real time."[14]

Laszlo's theory brilliantly points the way towards a truly new paradigm for material science and future research directions, but it is unfortunate that his use of the Vedic term *ākāśa* and the Theosophist term "Akashic record" serves only to undermine his theory among the scientific community. His occasional use of the terms "spiritual" and "yoga" in his essays would seem also to limit the dissemination of his work within a broader scientific community, as seen here:

> Our bodily senses do not register Akasha, but we can reach it through spiritual practice. The ancient Rishis reached it through a disciplined, spiritual way of life, and through yoga.[15]

The "Akashic record" is a phrase coined and widely used by Theosophists in the mid-nineteenth century, in particular by Alice Bailey, in discussing Patañjali's *Yoga Sutras,* "The ākāshic record is like an immense photographic film, registering all the desires and earth experiences of our planet."[16]

Laszlo's theories find a great deal of support in these writings and traditions outside of the scientific field of inquiry, based as they are upon participatory, experiential data, which is not normally of interest in the material sciences. He is not averse to discussing such participatory experience of his own, and using it to extend his theory:

> When we enter an altered state of consciousness images, ideas, and intuitions flow into our consciousness that transcend the range of our sensory perceptions. These elements are part of the totality of the information in the cosmic matrix: The Akasha. This information is in a distributed form, as in a hologram.[17]

The idea of information distributed as a hologram accords well with Karl Pribram's research-based speculation on holographic memory processes; and, in the following passage, Laszlo's insistence on the importance of the need for understanding the whole, rather than exclusively separate parts, reminds us of David Bohm's explicate "whole," connected everywhere by the implicate order:

> The crucial feature of the emerging view is space and time transcending correlation. Space and time do not separate things. They connect things . . . information is conserved and conveyed in nature at all scales of magnitude and in all domains.[18]

Laszlo refers to the Akasha field as a "fifth dimension," and points out that it was seen in ancient culture, much as Bohm views the implicate order, to be the foundational basis of the cosmos:

> The *rishis* (seers) of India viewed the deep dimension as the fifth and most fundamental element in the cosmos; they called it by the Sanskrit term *Akasha.*[19]

Laszlo's A-field hypothesis indicates that a shift in the material science approach to consciousness is occurring, and a new paradigm may be emerging:

> It is a paradigm where information rather than matter is seen as the basic reality, and where space and time, and the entities that emerge and evolve in space and time, are manifestations of a deeper reality beyond space and time.[20]

This deeper reality is said to be consciousness itself. Stephan A. Schwartz, executive director of the Rhine Research Center, put it succinctly when he wrote:

> Max Planck was correct when he said, "Consciousness is the fundamental." Spacetime emerges from consciousness, not consciousness from spacetime. I think spacetime is informational in nature and the product of intentioned consciousness creating informational architectures. We do not know what information is. The aspect of consciousness we think of as nonlocal is not physiologically based. It exists before we are born and continues after corporeal death.[21]

Another consciousness researcher is Dean Radin, chief scientist at the Institute of Noetic Science. Dean was on my dissertation committee several years ago, and, like myself, he was also initially trained as an electrical engineer (Dean earned his B.S. degree magna cum laude with honors in physics and went on to earn an M.S. in electrical engineering and a Ph.D. in psychology). Dean is quite clear here in his own description of consciousness:

> There's ultimately just one "substance" underlying reality. Historically that substance has been called Spirit, Advaita, Brahman, Tao, Nirvana, Source, Yahweh, God, and many other names. In recent times, to avoid religious connotations, the more neutral term *consciousness* is often used. By consciousness, I mean *awareness*—that which allows us to enjoy subjective experience.[22]

We have gone rather deeply in this chapter into cutting-edge theories in the physics of consciousness in order to lay the groundwork for an integral understanding of Tantric psychophysics. The primary assumption underlying all of these theories is that of panpsychism, the assertion that consciousness is primary in the universe and that consciousness "predates" and is the source of matter, space, and time. As our goal in this book is an effort to reconcile science and mysticism, physics and metaphysics, we next turn to several maps of consciousness that have arisen in Western culture, emerging primarily from the Judeo-Christian cultures of Europe. Subsequent chapters will explore traditional knowledge that has evolved from the efforts of countless contemplatives in Tibet and India over the past several thousand years. Each section will attempt to scientifically validate the wealth of experiential knowledge handed down to us by generations of contemplative explorers.

PART TWO

Western Tantric Psychophysics

4

On Christian Contemplation

That They May All Be One

In all major religions the predominant practice is that of following a prescribed liturgy on a regular basis. Individuals are taught to recite private daily prayers, and members congregate on a regular basis for group prayer. Each religion has its own language, prayers, rituals, and traditions, all primarily products of the particular culture from which it sprang, and each changing and evolving over time. But there are certain esoteric, nonpublic elements that can be found in each religion, special prayers and private practices that generally find interest only among priests, monks, hermits and the passionate few who are drawn to cultivate and explore deeper spiritual experiences than public prayer invokes. These private practices generally involve meditation (discursive cognitive focus upon prayer material) or contemplation (efforts to experience deeper states of consciousness). It is from these passionate few individuals, and their experiences of these deeper practices, that the mystical traditions of each particular religion arise. Christianity is no exception—there is a deep tradition of contemplation among Christian monks and hermits, and many Christian mystics have left written records of their experiences in support of their unique understanding of the cosmology of consciousness. In this part of the book, we explore the "Tantric elements" or the "mystical soul" of Christianity to discover traditional material that might be supportive of a new science of psychophysics.

At first glance the phrase "Christian Tantra" appears oxymoronic. However, the focus here is not on some kind of Tantric cult. Rather, the word *Tantric* is used here in the sense of "practical," "effective," "esoteric," or simply to connote "metaphysical Christianity." The focus of this chapter is the subject of Christian contemplative theory and practice.

The Latin word *contemplation* (from the root *templum* or "sacred place") was first used by Roman writers to translate the Greek word *θεωρία* (*theoria*). A dictionary definition of the word *contemplation* offers the following: "serious and quiet thought for a period of time."[1] In the Christian West during the Middle Ages, contemplation was often described as "gazing with love upon God," "the experience of union with God," or "a state of mystical awareness of God's being."[2]

As mentioned previously, with the East-West convergence of traditions and cultures, the term *contemplation* can now be understood not merely as a traditional method of Christian prayer, but more specifically as an introspective approach to a highly complex participatory experience that can be described variously as "non-ordinary awareness," "non-dualism," or "non-dual consciousness."

Contemplation has come to be seen as a wide range of practices for exploring other dimensions of consciousness through a variety of means. The oceanic dimensions of consciousness itself have become the "final frontier," and those who venture to sail into the strange, sometimes terrifying, and often overwhelming oceans of consciousness are called contemplatives, mystics, saints, or psychonauts. In a more secular context contemplation can be understood as the art and practice of discovering and exercising various faculties as necessary to arrive at a rich, direct, "non-dual" experience of the outer self with the vast inner self (Carl Jung's concept of the higher "Self") in contrast with the normal waking state, which has been called the "little ego-separated self."[3] In earlier cultures, contemplative techniques were the explicit domain of the monk or shaman, often in eremitical settings of silent forest or cave, far from the noise and bustle of village and city.

Unfortunately, the value of pursuing or even teaching the more contemplative dimensions of the religious experience seem to have been lost or discarded by modern Christian cultures. My own introduction to contemplation began fairly late in life, even though my religious instruction began when I was six years old, in a convent school near

London. We were required to study what is called "the catechism," a collection of fundamental Christian truths, according to the Roman Catholic Church, in question-and-answer format. This catechism was published by Cardinal Bellarmine, an Italian Jesuit priest, in 1597, and it consisted of a series of questions and answers children and catechumens were asked to memorize. I still clearly recall the struggle to memorize the following:

Question: *Who made you?*

Answer: God made me.

Question: *Why did God make you?*

Answer: God made me to know, love, and serve Him in this world, and to be happy with Him forever in the next.

Unfortunately the catechism taught us nothing about any actual approaches to prayer, contemplation, or meditation. In fact, I cannot recall ever hearing the words *contemplation* or *meditation* until well into my twenties. As children we simply learned that "to pray" encompassed the recitation of memorized prayers, aloud or silently, alone or in a group. To pray well was somehow to recite these prayers with what the nuns called "feeling" or "devotion." Years later, entering college to study science and engineering, I still had no concept of Christian mysticism, meditation, or contemplation.

Strangely enough, it was not the nuns or priests, but Dr. John Lilly, a medical doctor and researcher from Stanford, who first introduced me to the concept of contemplation and various techniques one might use for the experiential exploration of consciousness. In 1970, during my second year in New York, I came across an advertisement for a lecture to be given by Dr. Lilly on *programming and metaprogramming the human bio-computer,* which was also the title of a book he was about to publish.

Intrigued by the topic, I attended the lecture, which was presented to an audience of twenty or so in a small hotel room near Carnegie Hall on Fifty-Sixth Street. His talk made an enormous impression on me, perhaps because I had been so recently immersed in studying computer languages, electromagnetic theories, and exploring firsthand the effects of psychotropic substances upon my own consciousness. His talk involved all three topics each of which he viewed as central to several years of research that he had conducted in "interspecies communication." His theory was that the brain operates as a biocomputer, and that an individual can learn to program and reprogram the operations of the brain, and thus consciousness itself, through the practice of silent contemplative techniques in a soundproof, lightproof environment. Lilly's supposition that the brain can be "reprogrammed" is very much in accord with the currently accepted concept of neuroplasticity.*

In the late 1950s, Lilly had established a research center called the Communications Research Institute on St. Thomas in the U.S. Virgin Islands. There he conducted a series of experiments, condoned and financially supported by the National Institute of Mental Health. The experiments involved administering clinically pure LSD-25 to dolphins and their trainers and recording their audible and subaudible interactions as they floated in large indoor pools of water.[4]

Lilly's extensive knowledge of electronics and software made his ideas all the more fascinating, even more so when I discovered that, like myself, he had also become a licensed ham radio operator at an early age. His obvious enthusiasm for exploring the psyche in every way possible, through science as well as by direct introspective experience, was contagious. I was particularly encouraged by his assertion that individuals with backgrounds in physics and electronics, having developed the capacity to focus for extended periods upon abstract concepts, would find considerable success in applying the esoteric techniques of contemplation. In the future, he said, scientists will fill the ranks of a new generation of mystics.

In 1970, shortly after meeting Lilly, I began my first attempts to practice meditation and contemplation, guided mostly by what I was able to find in my books on Taoism, Buddhism, and Hinduism. I also attended the occasional lecture by Swami Satchidananda at his Integral

---

**Neuroplasticity,* also known as neural plasticity, or brain plasticity, is the ability of neural networks in the brain to change through growth and reorganization. These changes range from individual neurons making new connections, to systematic adjustments like cortical remapping.

Yoga Institute in Lower Manhattan, or weekend *satsangs* (spiritual talks) held by Chögyam Trungpa Rinpoche, a Tibetan Vajrayāna teacher who often visited New York City to give talks at the Cathedral of Saint John the Divine. For several years I followed and studied with Trungpa But during that time, I had no idea that there might also be a Christian dimension to contemplative practice.

Many years later, living in Saudi Arabia and trying to introduce my young son and daughter to their Christian heritage, I discovered, almost by accident, books written by Christian saints describing their own experiences of meditation, contemplative states, and "interior prayer." Among the works I found in the company library were *The Cloud of Unknowing,* the *Interior Castle* by Saint Teresa of Ávila, the *Dark Night of the Soul* by the Spanish priest known as Saint John of the Cross and especially his amazing poem, "En Una Noche Oscura," which describes the mystical journey of contemplation. I later learned that an early president of the oil company ARAMCO had been a Roman Catholic, and while Islam is the only religious practice legally allowed in Saudi Arabia, he had been able to circumvent the prohibition within the American-run compound in eastern Saudi Arabia.

To my amazement, the fourteenth-century text of *The Cloud of Unknowing* sounded much like the Asian writings on contemplative practices that I had devoured regularly years earlier. I soon found other Christian contemplative works, and was particularly surprised by a collection of four volumes called the *Philokalia,* written between the fourth and fifteenth centuries CE, consisting of essays for the guidance and instruction of monks in the art and practice of contemplation.*

For years I had felt like an "outsider," a contemplative without roots or tradition. Instead of being deeply focused within a single tradition (that of my ancestors), my private contemplative practice incorporated prayers from Christianity, Hinduism, and Buddhism, and I was guided by a mixture of teachings from Chinese, Japanese, and Tibetan sources. My spiritual life was thus "all over the

*The *Philokalia* is a collection of essays written between the fourth and fifteenth centuries by contemplative masters of the Orthodox Christian tradition and first published in Venice in 1782.

map," and I seldom discussed these topics with strangers, or even close family, yet I continued my daily silent contemplative period.

But it wasn't until 1990 that I made my first silent monastic retreat at a Christian monastery. While living with my family in the eastern desert of Saudi Arabia I had read Thomas Merton's autobiographical masterpiece, *The Seven Storey Mountain,* and immediately wanted to experience an extended silent contemplative retreat with monks. I contacted a Franciscan priest who recommended the Benedictine monastery of New Camaldoli on the Big Sur coast of California, and I soon made arrangements to leave my family for a week of silent prayer and meditation.

During the second day of my retreat I wandered into the small bookstore run by the monks for retreatants. To my absolute astonishment, here, in a Catholic monastery bookstore, were books on yoga, contemplation, and Asian religions, all subjects I had assumed would be taboo in such a deeply traditional Roman Catholic environment. It was a cathartic moment for me. Suddenly I felt much less isolated in my own enthusiasm for contemplation. On the shelf above the books on yoga I noticed a section on Russian Orthodox mysticism, and a four-book set of the *Philokalia* translated into English from the Russian and Greek. Suddenly I felt at home!

The next year, shortly after living through the Gulf War with my family in Saudi Arabia, I was able to visit the mother house of this particular Benedictine order, the Camaldolese, near Arezzo in Tuscany. There I had a moving experience while visiting the small cell of the founder of the order, Saint Romuald, in the chapel where he prayed. In 1992 I was accepted as a Benedictine oblate of the Camaldolese, vowing to practice prayer and contemplation every day for the rest of my life, and to visit one of their monasteries for retreat from time to time. A year later I found myself traveling to southern India for a long retreat with Father Bede Griffiths, a Camaldolese priest and monk originally from Great Britain, who presided over a Catholic-Hindu retreat center known as the Shantivanam on the banks of the Kaveri River, known as the "Ganges of the South," and especially sacred to Hindus.

During my week-long retreat at Shantivanam (which means "Forest of Peace"), I spent a great deal of time with Father Bede Griffiths, who presided over this Christian "ashram," originally founded in 1938 by a French priest, Jules Monchanin. There I was also able to live out my fantasy of sitting on my blanket on the banks of a holy river in India, practicing silent contemplation during the periods of dawn and dusk. All along the riverbank can be found small temples dedicated to God and the holy spirit of the Kaveri River, the source of water for much of the often-parched lands of South India. At dusk the silence was broken only by a strange slap, slap, slap sound which I soon discovered was made by local Indian women doing their daily washing by slapping their cotton saris on the water surface before hanging them on the bushes along the river to dry.

Father Bede Griffiths wrote extensively on contemplation, Eastern mysticism, and Christian faith. Educated at Oxford, the British-born priest left England in 1955 to spend the next forty years in India pioneering a Christian monastic presence in India that incorporated the customs of a Hindu ashram within a Benedictine Christian contemplative context. He welcomed people of different religious traditions to join him at Shantivanam, encouraging them to meet together in a monastic setting along the most sacred river in Tamil Nadu.

With his deep background in both Western theology and Indian metaphysics Father Bede Griffiths bridges both East/West and science/mysticism in his writing. In his book *A New Vision of Reality: Western Science, Eastern Mysticism and Christian Faith,* Father Bede Griffiths tells us that we use the names in the Trinity "to point to a reality which is beyond everything we can describe," and explains that:

> The spirit of man is a capacity for God. It is not God. My *atman,* myself, is not God, but rather it is a capacity for God which can be filled by God and can be transformed into God and this is a gift of pure grace.[5]

Father Bede Griffiths was a great proponent of ecumenism, an approach not fully appreciated by the local Catholic bishop who, though of Indian ancestry, did not readily approve of the ecumenical, transcultural approach to liturgy at Shantivanam, where elements of

Hindu symbolism, including traditional hymns to the Trinity in the Tamil language, were regularly incorporated into the Roman Catholic mass. Fortunately, the bishop was not in a position to censure what transpired at Shantivanam, as monks in the Catholic church are relatively free from local ecclesiastical authority. Father Bede Griffiths himself was actively interested in respecting and encouraging local Indian cultural traditions and sought to foster a healthy East/West dialogue. Here he explains his own view of ecumenism:

> In genuine dialogue we open ourselves to one another while being perfectly true to our own faith, our own religion, our own understanding—but at the same time open to the understanding of the faith, the religion of the other. Then growth can take place. This I feel is the task for humanity in the future.[6]

Another common theme in his writing is the discussion of nondualism, or *advaita* in Sanskrit. He felt that traditional Hindu metaphysical approaches to the Trinity offered rich possibilities for deepening Christian theological understanding:

> Every human being has the power to go beyond himself and to open to what is called the holy mystery. In the Hindu experience you go beyond your ego, your empirical self, the self by which you normally act, you touch the true Self which is the pure subjectivity beyond. . . . What I am suggesting is that in each tradition there is an experience of transcendent reality, of the transcendent mystery, which is interpreted in terms of non-duality. It has different expressions in each tradition but basically they are the same. . . . I seriously feel that this is the philosophy of the future and that we ought to be able to see how we can build our theology around this basic principle.[7]

REALITY AND THE TRINITY

Do we find a recurring trinitarian structure in major religions? Why do we find this view of three co-equally balanced elements as the basis of so many metaphysical world views? According to the renowned scholar of comparative religion Raimon Panikkar, "My surmise is that it is *reality itself* that discloses itself as Trinity—at least to me, and I am inclined to add to Christians and to an immense number of people seriously concerned with the problem of the Divine."[8]

The concept of a "Divine Trinity" as the matrix and sustainer of all reality is not exclusive to Christianity but can be found as one of the expressions and visions of an organizing structure to the manifest universe as recorded in some of the most ancient cultural records in existence. In India, the *Atharvaveda,* emerging at the end of the second millennium BCE, speaks of Agni, the King of the Gods, as "one energy whose process is threefold."[9] And in ancient Egypt, reference to the Trinity is explicit: "All gods are three: Amun, Re and Ptah, whom none equals. He who hides his name as Amun, he appears to the face as Re, his body is Ptah."[10] Only much later, during the Puranic period (c. 300–1200), arose the concept of the Trimurti, the widespread acceptance in India of the manifestation of the supreme God in three forms of Brahma, Vishnu, and Shiva.

The early Christian acceptance of God as Trinity is documented in the Nicene Creed still recited by most Christians. The wording of the creed was agreed upon during the First Ecumenical Council of Christianity held in 325 CE, one year after the transfer of the Roman Empire's government from Rome to the ancient Greek outpost of Byzantium on the Bosphorus Strait that now separates Europe from Asia. Panikkar, whose mother was Roman Catholic and father was Hindu Indian, is clear that "the symbol of the Trinity is not a Christian monopoly, but in fact is common in many other traditions."[11] If, as Panikkar says, this is "reality itself that discloses itself as Trinity," then we should be able to find this same Trinity disclosing itself in the realms of modern science.[12]

CHRISTIAN NON-DUALITY AND SAPIENTIAL WISDOM

Another Camaldolese Benedictine philosopher-monk, and a close friend of Father Bede Griffiths, was the American priest Father Bruno Barnhart (1931–2015). Trained as a chemist, Bruno Barnhart entered the remote monastery of the Sacred Heart Hermitage (also called New Camaldoli) in California at the age of twenty-nine. In his published writings, Barnhart suggests that Western Christianity has been living "in a sapiential vacuum" since the Renaissance and Enlightenment, in which the participative and unitive modes of consciousness have largely contracted to be replaced by the dominant rational-analytical approach. As a result, Western monasticism has become increasingly involved in pastoral, cultural, and educational activities, rather than in solitude, silence, and contemplative prayer. By contrast, he points out, Eastern Orthodox Christian churches have continued to focus on "a spirituality of interiority, of separation from the world, of asceticism and the quest for continual prayer."[13]

Barnhart calls for Western Christian churches to consider a new emphasis on "wisdom" which he terms "sapiential theology," and he views wisdom here as a form of participative consciousness, a *knowing* that surmounts the duality of subject and object. At the heart of this approach is what he called *non-duality* (the unitive principle which Indians would call *advaita*), that he points out is clearly expressed in the Gospel of John, where in the following passage (John 17:21–23, King James Version) Jesus states the reason for which he is praying:

> That they may all be one; even as you, Father, are in me and I in you, that they also may be in us, so that the world may believe that you have sent me. The glory that you have given me I have given to them, that they may be one even as we are one, I in them and you in me, that they may become perfectly one.[14]

Here, according to Barnhart, the central theological principle of *divinization* emerges, and it is in this mystery of the *incarnation* that the non-dual Absolute becomes present in humanity in a new way. Barnhart sees the multiple streams of Asian influence helpful to remind us of the importance of the efficacy of the practice of "contemplation, understood as non-dual consciousness and experience." He tells us that while faith itself is a dark unitive knowledge, faith itself can lead to the beginning of contemplation, which he has found to be a "direct experience of the ground of consciousness, of a depth from which we may live continually."[15] Barnhart affirms that, from the non-dual center outward, contemplation reveals the experience of a progressive *emergence of a person who is participating in a divine incarnation,* both individually and collectively. The problem of contemporary Western culture is that the individual and collective incarnation has not yet integrated.

> It is obvious today that the individual and collective progressions are not yet integrated. In the extreme individualism of the West—and the many-sided fragmentation of the modern Western world—we see an emergence of the individual person which has not yet been balanced by a growth of the collective person.[16]

Barnhart tells us that an antidote to this problem may be found through the contemplative cultivation of what is referred to, in Orthodox Christianity as well as in Roman Catholicism, as *purity of heart*, where the term *heart* is conceived of "as the central point or axis of the person where body, psyche, mind, and spirit are present together," and he goes further, providing a concise definition of contemplation:

> Contemplation is a direct experience of the ground of consciousness, of a depth from which we may live continually.[17]

Barnhart's direct experiential approach to this "central point or axis" clearly mirrors the vision of Pierre Teilhard de Chardin (1881–1955), another contemplative scientist-priest whose written ideas ranged beyond the conventional bounds of his religion.*

Teilhard de Chardin's concept of the Omega Point is congruent with Barnhart's "central point or axis" and is a major element in Teilhard's own "hyperphysics of consciousness," a rich and many-faceted geometry and dynamics of what he saw as an energy of consciousness

*Both were Catholic priests, however, Teilhard, whose written works on theology and consciousness were banned by the Church during his lifetime, was in the Jesuit order, while Barnhart was a monk in the Camaldolese order, an eremitical or "hermit" order somewhat more liberal in its East/West approach to ecumenical theology than the Jesuits.

that is constantly evolving as it approaches a culminating union in the Omega Point, a point of transformation at the center, everywhere, at the bottom of space.

While both of these Christian priests shared backgrounds of having been immersed in principles of science (Barnhart earned degrees in chemistry; Teilhard completed degrees in geology and paleontology), they also shared a common courage and passion for exploring ideas that often lay beyond the bounds of their own religion's theological dogma. In addition they were both practiced contemplatives whose writings reflect their own direct experience over many decades of prayer and introspection within deeply Catholic traditions. Considering that their published works reveal a cross-cultural focus upon the evolutionary transformation of consciousness, they can both be considered members of that rare group of Western thinkers who have contributed significantly to the advancement of psychophysics.

5

Pierre Teilhard de Chardin

Noosphere

> *In spite of all the theoretical objections that would seek to discourage the belief, our minds remain invincibly persuaded that a certain very simple fundamental rule lies hidden beneath the overpowering multiplicity of events and beings: to discover and formulate this rule, we believe, would make the universe intelligible in the totality of its development.*
>
> Pierre Teilhard de Chardin, "Centrology"

Marie Joseph Pierre Teilhard de Chardin* (1881–1955) was a rare combination of scientist, priest, and mystic whose profound legacy is revealed in his voluminous essays that, taken together, lay the foundation for a new science of spirit, a hyperphysics that maps and sheds light upon the dynamics of consciousness† in an evolving universe.

The import of Teilhard's work cannot be overestimated. It is a sad fact that, in our twenty-first century, the vast majority of physical scientists continue to show minimal interest in studying detailed maps of consciousness that have been handed down to us through generations of saints and introspective mystics. On the other hand, the mystics seldom

*In this book, I refer to him either as Teilhard de Chardin or simply Teilhard.

†Throughout Teilhard's essays, both the words *spirit* and *consciousness* are used interchangeably; throughout this book the word *consciousness* is used to emphasize Teilhard's more scientific approach to the phenomenon.

have had sufficient training or interest in science to model their discoveries in scientific language, while few scientists have found time and interest (under the tacit threat of ridicule or censure) to explore consciousness seriously, let alone to make any sustained attempt to articulate a hard-science basis for consciousness.

Teilhard was one of an exceedingly rare few: a priest, mystic, and highly trained scientist who wrote extensively and produced, in scientific terms and with great clarity, a complete model describing the evolution of consciousness in the universe. He left us a legacy that he hoped would forge a new mysticism, a science-based experiential analysis and mapping of the geometry and dynamics of an evolving consciousness. In an optimistic note, Teilhard, at the age of seventy-two, in sight of St. Helena on passage from New York, writes: "It is with irrepressible hope that I welcome the inevitable rise of this new mysticism and anticipate its equally inevitable triumph."[1]

THE HYPERPHYSICS OF TEILHARD DE CHARDIN

In 1934, Teilhard, pursuing a subject that he himself had been developing in relative isolation for many years, suggested a new term for the scientific study of consciousness. In naming this emerging field of study *hyperphysics* (from the Greek ὕπέρ or *hupér* meaning "beyond or above") Teilhard indicated that this science should be an extension of physics above and beyond its normal physical-science subject matter.[2] His intent was that this new discipline, hyperphysics, should encompass the study of both matter and spirit in order to construct an integral model of the physics and dynamics of consciousness within this evolving cosmos.

Teilhard's fascination with exploring the evolutionary arc of animals and humans early in his career can be seen in his chosen university specializations: geology, paleontology, and anthropology. However, his unexpectedly intense psychic experiences at the front in World War I of what he lucidly perceived to be an awakening collective consciousness (which in later years he termed a planetary *noosphere*) sparked the beginning of his lifelong fascination with the evolution of human consciousness as a subject for scientific exploration. As early as September 1917 he began to write a series of essays such as "Nostalgia for the Front," which closes with the following paragraph:

> The fullness of night was now falling over the Chemin des Dames. I rose to walk down again to our billets. And as I turned to take a last look at that sacred line, the warm, living line of the Front, it was then that in the flash of a nascent intuition I half-saw that the line was taking on the shape of a higher Thing, of great nobility, which I could feel was forming itself even as I watched. . . . And at that moment it seemed to me that as I was confronted by this Thing in process of formation I was like an animal whose soul is awakening and that can see groups of connected realities but cannot understand the unitive principle of what they represent.[3]

The article was published two months later, on November 20, 1917, in *Études*. However, the final paragraph, quoted above, was censored by his Jesuit superiors and removed at the essay's final printing. At a time when the Vatican had not yet reconciled the concept of evolution with theological doctrine, Teilhard's public focus upon evolution and spirit-consciousness was immediately frowned upon, and he was formally prohibited from publishing, teaching, or lecturing on any subject outside of anthropology. Yet he continued to articulate his ideas on consciousness and hyperphysics with a seemingly unquenchable zest to understand the nature and evolutionary role of consciousness in scientific terms. His efforts over the following four decades resulted in prolific essays that were widely (albeit unofficially) circulated by friends and colleagues during his lifetime. While Teilhard's many essays offer the foundation for a hyperphysics of consciousness, they were unfortunately completely banned during his lifetime by the Pontifical Biblical Commission at the Vatican.* Fortunately they had been preserved by his many friends and colleagues and eventually

---

*Official warnings against the thought of Teilhard de Chardin continued as late as 1962. Even the cautious (and incontrovertible!) statement of Pope John Paul II in 1996, that evolution is "more than a hypothesis," was met with considerable resistance among conservatives at the fringes of the church.

published subsequent to his sudden death at age seventy-three.

Teilhard argued that the stark rift that had grown to separate physics from metaphysics had impeded both subjects in any serious attempts to study the dynamics and evolution of consciousness as a phenomenon. It was Teilhard's conviction that this dysfunctional split could be healed through, as he said to a friend in a letter, "an *ultra-physics* in which matter and spirit would be englobed in one and the same coherent and homogeneous explanation of the world."[4] His first documented usage of the word *hyperphysics* can be seen in a 1934 letter to his friend Henri de Lubac[5] describing hyperphysics as a "kind of metaphysics" that would be built upon scientific laws and methodologies. He characterizes it as a "sort of metaphysics which would really be a hyperphysics."[6]

Almost twenty years after introducing the term *hyperphysics,* and in the introductory material to what is now regarded as his most important book, *The Human Phenomenon,* Teilhard makes an effort to ensure that his reader views his book as a *purely scientific treatise* in its approach to the evolution of consciousness, rather than as a theological or metaphysical work. In the book's English translation, Teilhard, in the first sentence of his "Author's Note" in *The Human Phenomenon,* states that the subjects studied in hyperphysics (human energy, consciousness, the noosphere, Omega, and the Christic) all can be found to have a scientific basis, "purely and simply":

> If this book is to be properly understood it must be read not as a work on metaphysics, still less as a sort of theological essay, but purely and simply as *a scientific treatise* . . . only take a closer look at it, and you will see that this "hyperphysics" is not a metaphysics.[7]

It can be assumed that, trained in the sciences of geology and paleontology, Teilhard would have been an astute observer, constantly seeking and discerning patterns in the natural world. His professional papers, published during his own lifetime (unlike his works on hyperphysics) led to significant recognition in the field of paleontology. When published in 1971, Teilhard's collection of scientific papers filled eleven volumes.[8] Yet, in spite of the time constraints on his triple career as priest-scientist-mystic, he was able to develop, through a long series of unpublished essays written over the course of his lifetime, a coherent and fully adequate theory describing a general physics and geometry of consciousness. Fueled by a lifelong practice of introspective observation, deep thought, and wide experience, and often alone in the silent vastness of nature, Teilhard articulated a detailed map in both word and diagram, outlining with clarity a vivid picture of the dynamics of consciousness. But how did Teilhard's passion for hyperphysics arise, what was it that steered his attention and inflamed his passion, igniting his zest for understanding consciousness?

TEILHARD: SCIENTIST AND MYSTIC

In numerous instances among his many essays Teilhard spoke of a "mystical sense," an unusual mode of perceiving that he himself was able to experience directly. While working in China during 1926 and 1927, Teilhard wrote *The Divine Milieu*. In the middle of this essay he describes a personal experience during deep contemplation in which, through a process of what he terms "increasing *centro-complexity,*" he began to travel consciously inward toward an encounter with heretofore unimagined depths of inner being experienced in progressively deeper levels of consciousness:

> And so, for the first time in my life perhaps (although I am supposed to meditate every day!), I took the lamp and, leaving the zone of everyday occupations and relationships where everything seems clear, I went down into my inmost self, to the deep abyss whence I feel dimly that my power of action emanates. But as I moved further and further away from the conventional certainties by which social life is superficially illuminated, I became aware that I was losing contact with myself. At each step of the descent a new person was disclosed within me of whose name I was no longer sure, and who no longer obeyed me. And when I had to stop my exploration because the path faded from beneath my steps, I found a bottomless abyss at my feet, and out of it came—arising I know not from where—the current which I dare to call my life. What science will ever be able to reveal to man the origin, nature and character of

> that conscious power. . . ? Stirred by my discovery, I then wanted to return to the light of day and forget the disturbing enigma in the comfortable surroundings of familiar things.[9]

Almost a quarter of a century later, in his 1950 essay, "The Heart of Matter," Teilhard discusses this "direct psychological experience," referring to it as the "Sense of Plenitude," the "Sense of Consummation and Completion," and the "Pleromic Sense."[10] Here he describes the phenomenon in a letter to his friend, Claude Cuénot:

> It is an essay on the reconstruction of the psychological genesis which historically has brought me (since my childhood) to pass from a vague and general *cosmic sense* to what I now call "the Christic sense."[11]

He describes his experience of this steadily expanding mode of conscious perception over the arc of twenty years as one of a "fundamental current constituted by my awakening to the Cosmic Sense" and goes on to say, "I found that I was gradually being invaded, impregnated and completely recast as the result of a sort of psychic metamorphosis into which, it would seem, there passed the brightest of the energies."[12] Again, he identifies the initial catalyst that invoked this new mode of perception as his time at the front in 1915–1916.

> I have no doubt at all (as I said earlier) that it was the experience of the War that brought me this awareness and developed it in me *as a sixth sense*. . . . Once I had acquired this complementary sense, what emerged into my field of perception was literally a new Universe.[13]

Coupled with his Jesuit training in logic and clear thinking, this rare "mystical sense" gifted Teilhard with the ability to explore his own consciousness directly and to write about it with growing conviction. In addition to eleven volumes of scientific papers published during his lifetime, since his death in 1955 an additional thirteen volumes of his essays have been published, revealing a science opening to his inner vision and his analysis of this evolving planetary consciousness he called the noosphere.[14]

While Teilhard's mystical sense first dawned within him during his protracted period as a stretcher bearer in the trenches during World War I, it was late in 1951 that he wrote a short essay entitled "Some Notes on the Mystical Sense: An Attempt at Clarification." The essay opens with the following:

> The mystical sense is essentially a feeling for, a presentiment of, the total and final unity of the world, beyond its present sensibly apprehended multiplicity: it is a cosmic sense of "oneness." It enables us to become one with all by co-extension "with the sphere": that is to say, by suppression of all internal and external determinants, to come together with a sort of common stuff which *underlies* the variety of concrete beings.[15]

At the end of World War I, Teilhard returned to Paris to complete his doctoral program, and in 1922 he defended his thesis on mammals of the Lower Eocene (56 to 33.9 million years ago) in France.[16] According to one biographer, "The board of examiners had no hesitation in conferring on him the title of doctor, with distinction."[17] He continued to write essays on the topics of consciousness, transformation, and evolution. In his unpublished (forbidden) essay "Hominization" written in May of 1923 in China, he included sections such as "The Human Sphere or Noosphere" and "The Psychic Essence of Evolution" in which he states "the Noosphere requires the presence *perceived by individuals* of a higher pole or centre that directs, sustains and assembles the whole sheaf of our efforts."[18]

In that same year, the British evolutionary psychologist Conway Lloyd Morgan (1852–1936) presented a series of radical new ideas as speaker at the Gifford Lectures in which he extended the then wildly popular ideas of Henri Bergson.[19] Morgan described how, rather than through the more gradual, steady processes of natural selection that had been predicted in the theories of Darwin, an observed increase of complexity in the evolutionary process often results in discontinuous leaps from the past.[20] Morgan's theory can be seen as a precursor to an expression of the dynamics of complexity-consciousness in Teilhard's own hyperphysics. The direct effect of centro-complexification, according to Teilhard, catalyzes transformation in the organization and functioning of consciousness, causing a phase shift, as when water crystallizes into ice or transforms into steam. It is the principle of *centro-complexity,* Teilhard tells us, that initiates and drives this catalysis.

Certainly, being forbidden to publish had its effect on Teilhard. To keep him from giving lectures in Paris, where the Church saw his ideas as attracting misplaced enthusiasm among young seminarians, shortly after receiving his Ph.D. he was effectively banished from Paris by being placed on assignment to China, his predominant home for the next quarter of a century. In 1946, after spending six years in Peking as a prisoner of the Japanese occupation forces, he returned to Paris but was soon sent to America for what were to be the last years of his life.[21] This pervasive censorship of the public expression of his most passionate ideas, coupled with the firsthand horrors and suffering he had endured during World War I, must surely have contributed to the frequent bouts of despondency and depression he experienced in his later years.

During his house confinement in Peking, Teilhard lived with two other priests. One of them, Father Pierre Leroy, had become Teilhard's close friend many years earlier in Paris while Teilhard was completing his doctoral dissertation. Here Father Leroy describes his firsthand account of Teilhard's bouts of depression during the war years:

> Many have rightly been struck by Pere Teilhard's great optimism. He was indeed an optimist, in his attribution to the universe of a sense of direction in spite of the existence of evil and in spite of appearances . . . but how often in intimate conversation have I found him depressed and with almost no heart to carry on. . . . During that period he was at times prostrated by fits of weeping, and he appeared to be on the verge of despair. . . . Six years thus went by in the dispiriting atmosphere of China occupied by the Japanese and cut off from the rest of the world.[22]

Teilhard persevered with his work, contributing steadily to a growing number of fascinating essays based upon his own direct experience, keen observation, and evolving theories of a hyperphysics. When Teilhard was finally able to leave China at war's end, he wrote, during the sea passage on his return to France: "These seven years have made me quite grey, but they have toughened me—not hardened me, I hope—interiorly."[23] Yet he managed to maintain the passion and motivation to write extensively in his later years, continuing the development of his observations and conclusions regarding consciousness as he mapped the dynamics of energy in what he was convinced to be an evolving universe.

THE SELF-OBSERVING SCIENTIST-MYSTIC

Teilhard's mystical sense merged with his deep knowledge of science and the scientific method, offering a powerful introspective tool for activating, exploring, and documenting the energies of consciousness within himself and the evolving cosmos. Teilhard, as a geologist and paleontologist, was in an ideal position for interpreting the direct experiences and inner life of Teilhard the contemplative priest and mystic. This unusually rich background conjoining Teilhard's personality and professional life provided the impetus and substance for the development of his "hyperphysics," his "physics of centration."[24]

That Teilhard's understanding grew over the arc of his lifetime is evident in the many essays striving to express his vision, beginning with those written in World War I and continuing until his death in 1955. Throughout his essays one discovers evidence of his passion to present with ever greater accuracy that which he himself experiences as a "seer," a contemplative scientist exploring consciousness directly through introspection. In his writing he strove to communicate the ineffable with scientific precision and worked tirelessly to model his discoveries, often with hand-drawn diagrams and lucid prose. He reflected:

> It seems to me that a whole lifetime of continual hard work would be as nothing to me, if only I could, just for one moment, give a true picture of what I see.[25]

After the end of his forced six-year isolation under the Japanese, Teilhard was invited to lecture at opening of the French Embassy in Beijing. Here, in his first public appearance in six years, it became clear that Teilhard's conviction in the value of "the mystical sense" had grown even stronger. He spoke about the "growing importance with which leading thinkers of all denominations are beginning to attach to the phenomenon of mysticism,"[26] and went on to describe mysticism in the perception of the Omega Point:

> Let us suppose that from this universal centre, this Omega point, there constantly emanate radiations hitherto only perceptible to those persons whom we call "mystics." Let us further imagine that, as the sensibility or response to mysticism of the human race increases with planetisation, the awareness of Omega becomes so widespread as to warm the earth psychically.[27]

During his confinement Teilhard had written some of his most profound technical essays, including "Centrology: An Essay in a Dialectic of Union," in which he describes his understanding of Omega and the "law of centro-complexity." Unfortunately, essays such as "Centrology" were never allowed to be published in his lifetime. Early in his career conservative elements of the Catholic hierarchy had become suspicious of his innovative ideas, in great part because the Church had not yet reconciled the science of evolution with doctrinal Catholicism. Strict censorship from the Vatican made it difficult if not impossible for Teilhard to publish his most creative ideas on evolution and consciousness, and yet many of his essays were widely circulated among friends and colleagues using mimeograph duplicators.

THE ZEST FOR LIFE

Teilhard himself characterized his gift of a "persevering energy of consciousness" with the term *zest,* which he defines here in a 1950 essay, immediately censored by the Vatican.

> By "zest for living" or "zest for life," I mean here, to put it very approximately, that spiritual disposition, at once intellectual and affective, in virtue of which life, the world, and action seem to us, on the whole, luminous—interesting—appetizing.[28]

It is almost as if the restriction placed upon him by the Vatican against publication and public expression became a challenge, offering him the unusual freedom to explore his ideas in a torrent of essays without the need to struggle with a publisher or a critic. In spite of Church censorship his groundbreaking theories quickly spread through the many unofficial copies of his writings reproduced by and distributed among friends. Many of these can now be found published in the aforementioned posthumous collections.[29]

Nevertheless, soon after emerging from his seclusion in China, Teilhard was again deeply disappointed when the Vatican forbade him to publish what he considered to be his most important major work, *The Human Phenomenon.* In a further setback, clerical authorities refused his request to accept the offer of a prestigious teaching chair at the Collège de France in Paris, across the street from the Sorbonne. Yet in spite of such sustained opposition to his visionary efforts to understand the energy of consciousness, he rose to the challenge, and it has been noted that "he wrote *more* religious and philosophical essays in the years 1946–1955 than during any other period of his life—his bibliography lists over ninety titles for this time."[30]

HYPERPHYSICS: ENERGY AND THE NOOSPHERE

Teilhard is critical of the one-dimensional approach to energy taken by contemporary research. He asks, "What is the relationship between this interior energy . . . and the goddess of energy worshipped by physicists?"[31] His answer is that there are two fundamental categories or modes of energy, and he implies that physicists deal with but one mode. In his own words, "We still persist in regarding the physical as constituting the 'true' phenomenon in the universe, and the psychic [consciousness itself] as a sort of epiphenomenon."[32]

Energy thus becomes the central element in Teilhard's technical model of a consciously evolving cosmos. He says that while "in metaphysics the notion of being can be defined with a precision that is geometric," things are not so clear in physics, where the notion of energy is "still open to all sorts of possible corrections or improvements."[33] Teilhard's essays on the energy of consciousness, spanning four decades, systematically introduce a coherent range of corrections and improvements. In the last page of his 1953 essay, for example, "Activation of Human Energy," Teilhard states, "there are two different energies one axial, increasing, and irreversible, and the other peripheral or tangential, constant, and reversible: and these two energies are linked together in 'arrangement.'"[34]

Thus, Teilhard's hyperphysics posits two modes, domains, or dimensions of energy. One is a *tangential component* of energy that operates within the regions of space-time, a domain that is measured and explored by modern physics, while the other, a *radial* or *axial component* of energy, is characterized by conscious experience (introspection). It is this axial energy that provides a direct link with that "center," which Teilhard terms Omega, and it is this modulated energy from Omega which guides, informs, and sustains the evolutionary process of transformation throughout the space-time cosmos.[35]

Teilhard describes this radial component of energy as "a new dimensional zone" that brings with it "new properties."[36] He describes how increasing *centration* along the radial component leads to increasing states of "complexity-consciousness" with a new mode of perception.[37] He tells us that what is missing in the efforts of modern science is the conscious drive to follow this radial axis inward toward the center, toward the origin and endpoint that he terms "Omega," an effort that he finds missing in the external methodologies of modern science in its efforts to map the material cosmos in space-time. He challenges science to regard the whole, both the external *and* the internal, in a way that reminds us of the approach taken by the maverick physicist David Bohm, author of *Wholeness and the Implicate Order.*[38] Teilhard here reiterates this in his magnum opus, *The Human Phenomenon*:

> Science in its present reconstructions of the world fails to grasp an essential factor, or, to be more exact, an entire dimension of the universe . . . all we need to do is to take the inside of things into account at the same time as the outside.[39]

Energy, for Teilhard, is not simply regarded as a mathematical abstraction or dead radiation. He views energy as the living matrix of consciousness, a driver of evolution, a conscious, dynamic, communicating flux. For Teilhard, energy is "a true 'transcosmic' radiation for which the organisms . . . would seem to be precisely the naturally provided receivers."[40]

In his 1944 essay, "Centrology: An Essay in a Dialectic of Union," Teilhard describes the integration of these two components of energy as both physical and psychic in nature: "*physical energy* being no more than *materialized psychic energy*,"[41] but he is not able to posit a mathematical or physical relationship between these two dimensions other than to express the hope that "there must surely be some hidden relationship which links them together in their development."[42] And yet this relationship is precisely what his new science of hyperphysics is meant to elicit.

One possible such relationship, congruent with Teilhard's hyperphysics and put forth by the physicist David Bohm and the neurosurgeon Karl Pribram decades after Teilhard's demise, may be found in the mathematical relationship modelled by what is called the *Fourier transform*. A transform equation is a powerful mathematical tool used to transform information from one dimension into another dimension (and usually back again). The Fourier transform is widely used in electronics, acoustics, and communication to transform information (audio or video) from our time domain into a pure frequency domain (imagine here the holographic intersection of pure frequencies outside of the time domain). The information now stored as pure frequency outside of space-time can now be manipulated, modified, and/or transmitted to some remote location or other dimension where it can be transformed back into the time domain by using an inverse Fourier transform.

Pribram and Bohm saw the Fourier transform as key to the consciousness and the storage of memory. They suspected that a component of an energy of consciousness residing outside of space and time (within a pure frequency domain) uses some type of a Fourier mathematical transformation *to project* everything that appears in our space-time cosmos from butterflies and zebras to galactic clusters. Yet simultaneously, every bit of information being generated in our space-time cosmos continually *flows back into* the frequency domain, where it is stored eternally, outside of space and time. These same ideas give support to

Teilhard's own unique concept of the noosphere, his vision of a kind of envelope of thinking consciousness girding the earth, the living consciousness of the planet.[43]

A THINKING EARTH: THE NOOSPHERE

Despite sustained clerical resistance to his ideas, Teilhard continued to be fascinated by what he saw as the emerging evolution of a collective human consciousness upon planet Earth, the emergence of a "thinking Earth." He had directly intuited this powerful collective awareness during several intense wartime experiences in the trenches at the front in 1917, going so far as to characterized it as "ultra-life."[44]

These wartime experiences seems to have led Teilhard to the perception of an emerging collective or planetary consciousness that he eventually referred to as the *noosphere.** In a 1918 essay, Teilhard described the phenomenon as "*an ultimate and inevitable sphere of evolution* . . . a scientific approach with a bridge to religion."[45] In the same essay Teilhard gave the name "The Great Monad" to his experience of this emerging singular collective consciousness.[46] But by 1920, having resumed his doctoral studies, he began using the term *Anthroposphere* (*anthropos*, ἄνθρωπος; Greek for human) in referring to this thinking sphere of the planet.[47]

In Paris in 1921, drawn together by similar interests, Édouard Le Roy (1870–1954) and Teilhard de Chardin met and became friends. A mathematician and philosopher by training, Le Roy immediately found in Teilhard an intellectual equal, and thus began a lifetime friendship, soon leading to the weekly discussions of a new concept, the noosphere.† Le Roy had studied at the University of Paris with Henri Bergson and had become known as his protégé; subsequently, he had been appointed successor to Bergson at the Collège de France.[48] The two soon began a series of informal weekly discussions:

---

*"Over and above the biosphere there is a noosphere"; see Teilhard, *The Human Phenomenon,* 124.

†Noosphere: from the Greek νοῦς (nous: "sense, mind, wit") and σφαῖρα (sphaira: "sphere, orb, globe"); Samson and Pitt, *Biosphere and Noosphere Reader*

> Punctually, at 8:30 p.m., on Wednesday evenings Teilhard would call at Le Roy's apartment in the Rue Cassette, and it was not long before the two men were thinking and speaking with a single mind.[49]

Though Le Roy was a decade older than Teilhard, their relationship appears to have been considerably more than simple mentorship. Teilhard wrote,

> I loved him like a father, and owed him a very great debt . . . he gave me confidence, enlarged my mind, and served as a spokesman for my ideas, then taking shape, on "hominization" and the "noosphere."[50]

Over their many months of frequent discussion, the two grew so close in their philosophical thought that Le Roy would later say in one of his books: "I have so often and for so long talked over with Pere Teilhard the views expressed here that neither of us can any longer pick out his own contribution."[51]

Their meetings soon included a mutual acquaintance, the brilliant writer Vladimir Ivanovich Vernadsky (1863–1945), a distinguished Russian geologist from St. Petersburg who eventually founded the field known as *biogeochemistry*. Vernadsky popularized his term "the biosphere" in a series of lectures at the Sorbonne from 1922–1923, which Le Roy and Teilhard frequently attended.[52] Although his ideas are not widely appreciated in the West, Vernadsky was the first to recognize the importance of life as a geological force, an idea that predates the more recent Gaia hypothesis.*

> James E. Lovelock, the British inventor and the other major scientific contributor to the concept of an integrated biosphere in this century, remained unaware of Vernadsky's work until well after

---

*The Gaia hypothesis, also known as the Gaia theory or the Gaia principle, proposes that living organisms interact with their inorganic surroundings on Earth to form a synergistic and self-regulating, complex system that helps to maintain and perpetuate the conditions for life on the planet.

> Lovelock framed his own Gaia hypothesis. Whereas Vernadsky's work emphasized life as a geological force, Lovelock has shown that earth has a physiology: the temperature, alkalinity, acidity, and reactive gases are modulated by life.[53]

On April 6, 1923, Teilhard departed from the port of Marseille for China, booking an inexpensive shipping route that gave him opportunity to spend time exploring the Suez, Ceylon, Sumatra, Saigon, and Hong Kong before arriving in Shanghai near the end of May. During his time at sea, he had ample hours to think about and to observe the biosphere:

> Teilhard spent his time aboard ship reading, writing, and observing nature. He liked to look at the stars at night—so clear and bright when seen from a ship far from the intruding lights of terra firma—and by day observe the state of the ocean, calm at times and stormy at others.[54]

On May 6, 1923, barely a month after departing from Marseille, Teilhard completed the essay that would later be titled "Hominization," putting forth his first extended discussion of the "noosphere" concept, which may be considered an outgrowth of his recent discussions with Vernadsky and Le Roy in Paris.[55] In the essay, Teilhard begins by making a subtle shift from the usual Cartesian linear approach to paleontological classification toward a more spherical, three-dimensional geometry: "We begin to understand that the most natural division of the elements of the earth would be by zones, by circles, by *spheres*."[56] In the last half of this essay, Teilhard expands upon his understanding of the "noosphere" concept, and in one section, "The Psychic Essence of Evolution," states the following.

> It has appeared as a possible element in a sort of higher organism which might form itself . . . or else something (Someone) exists, in which each element gradually finds, by reunion with the whole, the completion of all the savable elements that have been formed in its individuality.[57]

THIRTY YEARS OF NOOSPHERIC EXPLORATION

Teilhard's concept of the noosphere is indeed part of the phenomenal world even as it maintains links to the transcendent, but it is specifically associated with the planets in general and Earth in particular, with human consciousness evolving within a planetary sphere. Teilhard goes so far as to discuss the possibility of multiple, numerous noospheres, associated with distant planets, and speculates that there may indeed be communication between these multiple noospheres.[58]

Though there had been some controversy over the origin of the word *noosphere,* Teilhard confirmed shortly before his death that the word was his own. In a letter referring to the recent demise of his friend Édouard Le Roy, Teilhard writes:

> I believe, so far as one can ever tell, that the word "noosphere" was my invention; but it was he [Le Roy] who launched it.[59]

In a 1951 essay, almost thirty years after first using the term, Teilhard elaborates his mature understanding of the noosphere:

> It is an amazing thing—in less than a million years the human "species" has succeeded in covering the earth: and not only spatially—on this surface that is now completely encircled mankind has completed the construction of a close network of planetary links, so successfully that a special envelope now stretches over the old biosphere. Every day this new integument grows in strength; it can be clearly recognized and distinguished in every quarter; it is provided with its own system of internal connections and communications—and for this I have for a long time proposed the name of *noosphere.*[60]

THE DIVINE MILIEU

Teilhard, arriving in China in 1924, found himself in the Chinese city of Tientsin (today's industrial port city of Tianjin). He joined the French

"Paleontological Mission in China" founded by the Jesuit priest and natural historian Father Émile Licent, whom Teilhard soon discovered to be the sole other member of the "Paleontological Mission." After a two-week stay in Tientsin, he found himself departing on his first expedition into upper Mongolia and the mountainous Ordos Desert with his fellow priest, Licent, who himself had been exploring Mongolia for the past nine years. They were traveling to an area where Licent had discovered fossil deposit sites; he had previously shipped specimens from the Tertiary Period (65 million to 2.6 million years ago) to Teilhard in Paris.

The two priests traveled and camped for over a year in the vast silence of Mongolia. In an early 1924 letter Teilhard writes, "I looked over the steppes where gazelles still run about as they did in the Tertiary period, or visited the yurts where the Mongols still live as they lived a thousand years ago."[61]

It was here, during this extended period of solitude in the desolate Mongolian high desert plains, either on some silent bright day, or perhaps some cold crystalline night under the canopy of stars, that Teilhard experienced a new realization, a new communion with God and the universe. If we read carefully, we can even pick out expressions of these particular moments as they are recorded in *The Divine Milieu* (1927), when the young priest begins to establish this connection consciously—becoming one with the energies of the divine being in the surrounding landscape:

> On some given day a man suddenly becomes conscious that he is alive to a particular perception of the divine spread everywhere about him. . . . It began with a particular and unique resonance which swelled each harmony, with a diffused radiance. . . . And then, contrary to all expectation and all probability, I began to feel what was ineffably common to all things. The unity communicated itself to me by giving me the gift of grasping it. I had in fact acquired a new sense, *the sense of a new quality* or *of a new dimension*. Deeper still: a transformation had taken place for me in *the very perception of being*.[62]

The result of this transformation was a new level of written communication and communion, as his friend Father Pierre Leroy recounts: "It was during this expedition, in the stillness of the vast solitude of the Ordos desert, that one Easter Sunday he finished the mystical and philosophical poem, 'Mass upon the Altar of the World.'"

As to how Teilhard attained to this "new sense in the very perception of being," or precisely what occurred to establish the connection to this "hidden power stirring in the heart of matter, glowing centre," he does not give a clue; however, he personalizes it and gives it a name, "the *divine milieu*," characterizing it as a sound, a single note, an "ineffably simple vibration":

> Just as, at the center of the divine *milieu*, all the sounds of created being are fused, without being confused, *in a single note* which dominates and sustains them (that seraphic note, no doubt, which bewitched St. Francis), so all the powers of the soul begin to resound in response to its call; and these multiple tones, in their turn, compose themselves into a single, *ineffably simple vibration* in which all the spiritual nuances . . . shine forth . . . inexpressible and unique.[63]

Teilhard assures us that this *new sense* arises from a profound interior vision: "One thing at least appears certain, that God never reveals himself to us from outside, by intrusion, but from within, by stimulation, elevation and enrichment of the human psychic current."[64] Under the heading "The Growth of the Divine Milieu," he writes:

> Let us therefore concentrate upon a better understanding *of the process by which the holy presence is born and grows within us*. In order to foster its progress more intelligently let us observe the birth and growth of the divine milieu, first in ourselves and then in the world that begins with us.[65]

Teilhard gave four lectures on evolution during the winter months of 1925; and at the same time continued to develop his theory of the noosphere.[66]

LOCATING THE NOOSPHERE

At this point it may be useful to speculate as to where in the physical space-time universe the noosphere might be found. Does Teilhard's hyperphysics of the noosphere have any possible correlates known to the material sciences? To locate the possible locus of Teilhard's noosphere, let us try a thought experiment and construct a reasonable map of the noosphere. Picture in your mind the geometry of planet Earth. Imagine the intense heat due to compression and geothermic activity, approximately 7,200°C at the central core.[67] Place your consciousness at the absolute geometric-gravitational central point of this planetary core. Now, begin to slowly move (or rise) outward along a radial line toward the cold of space, noting the temperature drop as you move away from the center of the planet—and stop at the moment you arrive at the temperature 98.2° F, the average human core temperature.

By repeating the above procedure multiple times, with many different radii moving at various angular separations away from the core, a three-dimensional surface mapping, like a mathematical brane* or Teilhard's isosphere, will begin to emerge. Is it not conceivable that this infrared energy isosphere at 98.2°F may link in co-reflection with the energy of each human being through frequency resonance, much in the same way as electromagnetic energy links to an antenna?

The shape of this isosphere will likely be highly organic and fractal in appearance, sometimes hovering above the ground on thermoclimes where the "ambient temperature" reaches 98.2°F, while beneath the surface of the much cooler oceans and arctic regions it will be located hundreds of feet below the surface of ice or water.

But the noosphere is more than simply a dynamic location on the

---

*A brane is a conceptual tool used by mathematicians and cosmologists to visualize a theoretical higher-dimension such as Stephen Hawking's "micro black hole," David Bohm's "Planck holosphere," or Teilhard de Chardin's "Omega Point." Each of these concepts describes a "compact dimension" below that of the Planck length limit (10^{-35} meter) of our normally understood and visually perceivable three dimensions of what we term "space." A brane helps us to perceive and contemplate these concepts in a more visually geometric way as a boundary of higher-dimensional spaces. This concept is used in contemporary superstring theory and M-theory; see Susskind, *Black Hole War.*

surface of an isosphere at (or above or below) the rocky surface of the earth. It is energy at the same frequency band as the human body, which has been said to generate approximately 1.3 watts of radiant power with each heartbeat.[68] While we normally think of each heartbeat as simply a pushing of blood through the arteries, it is also radiantly generating infrared electromagnetic energy (the infrared being a range of the spectrum that we often hear dismissively described as "heat").

How then might this information be used to substantiate Teilhard's vision of the reality of the noosphere, which would manifest in some planetary energy of consciousness? A chart of global population growth (fig. 5.1) indicates that there are currently approximately 7 billion human beings living on the planet.

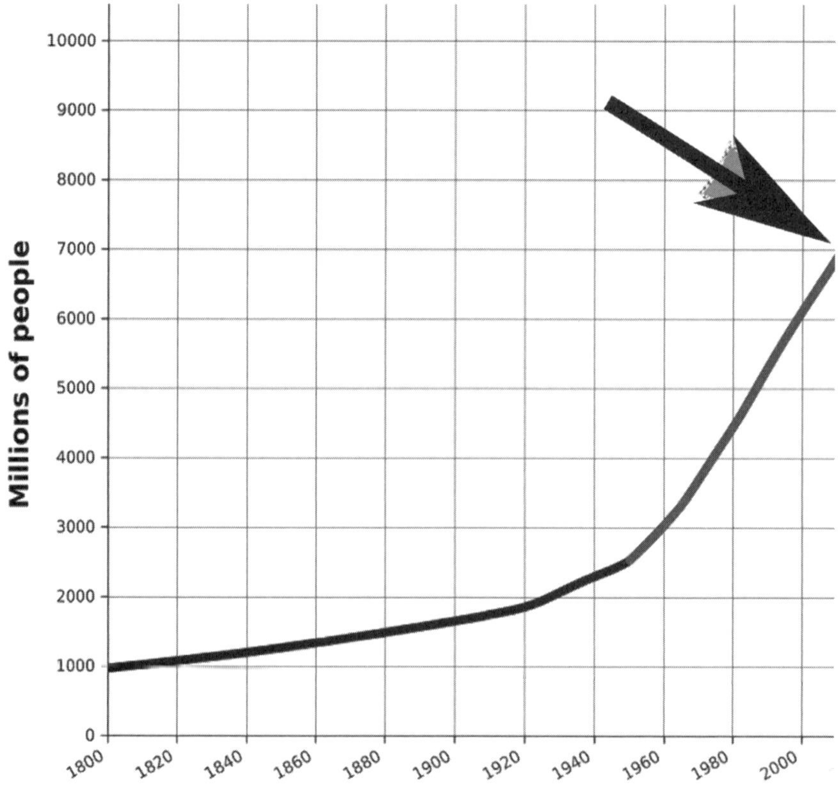

Fig. 5.1. Human population of the Earth since 1800. Adapted from the graphic by Aetheling, 2012.

Accordingly, when we multiply 7 billion humans by the average of 1.3 watts of radiation per human to find the current amount of energy being broadcast by all human hearts, this calculation gives us a result of more than nine gigawatts (9,100,000,000 watts). The table in figure 5.2 compares this amount with other major sources of radiant energy generated by humans. The combined output of human heartbeats well surpasses the output of the most powerful radio transmitter in the world[69] and even the maximum energy output of the infamous Three Mile Island nuclear power plant[70] when it was fully operational.

RADIANT ENERGY OUTPUTS, COMPARED

Source of Energy	Power
Most powerful radio frequency transmitter on planet	1,000,000 watts
Maximum output of Three Mile Island nuclear reactor	873,000,000 watts
Combined electromagnetic output of human heartbeats	9,100,000,000 watts

Fig. 5.2. Radiant energy outputs compared.

It is entirely possible that this nine gigawatts of electromagnetic energy that is being continuously broadcast by our collective heartbeats may be taking part in a vast energetic interactive resonance with Gaia. Our own collective energy, which transmits in the far infrared 10-micron wavelength range (predicted by Wien's law for our body temperature range), is the part of the geomagnetosphere that is us—the noosphere (the "us" sphere).

Evidence of direct interaction of the global electromagnetic energy of the geomagnetosphere with human consciousness can be viewed in figure 5.3 (p. 72). The figure presents a chart recording daily data from Geostationary Operational Environmental Satellites and weather satellites in geosynchronous orbit over the United States in the days before, during, and after the September 11, 2001 terrorist attacks. Continuous readings show a marked peak on September 11, 2001, followed by several days of marked disruption in the observed diurnal rhythm of the geomagnetosphere.[71]

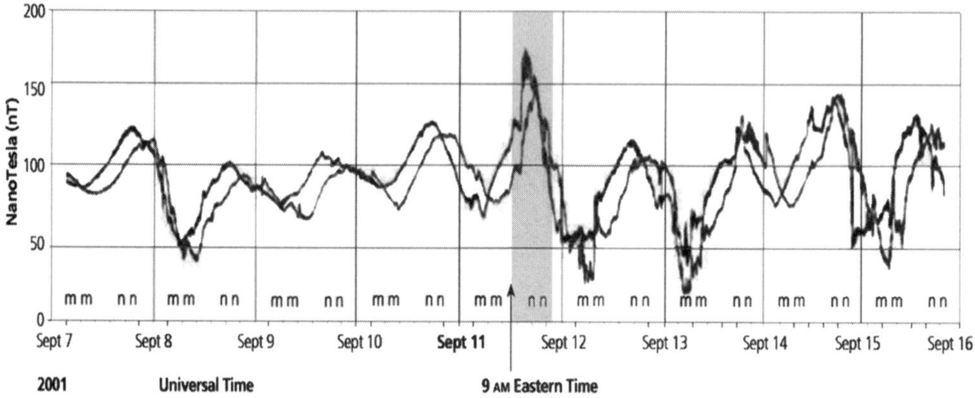

Fig. 5.3. Evidence of a coherent planetary standing wave. The data in this chart was recorded from the Geostationary Operational Environmental Satellites 8 and 10, weather satellites in geosynchronous orbit over the East and West Coasts of the United States in the days before, during, and after the September 11, 2001, terrorist attacks. Image from McCraty, Deyhle, and Childre, "The Global Coherence Initiative," 75, fig. 10. Reprinted with permission from HeartMath Institute.

In the conclusion of the paper, the authors state, "The study . . . supports the hypothesis that humanity is connected via a global field."[72] Perhaps the same hypothetical "global field" of radiation can be seen in the one Teilhard describes in a 1953 essay, "A Sequel to the Problem of Human Origins":

> Our minds cannot resist the inevitable conclusion that were we, by chance, to possess plates that were sensitive to the specific radiation of the "noospheres" scattered throughout space, it would be *practically certain* that what we saw registered on them would be a cloud of thinking stars.[73]

BREAKING THE DEATH BARRIER: REUNION WITH THE WHOLE

At the end of his life Teilhard sums up many of his thoughts on human consciousness, and particularly his own consciousness, in "The Death-Barrier and Co-Reflection," in which Teilhard describes a process by which each individual human, at least the "savable elements," transcends the physical death barrier to merge with the noosphere due to "the principles of the conservation of consciousness . . . conceived as the luminous attainment of *a new psychological stage*."[74]

On New Year's Day, several months before his own death on Easter Sunday, 1955, Teilhard finished his essay "The Death-Barrier and Co-Reflection, or the Imminent Awakening of Human Consciousness to the Sense of Its Irreversibility." In this essay he suggests that "breaking the death-barrier" is every bit as possible as breaking the sound-barrier, something that had been achieved in 1947. He tells us that his understanding of the energetics of a co-reflective consciousness (consciousness viewing itself) conflicts with the anticipation of a total death and that the ideas are mutually exclusive. He views the materialist's idea of death as a sort of brick wall or barrier as something that needs to be reassessed in light of our growing understanding of the reality of an evolutionary growth of consciousness. He emphatically states:

> And here it is important that I should be correctly understood. . . . I repeat, on the principle of the conservation of consciousness, that the reflective is evolutionarily irreversible. It [death] must be conceived as the luminous attainment of *a new psychological stage*.[75]

Teilhard had written previously of his own participatory experiences supporting his belief (as a scientist) in an immortality of consciousness. In a letter to his paleontologist colleague and friend, Helmut de Terra, he describes how he has come to understand personal immortality.

> My visible actions and influence count for very little beside my secret self. My real treasure is, *par excellence,* that part of my being which the centre, where all the sublimated wealth of the universe converges,

> cannot allow to escape. The reality, which is the culminating point of the universe, can only develop in partnership with ourselves by keeping us within the supreme personality: we cannot help finding ourselves personally immortal.[76]

Teilhard assumes that if there is a part, or region, or mode, or domain of our consciousness that continues beyond our bodies, beyond the death of our bodies, as he says in "The Death-Barrier and Co-Reflection," then *should we not then be motivated* to know and even to explore that domain even while still living? That is the real treasure Teilhard shares with us here: once specific memories are gone, the personality lives on, "keeping us within the supreme personality" whose locus is experienced when we pass through the Omega Point.

Teilhard's Omega Point, seen from the perspective of quantum physics, becomes the gateway to Bohm's implicate order, the sub-quantum region identified by David Bohm as the locus of additional dimensions beyond space and time. By passing through the Omega Point at the time of death, the former consciousness living in space-time transforms as it merges into the timeless domains of the implicate order. Geometrically at the center, everywhere, we can visualize micro black holes that correspond to Teilhard's Omega Points, as loci or gateways into the mysterious dimensions that string theorists have calculated to exist beyond our human space and time dimensions. Bohm goes so far as to suggest that the one consciousness itself (ourself), that fundamental base consciousness that underlies the cosmos of space and time, peers out from within the implicate order into our space-time cosmos. To Teilhard, through the Omega Point resides the supreme "personality," the "personality of the transcendent" that can be experienced, by mystics at least, even prior to their biophysical approach to the death-barrier.[77]

Thus Teilhard's concept of consciousness fusing with the noosphere through the Omega Point at death is supported by Bohm's quantum geometry of the implicate order's existence at the center, everywhere, at the extremely small dimension of the Planck length, and which spreads out in all of the ever-expanding holospheric shells of encoded information surrounding the micro black holes at the center of space.

Not only does Teilhard categorically reject the majority of contemporary humankind's tacit assumption that death is "the end" (i.e., the end of individual consciousness), but he worries that such a widely held popular but erroneous stance might delay what he saw as the natural growth and awakening of the planetary noosphere, a collective energy of modulated consciousness built upon the innumerable contributions of all *Homo sapiens* who have ever lived.[78]

TEILHARD'S REVOLUTIONARY UNDERSTANDING OF ENERGY AS CONSCIOUSNESS

We have examined a unique model of psychophysics describing an enormous energy that is consciousness itself evolving as a planetary noosphere. This model stems directly from the direct numinous experiences of Pierre Teilhard de Chardin, catalyzed by observations that began during his youth in the trenches at the front in World War I. Throughout the following five decades, his clear, incisive, and consistent efforts to map and to understand these rich perceptual experiences resulted in the articulation of a new field of observational inquiry that he termed "hyperphysics," a new scientific endeavour that he believed would lead to the reconciliation of material science and spiritual experience.

The phrase "spiritual experience" encapsulates Teilhard's efforts to fuse that which material scientists call "consciousness" with what priests call "divine personality." Teilhard worked to counter the stance of the material-science establishment that assumes the universe is 99 percent or more "dead stuff" and that consciousness itself is a recent accidental effect of hydrocarbon molecules coming together in various combinations over 3 billion years of interaction on our particular planet. Teilhard's view, shared with priests of all religions, sees the universe as a divine creation that springs out of a preexisting source, a transcendent consciousness with a personality, a divine being of pure awareness which is the primary substrate of all reality. As Teilhard said "We are not human beings having a *spiritual experience*. We are spiritual beings having a human experience."[79] It is understandable, then, that Teilhard, a material scientist as well as a priest, would see consciousness to be a divine energy, not a disenchanted accidental phenomenon emerging from a dead, unconscious universe.

Teilhard's revolutionary understanding of energy as consciousness and his insightful observations of an evolving collective human consciousness feeding an emerging "planetary noosphere" gives hope to all of those who contemplate the mysteries of life in the spirit after transitioning beyond what he termed "the death-barrier." The courageous efforts of this scientist-priest to reconcile spirit and matter have opened wide new avenues for scientific exploration and offered scientific support for religious doctrines. Even now, in the twenty-first century, a continuation of his work can be seen in academia's expanding interest in the establishment of formal programs of consciousness studies and research.

We now turn to another scientifically trained explorer of consciousness, Rudolf Steiner, born twenty years earlier than Teilhard de Chardin, whose extensive writings and lectures made great inroads into the exploration of a Western approach to the psychophysics of consciousness.

6

Rudolf Steiner

Supersensible Perception

Of the many Western scholars who developed a particularly effective articulation of such ideas in European terms through direct experience and years of study, one of the most notable was Rudolf Steiner, an Austrian professor whose doctoral dissertation dealt with Johann Gottlieb Fichte's philosophy of science. In 1904, Rudolf Steiner began his *Knowledge of the Higher Worlds and Its Attainment* with a sentence that well encapsulates the basic premise of his entire perception and teaching, which accords integrally with Tantra:

> There slumber in every human being faculties by means of which he can acquire for himself a knowledge of higher worlds. . . . There remains only one question—how to set to work to develop such faculties for this purpose.[1]

Steiner goes on to describe the development of these faculties for "supersensible perception," which becomes a recurrent theme in his life's work. In his lectures and books we find described methods and means by which a human being can work to discover ways to nourish, activate, and operate these latent systems of supersensory perception, and in these teachings we find a strong evidence of his exposure to Theosophy in general and Indian Yoga and Tantra in particular.

In *The Evolution of Consciousness,* Steiner states, "For higher knowledge the human being consists of four members: physical body, etheric body, astral body, and Ego-organization."[2]

Focusing upon Steiner's four domains of the human being (physical, etheric, astral, and Ego), figure 6.1 relates these four levels or domains within each human to four domains of energy. The table presents a bridge between Steiner's Theosophical four-domain approach and energy systems as mapped by psychophysics.

Four Domains of Human Being According to Steiner and Theosophy	Four Domains of Human Energy According to Psychophysics
Annamaya - **Physical body**	**Atomic energy** – Biochemical processes
Manomaya – **Etheric body**	**Electrical energy** – Nervous system
Prāṇamaya/Vijñānamaya – Liṇga Śarīra – **Astral body**	**Magnetic energy** – Blood plasma
Ānandamaya – **Causal body (Ego, 'I')**	**Radiant energy** – Cerebrospinal fluid

Fig. 6.1. Psychophysics of the four domains.

Tantra, being a tacit methodology for adopting and practicing that which has been found to give results, accumulated over the centuries numerous specific exercises and rule-of-thumb injunctions for what one ought and ought not to do in order to acquire new modes of perception and perhaps, above all, to reach the one true Self from which the universe of butterflies and zebras is projected into space-time. Thus we have been handed down teachings for human development of a range of new perceptual organs discovered to be evolutionarily emergent within the locus of what Tantrics themselves termed the *chakras* (wheels or, more accurately, spherical regions), located within the body in specific locations along the spinal column. These chakras have been detected and developed by mystics in many cultures through directly focusing awareness within one or more of these areas to energize and activate specific systems of what is often called "higher consciousness." The activation of these chakras will be discussed in detail in a later chapter, but we now view Steiner's four domains in greater detail by examining perspectives both classical and contemporary. In the process we will construct a simple model fully congruent with paradigms of modern physical science.

THE PHYSICAL-MOLECULAR DOMAIN

The first domain is primarily concerned with the physical and biochemical aspects of the human body, and the first stages of yogic progress focus upon hatha yoga and other physical exercises, diet, and relaxation in order to develop a strong and healthy physical body as the platform from which to develop higher stages of conscious awareness; this first domain has been the primary focus of the modern physical sciences and is already well explored.

This is the dimension in which energy vibrationally resonates in the orderly geometric alignment of molecular structures in space-time. In this configuration energy manifests macroscopically as particle, atom, organic or inorganic molecule, galactic cluster, liver, spleen, brain, and the seemingly infinite variety of complex semi-permanent geometrical systems that manifest as the human body, the biosphere, and the lithosphere of Gaia.

Modern physical science deals exclusively with this physical realm, but physical science has largely ignored a supersensible world. Professionals have been ostracized for exploring beyond the boundaries of their fields of existing physical science as currently defined, and those who would explore without the backing and funding of a scientific establishment find that much exploration has even been prohibited by law.

THE ETHERIC-ELECTRICAL DOMAIN

This second domain, Steiner's etheric, consists of the electrical nervous system and brain/memory/logic mechanisms that act much like a modern computer system. In the human body this nerve-impulse system (in the brain and throughout the body) currently dominates many of the resources of consciousness in its activities of remembering, comparing, articulating, and forming abstract thought into language tokens. In the modern human this system predominates and tends to mask or hide the higher levels of psychophysical activity found in the blood and cerebrospinal systems.

Steiner tells us that even though "our ether body goes back to the earlier evolutionary stage," it is highly evolved and "in reality, the paragon of all *wisdom* in the earthly sense."[3] The etheric body differentiates itself from the physical body but is linked with the physical, most closely associated with the nervous system and brain. However, the etheric has a counterpart in the physical: "If the ether body did not have a counterpart in the physical body, we could not live in our ether body. The ether body's inner life would float suspended in the air."[4]

In 1925, the year of Steiner's death, a book titled *The Etheric Double* was published by the Science Group of the Theosophical Research Centre in London. It was a compilation of work by Annie Besant (1847–1933) and C. W. Leadbeater (1854–1934) up to that time.[5] The material within the book would have been familiar to Steiner, who himself had been acting head of the Theosophical Society in Germany from 1900 to 1910. In the opening of the book, a concise description of the etheric body is given as follows:

> Every solid, liquid and gaseous particle of the human body is surrounded with an etheric envelope . . . it acts as an intermediary or bridge between the dense physical body and the astral body, transmitting the consciousness of physical sense contacts through the etheric brain to the astral body, and also transmitting consciousness from the astral and higher levels down into the physical brain and nervous system.[6]

This description provides a clear view of the relative position of the etheric in its functional role within the four levels of the human being. As we can see in figure 6.2, the etheric forms a bridge between the physical and astral.

Steiner's use of the name *etheric* reminds us of the term for luminiferous *ether,* the hypothetical substance through which electromag-

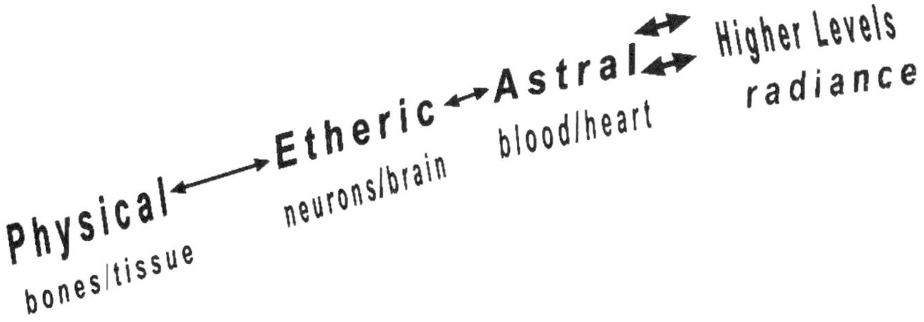

Fig. 6.2. Rising arc of the four domains.

netic waves travel. Physical science describes how the nervous system and physical brain manifest current flows of electrical energy throughout the body.

If we make the assertion that the etheric lies in this electromagnetic system or energy matrix of electrical activity, we can see how the etheric could arise, continuously activated and powered by hundreds of millions of simultaneous electrical impulses fired by interconnected neurons, and how our modern human ego or sense of individual personality could be operational within this etheric-electrical body. Active capabilities of such an electrical body would need to include memory storage and retrieval, and the ability to generate new thought patterns by searching among multiple memories. The system would also need to be capable of applying logic and the ability to self-program capabilities to solve and anticipate problems. In short, this etheric-electric body would include most of the activities and capabilities that we commonly identify with our ego and daily identity.

From this perspective the etheric body can be seen as a sophisticated machine-like computer running within the electrical activity of the nervous system and brain—a system that, when fully operational, we take to be our accustomed selves as human beings. The center of gravity of our consciousness remains largely centered within this avatar-like etheric-electric body, masking the deeper levels which, Steiner says, are to be developed for acquisition of supersensible perception. Steiner points out that the etheric body itself, consisting of neural system and brain, has already evolved the following perceptual systems:

- *sight*: its color, form, and brightness, ranges from hummingbirds to whales
- *sounds*: with their rich ranges of pitch and volume, yield murmuring brook and bomb
- *smells*: with their range of scent and intensity from rose to skunk
- and *touch*: that moves us from gentle caress to fiery burn

Other perceptual systems lie beyond the etheric body in another body, the astral body, for which the etheric functions as a "bridge . . . transmitting the consciousness of physical sense contacts through the etheric brain to the astral body."[7] It is in this astral domain that we evolve organs of supersensible perception with which to perceive the supersensible.

THE ASTRAL-MAGNETIC DOMAIN

In its focus upon acquiring new *siddhis* or powers of consciousness, traditional Tantra is primarily concerned with the third domain, termed the astral body by Steiner and the Theosophists. It is within this third domain that normally integrated human consciousness operates, within a system of polarized magnetic flux coursing throughout the flowing blood plasma of the human body. These magnetic fields link with the electrical fields of the nervous system forming a system that receives and processes external sensory input and presents it for internal perception by the Ego (the "I"). In particular, it is in this domain, predominantly operative within the human blood system, that we find the development of the initial stages of supersensory perception: the siddhi of "Yogic vision," or in Sanskrit, *Yoga-dṛṣṭi*.[8]

One basic objective of meditation is to quiet down the electrical cognitive activity in the etheric body so that one may become more directly aware of the magnetic sensations within the astral body, primarily within the heart center and throughout the bloodstream. This magnetic component of consciousness resonating in the blood is called *prana* by yogis in Tibet and India and *chi* by Taoists in China. The traditional healing arts of acupuncture work to remove obstructions to facilitate the free flow of this plasma-induced magnetism throughout the bodily systems.

Steiner discusses this third domain of the human being at great length, and it is to this astral domain that one's attention is directed for the development of supersensible perception. The term *astral body* (from the Greek *σώμα αστέρι* for "star body"), widely used by Neoplatonists (third century CE), is referred to as early as Plato's *Republic* (fourth century BCE). At the conclusion of chapter 10, a fallen hero, Er, suddenly revives just as he is about to be burned on a funeral pyre after being seemingly dead for twelve days. He relates that he was told by a certain "judge" there that "he had to become a messenger to human beings of the things there."[9]

Er continues to relate his experiences in traveling through eight planetary spheres, a journey which, Plato tells us, leads all human souls, after death, through a process of reincarnation culminating at the moment the waters of forgetfulness are drunk. At that moment of transformation, what remains of the previous soul is carried away as a soon-to-be-reincarnated being, and seen "shooting up to the stars."[10]

In the fifth century CE, Proclus Lycaeus, an attorney in Constantinople, fated to be perhaps the last of the great Greek philosophers in the classical style, published an elaborate exposition of Neoplatonism. He described two subtle bodies or "carriers," intermediate between the individual physical human body and the immortal spirit: one carrier, the astral vehicle, was, he claimed, the immortal part of the soul, while the second carrier, which he considered transitory and not meant to survive death, he aligned with the breath (*pneuma*).[11]

It is interesting to note that three major Western thinkers (Plato, Proclus, and Steiner) over the span of the past two thousand years have observed that the third level or domain of the human being is termed "the astral" (fig. 6.3, p. 84). Having differentiated the two adjacent and interpenetrating levels referred to by Western writers as the etheric and the astral, it is now possible to examine potential physiological correlates of these components within human physiology.

	Domain 1	Domain 2	Domain 3	Domain 4
Plato (4th c. BCE)	Physical Organs	Brain/ Nerves	Astral/ Starry	Immortal Spirit
Proclus (4th c. CE)	Physical	Breath/ Pneuma	Astral	Immortal Spirit
Steiner (20th c. CE)	Physical (*molecular domain*)	Etheric (*electrical domain*)	Astral (*magnetic domain*)	"I" or Ego (*frequency domain*)

Fig. 6.3. The four domains of Plato, Proclus, and Steiner.

THE EGO-FREQUENCY DOMAIN

Steiner's fourth domain is the *ānandamaya* body (recall fig. 6.1, p. 78), the Theosophical "causal body," or as indicated by Steiner, the Ego or "I." It is this domain that is the primary focus of contemplatives in their efforts to create and maintain a bridge to the deeper Self that resides in the frequency domain and other dimensions within Bohm's implicate order at sub-quantum dimensions.

It is the fourth domain in figure 6.3, the Ego-frequency domain, variously characterized as "immortal spirit," "Ego," or the "I," that corresponds to what we consider to be our real unique self in space-time, and yet a projection of the one big Self out of the transcendent implicate order. In this Ego domain we maintain the sense of "I." Each human Ego can be visualized as a unique electromagnetic flux entity, a plasma that holographically projects the individual "I" into space-time and directly links with each of the additional dimensions that transcend space-time and lie within Bohm's implicate order. In space-time we see how energy becomes a conscious center, an Ego or an "I," both consciousness and energy, a unique energy "personality" that generates experiences in space-time that are then stored eternally within the implicate order. But at its heart this is a feeling energy-plasma being that links to its source in the transcendent, a feeling being that can experience the delights of love and beauty, or as the poet William Blake wrote, "Energy is Eternal Delight!"[12]

LINKING ANATOMY TO THE ASTRAL AND ETHERIC BODIES

Physiologically, Steiner differentiates the activity of the astral from the etheric through their carriers, the blood circulatory system and the nervous system. They are further differentiated by the ninety-degree geometric relationship between the two that is observed by Steiner in his discussion of human duality in *An Occult Physiology,* where he gives a description, replete with diagrams, of how "nerve-activity" is at right angles to the alignment of the "blood-tablet."[13] This description accords well with the established physics of the electromagnetic field: the electric field and the magnetic field are always at ninety-degree angles to one another as energy flows through space-time.

After establishing this ninety-degree relationship of consciousness between nerves and blood, Steiner provides a key to access supersensible perception:

> It is, therefore, possible purely through processes of inner concentration, to separate the blood-system from the nerve-system. . . . Now, the peculiar thing is that when the human being once actually brings this about through such inward exertion of the soul, he has then an entirely different sort of inner experience . . . when, through inner concentration, he separates his nerve-system, lifts it, that is to say, through inner soul-forces out of his blood-system, he does not then live in his ordinary ego but another Self. He feels a supersensible world uplifted within him.[14]

It is this "process of inner concentration, to separate the blood-system from the nerve-system," Steiner says, that is a developmental result of sustained contemplative practice: it is the fruit of the development of skill in silencing mental activity in the nervous system at will and for sustained periods. The energy that would otherwise have been used up during the cognitive neuronal activities instead accumulates, reaching sufficient cumulative power to cross a threshold for transformation into the next level or holism of consciousness. According to Lilian Silburn, a French Indologist who spent much of her life translating and interpreting more than a dozen Kashmiri Tantric texts, "The retraction of energy into the Self is an interiorization due to a sudden reflux of the energy which, in ordinary life, escapes through the sense organs."[15] Professor Silburn goes on to reference the eleventh-century CE Kashmiri mystic Kṣemarāja, who himself compares this process to that of a frightened turtle contracting its limbs, drawing them into its shell. Quoting his *Pratyabhijñāhṛdayam* (Doctrine of Recognition): "Withdrawn from the outside, one becomes firmly rooted in the ever-present Self."[16] Silburn goes on to stress the prime importance of the *sense of touch* in this process, and this time quotes Kṣemarāja's teacher, Abhinavagupta.

> The organs of sight, hearing, taste and smell belong to lower levels of reality . . . the highest among them being still within the sphere of illusion, whereas touch resides at the superior level of energy as an indescribably subtle sensation ceaselessly yearned for by the yogin; for this contact leads to a consciousness identical with the self-luminous, pure firmament.[17]

In psychophysical terms, the ensuing silence within the electric self of the etheric body allows energy charges to build, facilitating the transforming shift of consciousness into the magnetic self in the bloodstream, which in turn triggers the organs of supersensible perception to begin opening, to become active, and to communicate with the various previously unknown dimensions of awareness.

But how does this model that identifies the bloodstream with the magnetic astral body reconcile with physical science? We must first note that human blood, with its billions of hydrogen ions (of which pH is a measure) flowing throughout the circulatory system, generates a magnetic field, a charged plasma. This plasma, composed of hydrogen ions and heated, magnetically polarized water molecules, flows throughout the body at an average velocity of 25cm/s. With each heartbeat this magnetic plasma undergoes powerful acceleration spikes, visible in EKGs. The composite magnetic field created by the flow of ionized blood within the circulatory system is distinct from and at right angles to the electric field created by the flow of electrons in the neuronal system near and along arterial walls.

The importance of Steiner's emphasis on this ninety-degree relationship between etheric and astral energy is reinforced when mapped upon Teilhard de Chardin's observations on radial and tangential (psychic) energies. Teilhard's model of energy has two components perpendicular to one another: a tangential component, and an axial, radial component. The tangential component of energy is described in familiar terms as movement within space and time, while the radial component, which Teilhard links to the process of "centration" or a thermodynamic heating up of consciousness, is also referred to as "soul" and "spirit" in his essays. He talks about the radial component of energy as "a new dimensional zone" that brings with it "new properties,"[18] and he describes how increasing centration along the radial component leads to increasing states of complexity-consciousness.

In language amazingly Steinerian, Teilhard talks about "*physical energy* being no more than *materialized psychic energy*,"[19] but he is not able to posit a mathematical or physical relationship between these two dimensions other than to express the hope that "there must surely be some hidden relationship which links them together in their development."[20]

The Frequency Domain (Implicate Order)

Eventually, through the practice of quieting the nervous system so as to enter and gain experience within the magnetic plasma bloodstream mode of awareness, Steiner insists, "we give birth to a new, higher being within us . . . something comes to life in us that transcends the personal or individual."[21] Supersensible perception becomes the bridge to what Steiner calls the fourth body or fourth domain, known by Theosophists as *turiya,* the Sanskrit word "fourth:" a realm identified by the Upanishads as the highest domain of human consciousness. It is in this fourth domain, also referred to by Steiner as "Ego" or "I," that the organs of supersensory perception are fully activated, providing a bridge that establishes communication links beyond the individual with previously unknown networks of experience.

Finally, Steiner says, we begin not only to see but to hear the supersensible, and he challenges us to go even further, into what he strikingly terms the *zero-point* of silence:

> There would be not only the absolute peace of the zero-point of silence but it would go further and come to the negative of hearing, quieter than quiet, more silent than silence. And this must in fact happen when we are able through enhanced powers to reach this inner peace and silence. When, however, we arrive at this inner negative of audibility, at this peace greater than the zero-point of peace, we are then so deeply in the spiritual world that we not only see it but hear it resounding.[22]

Through Steiner, we see that harnessing the four domains of the body is another example of "what works" as a key to unlocking supersensible perception. Next, we'll explore the ideas of the Armenian philosopher and mystic G. I. Gurdjieff (1866–1949), a contemporary of Steiner. Gurdjieff created a school of esoteric studies somewhat similar to Steiner's that Gurdjieff called "The Work" or "The Way" and which spread widely across Europe during the early twentieth century.

7

G. I. GURDJIEFF

"Remembering the I"

THE THREE-BRAIN MAP OF G. I. GURDJIEFF

Another early explicit map of consciousness can be found in the intuitive perception of a triadic structure of consciousness developed in the writing of the early twentieth-century philosopher and mystic G. I. Gurdjieff, who developed an extensive model of consciousness in which he perceived humans to be "three-brained beings." In his 1,248-page *Beelzebub's Tales to His Grandson, or An Objectively Impartial Criticism of the Life of Man,* Gurdjieff describes the experiences and observations of an extraterrestrial being among the "three-brained beings" of Planet Earth.[1] Gurdjieff's Beelzebub, an alien cosmonaut, reports that each of the three brains operates quasi-independently within one of three modes of consciousness, and to complicate matters, one of these brains (the electric) consists of many microbrains, microegos, and micro "I"s—often competing for dominance.

The electromagnetic field theory model of consciousness* supports Gurdjieff's "three-brain theory": it proposes that consciousness is

*The electromagnetic field theory of consciousness is an integral part of the psychophysics of consciousness discussed in chapter 3. It posits that each conscious entity consists of a unique holoflux of electromagnetic energy (a plasma entity that has both electric and magnetic fields resonating in space-time) that links the implicate order with the space-time cosmos. Thus in our space-time universe, an individual conscious being is essentially a holonomic electromagnetic flux-entity that animates biomolecular structures in space and time. See my previous book *The Electromagnetic Brain.*

operational within each of three distinct primary domains. These three hypostases* of the one and same energy can be visualized as operating in three different dimensional "regions," separate yet interconnecting, interpenetrating, and intercommunicating.

In a parallel way, it is feasible to associate Gurdjieff's three "brains" with the three domains of the electromagnetic field theory of consciousness:

- "Gurdjieff's Brain 1" = the electric field domain (e_d)
- "Gurdjieff's Brain 2" = the magnetic field domain (m_d)
- "Gurdjieff's Brain 3" = the frequency field domain (f_d)

First Brain: Consciousness within Brain Neurons

Gurdjieff 's "first brain," currently the sole focus of consciousness research, operates through the electrical activity of neuron cells firing within the electric domain of the electromagnetic field of energy. Neurons making up the human nervous system have evolved to work primarily with sparks in the electric domain of the energy field. "Brain 1" thus resides in the actual wet, neuronal meat tissue. It is dominant over the other two brain modes in our contemporary, hyperverbal society, and operates within the electric domain. This domain was labeled the "etheric" body in the writings of nineteenth-century Theosophists such as Annie Besant, Madame Blavatsky and C. W. Leadbeater.

The electrical-impulse fields within the brain operate in the time domain, relying upon memory-storage operations that can address and recall, compare, and evaluate. The nervous system is designed somewhat like a network of laptop computers. With its bifurcated architecture (two separate hemispheric systems), the electrical wet brain system has excellent potential for generating electromagnetic holograms within the three-dimensional space of the cranium.

Recording and/or playing back a hologram uses interference patterns caused by two slightly differently sourced electromagnetic fields

*The word *hypostases* has different meanings in theology, metaphysics, and medicine. Integrating the three gives the following definition: the warm blood that is the underlying foundation of the threefold essence of God.

interacting, creating shadow patterns on an imprintable medium, which are perhaps viewed or projected by the solitary pineal gland onto the cavernous walls of the ventricular cavity. In the physics laboratory, two offset source beams are provided by a beam splitter, usually an optical prism. This produces a primary beam and a secondary beam that split off from the original. However, in our real space-time universe these beams come from myriad directions, not just two, and the intersection of literally billions of beams of radiation form the three-dimensional shadows that we call objects in space and time.

In the "first brain" system described by Gurdjieff, multiple centers of cognitive processing are developed, often competing with one another. The "first brain's" architecture and activity are similar to those of twenty-first-century computers. The multiple centers, registers, or Gurdjieffian "I" subprograms, or sub-egos, can do advanced pattern recognition, logic, develop language, and give this "first brain" the capability to self-program (an ability called neuroplasticity by brain researchers). Concurrently, this "first brain" functions to operate all physical peripherals (arms, legs, organs) through a complex wiring system of neuron cell fibers, and works to process the incoming sensory information picked up by each of the five normal human sensory peripheral systems.

Second Brain: Consciousness within Blood Capillaries

The "second brain" operates within the blood system and has been called the "astral" by Theosophists. This second brain is not made of neurons or tissue; instead, it is the magnetic component of the electromagnetic energy field resonating throughout blood in the body. This magnetic field is generated by the relatively hot ionic streams of swiftly coursing blood moving resonantly through the estimated 60,000 miles of vessels in the adult human. The moving ions resonantly generate a magnetic field, further polarizing the billions of water molecules in the bloodstream. This polarization has the effect of creating one giant polarized water molecule, with a polar magnetic axis running parallel to the spinal column and out through the fontanelle at the top of the skull, resonating with peak electromagnetic energy at 10 microns wavelength at a temperature of 98.6° Fahrenheit. The source of power for the magnetic flux of energy powering this "second brain" is the human heart, as Joseph Chilton Pearce writes:

> In some sense everything has an electromagnetic element or basis, but a heart cell's electrical output is exceptional. That congregation within us, billions of little generators working in unison, produces two and a half watts of electromagnetic energy with each heartbeat at an amplitude forty to sixty times greater than that of brain waves—enough to light a small electric bulb. This energy forms a magnetic field that radiates out some twelve to fifteen feet beyond our body itself.[2]

Thus, whereas the "first brain" operates in the neuronal system within the electric domain, dominated by the brain, this "second brain" operates in the magnetic field, in the blood, through the cardiovascular system, sustained and generated by the rhythmic beating power of the heart.

Quantum field theory, applied to the electromagnetic field, describes all physical phenomena involving electrons and photons* and is called *quantum electrodynamics,* abbreviated QED. As early as 1978, Stuart, Takahashi, and Umezawa proposed a mechanism of human memory and consciousness, consistent with quantum field theory, which they have called quantum brain dynamics (QBD).[3] Building on this paradigm, Jibu and Yasue in 1995 described the creation and annihilation dynamics of corticons and their proposed higher level electromagnetic structures of awareness in the human body, as follows:

> Energy quanta of the water rotational field extending to the whole assembly of brain cells, and photons, that is, energy quanta of the electromagnetic field.[4]

They go on to describe a theory in which the polarization of water molecules plays an exceptional part by producing, on a macro level, a single resonant magnetic water "macromolecule" in bodies of living, water-based creatures. Within this polarized, nonlocal H_2O quantum

---

*In *Physics for the Rest of Us,* Roger Jones refers to photons as "the so-called quantum of the electromagnetic field" (289).

field is embedded an electromagnetic field in the form of a plasma field.* Quantum brain dynamics thus supports a potential locus of consciousness other than the electrical neuronal locus, a possible "second brain" or consciousness manifesting within the quantum mechanical plasma of the bloodstream system, perhaps the source of a living network of high-frequency information flow.

Third Brain: Consciousness within the Frequency Domain

It is possible that the "third brain" catalogued by G. I. Gurdjieff operates within the third vector of a modulated (information encoded) energy field, the *frequency domain* (f_d). Information encoded in the frequency domain manifests in a fifth dimension "outside of" the four-dimensional domain of space-time. Each of these five dimensions intersects directly with every other dimension (eleven or more dimensions exist according to string theory mathematical proofs and recent experiments at the Large Hadron Collider near Geneva, Switzerland). The frequency domain is definitely an essential part of the "the holographic paradigm" introduced early in the 1980s by physicists Karl Pribram of Stanford and David Bohm of the University of London.[5] The frequency domain is described here by Pribram:

> Time and space are collapsed in the frequency domain. Therefore the ordinary boundaries of space and time, locations in space and in time become suspended and must be "read out" when transformations into the object/image domain are effected.[6]

This transformational "read out" from the frequency domain that Pribram mentions uses the mathematical relationship of the Fourier transform to translate between each of the domains. Bohm expressed his own belief that the transcendent frequency domain or "implicate

*"A plasma is a state of matter in which a significant portion of the particles are ionized. Plasmas are by far the most common phase of matter in the universe, both by mass and by volume. All stars are made of plasma, and interstellar space is filled with plasma. Common forms of plasma include lightning, St. Elmo's fire, the polar aurorae, the solar wind, neon signs, and plasma displays in modern home television." Chen, *Introduction to Plasma Physics,* 56.

order," as he called it, is the locus of primary consciousness within the universe and that this single consciousness-being projects into space-time all of what we call material objects and individual seemingly separate conscious selves. This frequency domain can be viewed as Gurdjieff's "third brain," a consciousness that interconnects all life and evolutionary process in the cosmos, linking and interlinking all electric and magnetic energy plasma through what Rupert Sheldrake calls morphic resonance. This single primary Self or consciousness singularity (called God, Brahma, Yahweh, and so on, within religious traditions) exists within a nontemporal field in a dimension other than (for you cannot say "outside" in nonspatial dimensions) time and space.

The quantum theorist David Bohm supports this proposition in his description (supported by mathematics) of two coexisting, interpenetrating states of quantum energy: a physical configuration of energy, expressed in time and space, and a transcendent configuration of energy called "the implicate order,"[7] synonymous with the frequency domain (f_d). Bohm here presents examples of this implicate order:

> It will be useful in such an exploration to consider some further examples of enfolded, or *implicate* order. Thus, in a television broadcast, the visual image is translated into a time order, which is "carried" by the radio wave. Points that are near each other in the visual image are not necessarily "near" in the order of the radio signal. Thus, the radio wave carries the visual image in an implicate order. The function of the receiver is then to *explicate* this order, i.e., to "unfold" it in the form of a new visual image.[8]

Gurdjieff's hypothesized three brains may be functionally mapped into three domains of the electromagnetic energy field:

- We remember, compare, reason, and verbalize through means of the electric domain (e_d). We "think" in the electric domain.
- We experience emotion, joy, pain, fear, and wonder through means of the magnetic domain (m_d). We "sense" in the magnetic domain.
- We empathize, resonate, understand, communicate, and transfer knowledge from one generation to the next through morphic res-

> onance between space-time and the frequency domain (f_d). With luck we learn to "intuit" information from the frequency domain into our space-time consciousness, and thus gain what we term "insight."

Unfortunately recent scientific and academic research has been trying to understand consciousness solely by studying electrical activity in the interaction of neurons within the brain, and few have attempted to explore the possible connection with the other dimensions that have been recently discovered by particle physicists. Nor has there been any discernable research interest in exploring the possibility that consciousness may manifest in multidimensional electromagnetic fields both within and outside of the body.

Words definitely dominate our present cultural civilization, and our brain, and much of our consciousness, is dominated by the processing of words. We think, talk, chatter, read, tweet, and text incessantly, keeping consciousness within the boundaries of verbal, linear, neuronal electrical activity within the cranium. In general, little time and conscious focus is spent within the other two of Gurdjieff's "brain" domains of consciousness, except during periods of escape from electric neuronal mind chatter. Such periods only occur when the center of gravity of consciousness shifts out from the first brain: during nonverbal aesthetic experience, sleep, contemplation, sex, wandering in nature, or during entheogenic experiences. The dominant paradigm for consciousness among neurophysiologists, and within the scientific materialist community in general, continues to hold that consciousness resides within the operation of, or as an epiphenomenon of, the activity of neurons in the brain.

To summarize our brief exploration of Western approaches to psychophysics and before exploring traditional Tibetan and Indian psychonautical techniques, it may be useful to highlight what has been covered thus far. The theories of consciousness discussed in this chapter have been based in large part upon the introspective experiences of several highly intelligent and scientifically trained twentieth-century European priests, contemplatives, and mystics. Their accounts and conclusions appear to be in substantive agreement, and yet their ideas have been ignored by the highly conservative hard-science community which itself has made little headway in understanding the nature of consciousness.

The following six considerations support the contention that human consciousness might even now be continuously evolving and that higher levels of consciousness operate beyond physical neurons within the brain:

- The human body broadcasts radiation: electromagnetic energy centered in the infrared frequency band can be observed radiating from the human body when viewed with optoelectronic night-vision devices, and recent experiments conclude that all living cells generate photons.
- Recent high-energy particle experiments at the Large Hadron Collider near Geneva confirm the existence of at least seven dimensions beyond those of space and time. By including these seven distinct additional dimensions, string theorists have now developed a reasonable model that can mathematically account for these previously unexplainable particle collision results; however, these dimensions are said to be too small for current technologies to detect them directly (it is assumed that these dimensions are "rolled up" below the bottom limits of spatial dimensions).
- The existence of a planetary noosphere of consciousness: Teilhard de Chardin and Vladimir Vernadsky have written extensively on the existence of a collective consciousness they called the noosphere, a "layer" of the planet in addition to the geosphere, lithosphere, and biosphere. Their noosphere is similar to that which Carl Jung called the collective unconscious, an integrated, dynamic storage repository of all consciousness generated within the biosphere.*

*Jung writes: "My thesis then, is as follows: in addition to our immediate consciousness, which is of a thoroughly personal nature and which we believe to be the only empirical psyche (even if we tack on the personal unconscious as an appendix), there exists a second psychic system of a collective, universal, and impersonal nature which is identical in all individuals. This collective unconscious does not develop individually but is inherited." Jung, *Collected Works, Vol. 9,* 112.

- The existence of a frequency domain/implicate order/Akasha: Bohm and Laszlo are convinced that there exists a transcendent, "nonlocal," coherently unified field of conscious information outside of space-time. This frequency domain is filled with intersecting holographic doppelgänger mirror-images of everything that exists in space and time, and information regarding everything that occurs in space-time is enfolded back into this frequency domain where it is stored eternally, outside of space and time.
- Multiple centers of consciousness exist spatially throughout the human body: termed chakras in Tibet and India, these regions of high neuron density and endocrine cells can be energized, cultivated, activated, and utilized through various contemplative and entheogenic techniques.
- The existence of black holes: recent cosmological observations have proven the existence of black holes as predicted by the quantum physics of Einstein. These black holes contain dimensions beyond space and time and are likely to exist everywhere in the universe. While enormous, continually growing black holes have been seen to exist at the center of galaxies. Pribram and Bohm suggest that the basis of the space-time universe is a plenum of extremely small micro black holes called holospheres. These holospheres, of Planck length diameter, project the space-time universe (much as pixels on a flat video screen project a two-dimensional image) using the accumulated information stored within the black hole.

Before exploring Indian and Tibetan maps of consciousness, let us try to form an initial map of consciousness based upon these significant Western ideas. To do this, imagine viewing energy fields swirling around the human body and continually interacting with external energy fields that blanket the planet. A subset of these fields of electromagnetic energy that flow through our bodies are the thousands of AM/FM/shortwave-station frequencies being continually generated within our biosphere. Within the human body itself is a distributed network of sub-centers of consciousness (chakras), somewhat like separate brain centers, that control and regulate various physiological systems and which, depending upon their various stages of development, are also capable, say the mystics, of sensing and interacting with unique channels (electromagnetic bands) of the noosphere. Much like a distributed system of cloud-computing servers, these chakras comprise integrated networks of radiant energy flowing throughout the body, and they most likely flow through pathways in the body known as acupuncture meridians. Certainly the methods of information encoding, modulating, and communication interchange must have developed during 4.5 billion years of evolution in Earth's history.

Numerous individuals throughout history have recounted stories of their supersensible experiences and described ways to expand one's consciousness in order to interact with these normally invisible networks. Though contemporary science seems to have neglected the information that has been left to us by many of these rare pioneers of consciousness, particularly those in India and Tibet, it is to these traditions that we now turn in order to gain another perspective of the psychophysics underlying supersensible perception with which we might begin to open our inner eye to these higher networks of consciousness that fill the planet and the stars.

PART THREE

Hindu Tantric Psychophysics

8

Patañjali

Samādhi and Jñāna Yoga

During the past several millennia generations of Indian thinkers have explored consciousness through direct participatory experimental methods of their own, though they would not have used such terms. These sages discovered numerous techniques for modulating and expanding consciousness in their search to understand God, the universe, and the human mind. Many passed down their discoveries to students and future generations, though almost always couched in the language and symbolism of their local culture and religious traditions. In the region of northeastern India (in what is now the modern state of Bihar), geographically close to Tibet, a great university called Nalanda sprang up in approximately 1500 BCE. Nalanda, now a UNESCO World Heritage Site, became a particularly important center of learning, a confluence of the rich and evolving knowledge accumulated through experiential research into consciousness and Tantric cosmology, both Buddhist and Indian. Nalanda was one of the greatest centers of learning in the world between the fifth century CE and 1200 CE, during which over a thousand full-time students studied and practiced contemplation and made copies of instructional texts called Tanta Shastra. These texts were disseminated widely throughout India from Kashmir in the northeast to South India.

The word Tantra is almost completely misunderstood in the modern world. Beginning with the misconception of early British missionaries in India that Tantra is primarily concerned with sex, many in the twenty-first century continue to believe that Tantra is "the yoga of sex."

It is common to find advertising for weekend Tantric sex workshops in the more liberal countries of the world, primarily in the West. A quick Google search on the internet using the words "Tantra and sex" returned over 52 million results! Indeed there are various Tantric teachings that involve the integration of contemplation and sexual activity, yet the vast majority of Tantric texts and practices deal with exploration of deeper states of consciousness that break the boundaries of space and time and external physical sensation.

But a broader and more accurate understanding of Tantra lies in the extraordinarily precise detail with which the traditional texts describe interior transformations of conscious energy, along with numerous techniques for modulating and transforming the consciousness of the perceiver. It is from these re-creatable Tantric methodologies and models explaining the dynamics of conscious energy that a possible coherency emerges upon which to develop a new psychophysical view of consciousness itself, a new psychophysics, and perhaps new ways of applying such psychophysical principles in a sort of Tantric engineering approach.

PSYCHONAUTICS AND PATAÑJALI

Perhaps the most practical and comprehensive mapping of states and stages of contemplative practice can be found elaborated in the *Yoga Sūtras,* attributed to the fourth-century CE Indian sage Patañjali. A contemporary teacher describes the relationship of Patañjali's *Yoga Sūtras* to Tantra:

> Most yoga scholars draw a distinct separation between Patañjali's *Yoga Sūtras* and the teachings of the Tantric texts, basically claiming that Patañjali's *Aṣṭāṅga Yoga* and Tantra are entirely different schools of yoga. But not everyone draws such a distinct separation between the two systems, especially not the indigenous teachers of the tradition.[1]

Almost two thousand years ago, Patañjali, an inheritor of the experiential knowledge gathered from previous generations and a master navigator of consciousness himself, composed the integrated set of aphorisms now called the *Yoga Sūtras.* This interconnected thread of 196 *sūtras** describes in great detail the structure and dynamics of consciousness within the human being and the states and stages experienced on the way to *samādhi* (समाधि in Sanskrit, pronounced "sum-ah-dee"), the gateway to the supersensible. More than simply a descriptive map, however, Patañjali's *Yoga Sūtras* provide a theory-practice continuum that includes "effective definitions, explanations and integration of key concepts and terms relating to *theoria* and *praxis* in Yoga."[2]

Patañjali was steeped in a culture that valued observational experience and recorded collections of verbal instruction and guidance for navigation within the vast oceans of supersensible consciousness, much in the same way as Portuguese navigators created *rutters*—the written compilations of collected sailing experiences used to cross oceans to mysterious new lands prior to the development of scientifically calibrated nautical charts in the fourteenth and fifteenth centuries. Portuguese *rutters* contained not only sketches, charts, and maps from firsthand accounts and direct observation, but also a wealth of sailing tips, such as dangers to avoid, steering directions, and other practical instruction. Patañjali's *Yoga Sūtras* can be viewed much in the same way as a Portuguese *rutter.*

Patañjali's work was compiled to guide the navigation of a human psyche in its exploration of an ocean of consciousness, while a Portuguese *rutter* was compiled to guide the navigation of a wooden ship in its exploration of an ocean of water. The late German scholar and practitioner of the *Yoga Sūtras,* Georg Feuerstein (1947–2012), describes here how the *Sūtras* are a guide:

> These models were originally and primarily maps for meditative introspection intended to guide the *yogin* in his exploration of the *terra incognita* of the mind. These "maps" are records of internal experiences rather than purely theoretical constructions.[3]

But navigation technology has changed since the fifteenth century,

*The Sanskrit word *sūtra* is related to the English word *suture* or *thread,* indicating that the terse sentences are strung together like beads on a string, a comprehensive teaching woven with coherent meaning. Each *sūtra* was meant to be chanted as a mantra until the full meaning was understood in the context of previous *sūtras.*

and much in the same way as the *rutter* navigation has evolved in five hundred years to include modern-day navigation aids (radio, internet, the Global Positioning System, AI navigation, etc.), so too the navigation *rutter* of consciousness in the *Yoga Sūtras* could use an upgrade or makeover.

Recorded by Patañjali over 1,500 years ago, the rich map presented in the *Yoga Sūtras* did not enjoy the advantages of the many advances in the sciences that have occurred since Patañjali's era. It is time to support and supplement Patañjali's early map of consciousness with new material and technological terms that have evolved since his day. The balance of this chapter is an attempt to articulate a pragmatic model of consciousness that will both clarify and extend Patañjali's model of the structure and dynamics of consciousness through the application of contemporary concepts expressed in the language of science.

The model will be shown to be supported by recently hypothesized theories of consciousness put forward by the Cambridge molecular biologist Johnjoe McFadden,[4] the New Zealand neurobiologist Susan Pockett,[5] the Stanford physicist Frank Heile,[6] the theoretical physicist, David Bohm,[7] and the author's own holoflux hypothesis.[8]

The psychophysical model developed in this book posits human consciousness as operating in three distinct modes:

1. As a fluctuating process of time-based organic memory and symbolic reasoning operating within the constraints of the human brain and neuronal systems (acting much as a computer system operates in space and time); primarily neuron-based electrical activity
2. As a distributed nexus of frequency-communication bands active within the electromagnetic plasma (ionized blood) resonant within the waveguide that is formed by the capillary system of the human body and the microtubules that fill every cell (acting much as our global information internet)
3. As electromagnetic holoflux within the ventricular cavities in the brain and down through the center of the spinal cavity where the transcendental observer (the Self) interfaces with the projected individual avatar self

While it is understandable that at first glance this tripartite model of consciousness may be somewhat opaque to the reader, a grasp of the model should become increasingly clear as this chapter progresses.

This model can be seen to be congruent with Patañjali's map if we assume the following

1. That the activities of the cognitive human mind are *citta*
2. That radiant individual consciousness is *puruṣa*
3. That the transcendental Self (*Puruṣa* or *Brahman*) interfaces with the isolated individual consciousness (*puruṣa*)

Figure 8.1 offers an abbreviated comparison of the three modes of consciousness in the two models. The term *Brahman* in Mode #3 should be understood as equivalent to the terms *Puruṣa* (with a capital *P*), Carl Jung's *Self*, and the Christian-Judaeo word *God*.

	Consciousness **Mode #1**	Consciousness **Mode #2**	Consciousness **Mode #3**
Yoga Sutras	*citta* (brain-mind)	*puruṣa* (individual self)	*Brahman* (the One Self)
Tantric Psychophysics	Electromagnetic fields in brain and nervous system	Ionized plasma fields in capillaries and microtubules	Cerebrospinal fluid in the ventricular cavities

Fig. 8.1. Comparison of the two models of consciousness.

The focus in the remaining material presented in this chapter is upon the intersection of psychophysics and contemplation. We support Patañjali's map with the geometry of mind offered by the "implicate order," a domain explored by the quantum physicist David Bohm. But first we will go a bit deeper into the *Yoga Sūtras*. On this journey, we will see how science and metaphysics clearly support one another.

In Patañjali's work we find a map describing in exquisite detail a comprehensive and practical approach to contemplative stages of meditation. Patañjali's more technical instructions on meditation are the focus here, and the emphasis is upon a clarification of his practical techniques for applying these theories during daily meditation. The *sūtras* taken together explore the heart of Patañjali's map that leads to awareness of the distinction between the isolated individual ego self and the transcendent "One Self." With sufficient knowledge of the states and stages of psychonautic contemplation, one has the potential to leave the ego behind and to link with that "One Self." In a clear step-by-step manner, the lessons found in these *sūtras* of Patañjali offer valuable guidance in one's efforts to activate and develop supersensible perception.

While a rare few humans are born with these supersensible faculties fully developed and functioning, most of us must apply other steps in order to activate and cultivate these evolutionarily emergent capabilities of perception. Only then can we open up our "inner eyes" in order to interact with supersensory multidimensional webs of awareness both to receive information and to dialogue with those on the other side. The first step is to understand what may be an astonishing idea to many: there are indeed other ways of thinking, other ways of operating our conscious mind-stuff. The first step toward development of supersensible perception is to accept the possibility that there are indeed other operational modes of our conscious mind if we only know how to activate them. Throughout the *Yoga Sūtras* pithy aphorisms are presented that, when woven together, provide a detailed and experientially accurate picture of the states and stages of consciousness. Being able to identify the stage from which one's center of consciousness is currently operating within gives the psychonaut information on how best to navigate experiences that might arise in that state as well as how best to shift to the next higher stage of awareness.

PATAÑJALI'S PSYCHOPHYSICS

As previously mentioned, in Patañjali's *Yoga Sūtras,* dating back to the second or third century CE,[9] we find an elaborate map of human consciousness as well as explicit methods for traveling through and among the various regions described in that map. The most important element in interpreting the *Yoga Sūtras* is the element of introspection, an "experiential dimension" of inquiry inclusive of the observer within the observation—*introspection* as championed by William James over a century ago. The *Yoga Sūtras* contain a collection of experiential wisdom distilled over the lifetimes of generations of Indian sages, which has been compiled with a stamp of authenticity—a great deal of real, enduring, and practical validity to Patañjali's map can be inferred by the many translations and written commentaries that have sprung up beginning with the legendary Indian sage Vyāsa, as early as the seventh century CE.

In a series of terse *sūtras* (mnemonic threads, from the root *siv,* "to sew"), Patañjali constructs a pragmatic model for human access to states of awareness rarely found in daily human waking experience. The descriptions of these states and dimensions of consciousness, and the instructions given for maneuvering among them, are the outgrowths of direct observations contributed from age to age through a long lineage of contemplative seekers in India. Patañjali has not only compiled this treasure trove of experiential wisdom, but he has organized the material in such a way that each new concept builds upon an understanding of the previous *sūtra.*

The word *yoga* can be translated as "a yoke," "to link," or "to unite."[10] In contemporary societies, yoga is commonly misconstrued to indicate a form of physical exercise consisting of traditional Indian body-stretching poses. But Edwin Bryant, a Harvard professor of Hindu philosophy and religion, tells us otherwise:

> When it is used by itself without any qualification, it refers to the path of meditation, particularly as outlined in the *Yoga Sūtras*—the Aphorisms on Yoga—and the term yogi, a practitioner of this type of meditational yoga.[11]

The word *yoga* is often used incorrectly as being synonymous with the word *samādhi,* but *samādhi* is actually an "ego-free, distraction-free" state of consciousness that is eventually acquired through practicing the various techniques of yoga as described not only in the *Yoga Sūtras,* but as taught in even greater detail in numerous other texts and schools of Indian and Tibetan Tantra. While *samādhi* is the goal of yoga, it is not the end, but only the entry into the world of psychonautics. As a professor of Tibetan studies in Varanasi, India, states:

> Patañjali emphasizes the goal called *samādhi* which one has to attain through practice and make it a matter of experience. The vision which one attains through the practice of *samādhi* is again a direct vision. It is not of an abstract or speculative kind.[12]

The *Yoga Sūtras* offer detailed instruction for an experiential, introspective approach to achieving the state of *samādhi* in order to navigate the flow of sentient energy within the human *citta*, the brain's psychocognitive mental subsystem, with the tacit goal of shutting down the normal cognitive activities of the brain-mind (*citta*). When the normal activities of the mind are attenuated, or even halted, a radically non-dual mode of conscious awareness is experienced—an astonishing perception of an entirely new world of consciousness floods in to fill the cognitive vacuum. Patañjali gives us numerous ways of controlling, redirecting, and modifying normal mental activities to establish new transcendent* links, unions, and communions with a wide range of disparate centers of conscious awareness.

Patañjali's *Yoga Sūtras* is divided into four sets of aphorisms, four chapters, parts, or *pāda* described by Whicher[13] as:

1. ***Samādhi-Pāda***: a discussion of *samādhi* and the general approach of yoga as a practical method of activating *samādhi*; 55 *sūtras*
2. ***Sādhana-Pāda***: a discussion of the "path" as eight major "external practices" of yoga that lead to an activation of *samādhi* (these include the physical exercises of *hatha yoga*); 55 *sūtras*
3. ***Vibhūti-Pāda***: The first 4 *sūtras* encapsulate the most powerful series of techniques that must be mastered for entering *samādhi*; the remaining 51 sutras discuss the numerous skills and powers that arise through the practice of samādhi; 55 *sūtras* total
4. ***Kaivalya-Pāda***: A deep discussion of the non-dual experience of "Oneness" (i.e., the experience of congruent non-dualism with what Carl Jung calls "the Self"); 34 *sūtras*

**Transcendent* as used in this work is to be contrasted with "ordinary everyday waking" consciousness: a state or condition of awareness beyond verbal-emotional ego boundaries, numinous, sublime, inexpressible, elaborated by Patañjali in his descriptive injunctions defining the various stages and states of *samādhi* and *kaivalya*.

The initial goal of yoga is attainment of the state of *samādhi,* an initial experience of supersensible perception from which deeper psychonautical voyaging may proceed. Contained within the four collections of *sūtras* is a comprehensive and succinctly presented map with various proven methods for navigating consciousness, the ultimate goal of which being attainment of the state of *samādhi.* It is in the final chapter, *Kaivalya-Pāda,* that *Patañjali* describes various experiences and realizations that lie beyond the initial attainment of *samādhi.* However, until a psychonaut has begun to explore dimensions of super consciousness using *samādhi,* much of the material in this final chapter will not be easy to grasp. Once an individual is able to use *samādhi* to explore these higher worlds directly, much of the final chapter will become clear. It will be found that the same territory is clearly described in Tibetan Buddhist texts that map states and stages of Vajrayāna contemplation, though in this Buddhist context, different terms are frequently stressed. The Tibetan approach is discussed and reconciled with Patañjali's work in part 4, "Tibetan Tantric Psychophysics."

The short Sanskrit aphorisms of the *Yoga Sūtras* were composed during an era when written records (often on palm leaves) were scarce and fragile. Memorization of material was of utmost importance, and the *sūtras* were composed to facilitate the recitation of individual *sūtras* in mantric form (often counted on a *mala* consisting of 108 beads on a string). Repetition of an individual *sūtra* allows the meaning to develop, slowly revealing itself, and each *sūtra* builds methodically upon previous *sūtras,* while often prefiguring the appearance of future *sūtras* to amplify and extend their meaning.

The model of human consciousness that is methodically described by Patañjali is constructed using many concepts that are found to be basic components from the older *Sāṃkhya,*[14] a philosophy thought by some to have arisen as early as 500 BCE. The *Sāṃkhya* cosmology regards the universe as consisting of two independent realities, *puruṣa* (consciousness) and *prakṛti* (matter). These two realities coexist in parallel, intermixing with one another. In a human being the ratio of "matter and spirit" can be affected through the practice of yogic techniques, which work to separate and refine spirit (consciousness) through identifying it and extracting it from matter, much as gold can be mined and separated from rock.

If we take the view that successful practice of Patañjali's yoga leads not only to a liberation of *puruṣa* from *prakṛti* but a freeing up of *puruṣa* that allows movement into progressively deeper states of *samādhi* that lead to eventual direct non-dual experience of *Puruṣa* (Self, Brahman, Yahweh, God), it is even more important to realize that this is *not* an escape from the mind, but an evolution of consciousness both within the individual and collectively within the species; operationally, this is an entirely new functioning of *puruṣa* within *prakṛti,* a new mode of awareness and a gateway to the implicate order.

For contemplatives of all persuasions, the *Yoga Sūtras* provides a wealth of both practical and theoretical material that can greatly help one to grasp an overview of the subject and to visualize the territory that opens up to new modes of perception as one enters higher states of consciousness. To begin with, it is worthwhile to understand the general purpose of each of Patañjali's four parts or chapters (*pāda*) of the *Yoga Sūtras.*

I. *SAMĀDHI-PĀDA:* TUNING THE MIND

The concept of *samādhi* finds parallels in the experiential metaphysics of other cultures in such terms as "the uncreated light" (Hesychasm), "Nirvana" (Hinayāna Buddhism), "the Void" (Tibetan Buddhism), and even earlier in the "ecstasy" (ἐκ-στασις) of Plotinus. A diagram of the first section of the *Yoga Sūtras* is given in figure 8.2 (p. 110) that reveals the relationships among the first eighteen *sūtras* within the *Samādhi-Pāda.*

In all schools of yoga, it is believed that a richer, more unitive state of consciousness (beyond ordinary everyday awareness) can be reached through practicing techniques that have been found efficacious for developing the acquisition of the state of *samādhi,* a state of unbroken, undistracted concentration of consciousness. *Samādhi** is clearly identified as the primary goal of practicing yoga, and it is the subject of

**Samādhi*: from the Sanskrit word *sam,* meaning "together," "union," "perfect," "integrated," and *adhi,* meaning "unbroken," "whole"). It is the eighth and final step of what Patañjali calls *aṣṭāṅga yoga* or the "eightfold path." Similarly, in Buddhism, it is the eighth and final step of the Noble Eightfold Path.

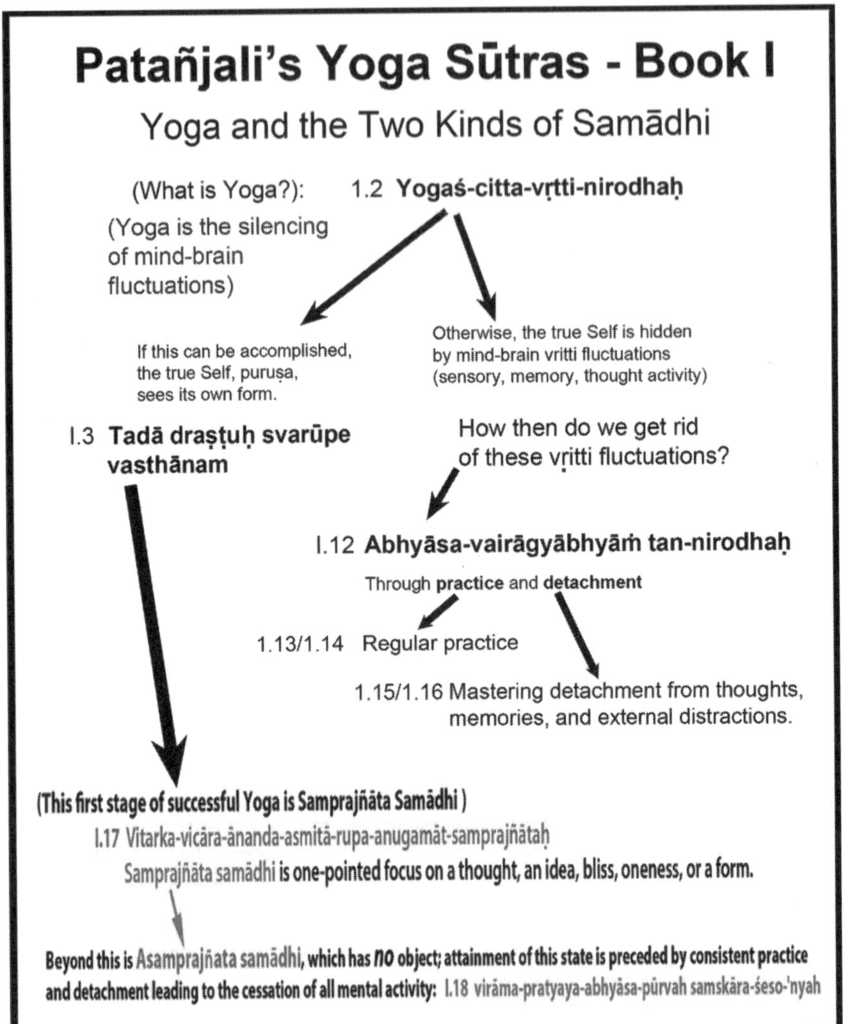

Fig. 8.2. Diagram of *Yoga Sūtras* part I.

the first section of the *Yoga Sūtras*. Through mastery of the fluctuations of the cognitive mind-brain (*vṛttis*) one is able to reach the state of *samādhi* within which it is possible to experience conscious identity with the *Puruṣa,* also described as "one's true Self."[15] This state is eventually realizable through persistent and regular efforts in following the various practices described in the *Yoga Sūtras*.

Quieting the Mind to Bring About *Samādhi*

The Yoga Sūtras are often summarized in a relatively simplistic translation by focusing exclusively upon the second sūtra:

Sūtra I.2. Yogaś-citta-vṛtti-nirodhaḥ.
Yoga is the stilling of the changing states of the mind.[16]

Numerous translations and commentaries have been made of the *Yoga Sūtras,* and it is surprising to find such an enormously wide range of interpretations of even this first *sūtra* (fig. 8.3), making it quite difficult to extract Patañjali's true intentions without a great deal of contemplative

Various Translations of Yoga Sutra I.2	Translator	Date Published
"Yoga is the **stilling** of the changing states of mind."	Bryant	2009
"Yoga is the **control** (*nirodhaha,* regulation, channeling, mastery, integration, coordination, stilling, quieting, setting aside) of the modifications (gross and subtle thought patterns) of the mind field."	Jnanesaa	2004
"The **restraint** of the modifications of the mind-stuff is Yoga."	Satchidananda	1990
"Yoga is the **restriction** of the fluctuations of consciousness."	Feuerstein	1989
"Yoga is the **cessation** of the waves (arising in) (or) activities of mind-stuff."	Arya	1974
"Yoga is the **control** of thought-waves in the mind."	Prabhavananda	1969
"Yoga is the **inhibition** of the modifications of the mind."	Taimni	1961
"Yoga is **restraining** the mind-stuff (*Chitta*) from taking forms (*vrittis*)."	Vivedananda	1955
"This union (or Yoga) is achieved through the **subjugation** of the psychic nature, and restraint of the citta (or mind)."	Baily	1955
"Yoga is the **control** of the ideas of the mind."	Wood	1948
"Yoga is **suppression** of the activity of the thinking principle."	Dvivedi	1930

Fig. 8.3. Alternate translations for *nirodhaḥ*

practice itself. The figure on the previous page reveals this problem in the interpretation/translation of the word *nirodhaḥ* in this first *sūtra,* taken from an excellent compilation by Salvatore Zambito.[17] The translations of *nirodhaḥ* shown on page 111 reveal a somewhat heavy-handed aggressive translation taken by these English translators (e.g., their use of the words *suppression, subjugation, inhibition, restriction,* and *restraint*), as if the *citta* (translated variously as "mind," "mind-stuff," "thinking principle," "thought-waves," "consciousness," "mind-field") were somehow an insurrection needing to be put down with the firm authoritative commands of "suppress," "restrain," "inhibit," and "halt" the flow of the cognitive brain-mind.

Along with Bryant, who translates *nirodhaḥ* as "stilling," Jnaneshvara, an American disciple of my own teacher, Dr. Rammurti Mishra, comes in with the second least aggressive translation in the table with "control." My own translation would be "Yoga is the attenuation of activities of the mental subsystems." Here the word *attenuation* implies a less aggressive exercise, the application of knowledge and skill gained through practice in modulating the various subsystems of the human mental processes. Thinking in words, remembering, conceptualizing, allowing ideas to arise and develop—all of these normal activities and skills of what we call mind must be attenuated, turned down, and allowed to taper off so that awareness can enter into a new state.

The internal silence opened up through the successful quieting and detaching from the normal operations of mind allows awareness to flow into alternate configurations, opening up new modes of sensory and cognitive perception. In fact, the word "quieting" might be a good translation for *nirodhaḥ,* and it is not a coincidence that it also appears as a major concept in the early Christian contemplative practice of *hesychia* (ἡσυχία), the "stillness, quiet, silence" found in the writings of Evagrius Ponticus[18] and other eremites in Egypt as early as the fourth century CE. For example: "Antony said, 'He who sits alone and is quiet has escaped from three wars: hearing, speaking, and seeing.'"[19] And in the fourteenth century CE a monk on Mount Athos, Gregory Palamas, wrote extensively on the practice of inner silence and defended this contemplative practice against a Calabrian priest who attacked hesychasts as "navel gazers" and abandoners of the material world and its responsibilities.

Sūtra I.2 of the *Yoga Sūtras,* taken alone without an appreciation for its context within the entire collection, has similarly led to criticism for appealing to what seems to be an abandonment of the material world and its responsibilities, the popular "escape from reality" epithet. More recent views have rescued Patañjali from this criticism. Many now view Patañjali's yoga *not* as "a withdrawal from the world" but as a program of contemplative exercises leading to a transformation of consciousness beyond what is considered to be the normally discursive, isolated, outward-looking human psyche.

In Patañjali's yoga, the initial objective is to train the mind (*citta*) to enter into a state of deep quiescence or silence, to remain as dormant as possible, and to learn techniques to attenuate the various physiological systems of the body to idle at their lowest levels.

What is the objective in shutting down these normal waking-state active cognitive mental systems? In that quiescent state the energy of consciousness, thus freed, will be available to flow into a new mode of consciousness, powering the supersensible perception of dimensions that are normally hidden, masked by what are called the *vṛttis* (literally, whirlpools), the incessant gyrations of the cognitive mind's inner dialogue and memory retrieval activities. This leads us to the next *sūtra,* I.3.

Sūtra I.3. Tadā draṣṭuḥ svarūpe vasthānam.
Then the Seer [Self] abides in His own Nature.[20]

At this point Patañjali tells us that this Seer (or Self) then wakes up and "abides in His own Nature." With the additional energy available from the suspension of normal mental activities a threshold is crossed into the pure self-resonant, self-reflecting Self.

Nirodhaḥ: How to Quiet the Mind

In subsequent *sūtras,* Patañjali teaches how progress can be made in controlling the mind to reach *nirodhaḥ* (cessation or attenuation of the fluctuations of the *vṛttis*), which then opens up access to the *samādhi* states. For "shutting down the mind," the student is advised to rely upon and to cultivate two primary tools: *practice* and *detachment.*

Sūtra I.12. Abhyāsa-vairāgyābhyāṁ tan-nirodhaḥ.
Through practice and detachment, quieting of the mind.[21]

The state of *nirodhaḥ* has been attained through crossing a threshold into *samādhi* and might be likened to rebooting the mind (*manas*) with a new operating system that is less linear, has more capabilities, and offers fewer distracting limitations. Commentators have advised that it is only with sustained practice (*abhyāsa*) and detachment (*vairāgya*) that the first glimpses or tastes of *samādhi* dawn on the practitioner; however, eventually the fluctuations of cognitive mind and memory, the many types of *vṛttis,* subside and are replaced with an opening up to a more complete identification with one's primordial baseline self, the *puruṣa*. The dawning sense of congruence with the *puruṣa* allows the contemplative to have an initial experience of *samādhi.*

But simply attaining an initial *samādhi* experience is only the beginning, not the final goal. The first experiences of *samādhi* are almost always quickly lost when the individual returns from silent meditation, "reboot" their cognitive brain-mind, and return to the habitual state of an ego active within a body-biosuit.* The objective of Patañjali's yoga is to acquire the skills to maintain *samādhi* for as long as possible in an unbroken time sequence. The ultimate goal is to be able to enter and maintain the state of *samādhi* at will, even during normal waking cognitive activities.

Patañjali tells us that there are two major categories of *samādhi,* and there is a specific sequence in which these two *samādhis* typically develop, prior to "enlightenment" (a state of experiential knowledge of reality attained when one's little separate "self" is finally able to merge and identify with the one "Self" of the Whole).

The two *samādhis* are categorized broadly into two ontological regions. The first, being the practice of "*samprajñāta samādhi,*" translated as "with seed" or *sabīja samādhi,* is attained through such contemplative exercises as mantra. Such a focal "seed" acts as an object for consciousness to dwell upon as the ordinary activities of the brain-

*A term coined by William Tiller, professor emeritus of materials science and engineering at Stanford.

mind begin to attenuate. At some point the mantric "seed" sprouts into deeper states of conscious experience.

During the state of *sabīja samādhi,* since the fluctuations or *cittavṛttis* (verbal cognition, arising trains of memory, emotional impulse, etc.) are attenuated (through much practice and detachment, *sūtra* I.12), as the contemplative is able to practice one-pointed attention (*saṁyamaḥ*) on a single categorical element, a *bīja* ("seed"), in this case a mantra though there are a number of other *bīja* objects beyond a mantra, for example, visualization of the symbolic figure of a yantra, or focus upon a specific locus (chakra) within the human body.

The second and more advanced *samādhi* experience is typically *asamprajñāta samādhi* or "without seed" during which all external sensory systems are shut down and consciousness focuses on pure consciousness without an object with the intent of liberating consciousness from the bounds of sensory input and brain-mind cognition and thus allowing psychonauts the freedom to sense, enter, and explore new worlds of awareness. The two approaches to *samādhi* are further explained in the following sections.

Samprajñāta Samādhi: Consciousness with "Seed" Object

The movement from ordinary, isolated, human brain-mind consciousness to the experience of the non-dual *puruṣa* is possible, according to Patañjali, through the knowledge and mastery of two states (or stages) of *samādhi,* not necessarily practiced in sequence.*

- *sabīja samādhi* > "consciousness with seed"
- *nirbīja samādhi* > "consciousness without seed"

So what are these "seeds?" The root of the word *bīja* is *bij* meaning "seed," "origin," "cause." It is frequently used as a metaphor for the origin and root cause of things. The earliest use of the word *bīja* can

*Though most people require training and practice (as in the development of any sport/skill) to acquire these *samādhis,* some individuals are born with the innate proclivity to shift their consciousness into one or both of these *samādhi* states at early ages, without the need for many months or years of regular developmental practice.

be found 3500 years ago in the Vedas.* The most famous *bīja* is *Om* ("aum"), what is called a "seed mantra" that appears many times in Vedic chants.

The word *bīja* is at the heart of understanding the function and objective of mantra, which can be understood as much more than words, even sacred words, though all prayer can be mantra. Single words or a single syllable (i.e., a *bīja*) repeated over and over, are mantra when practiced with as continuous a focus of awareness as possible. Of course, the mantra does not have to be audible; it can be a silent repetition, which is internally audible only within the brain-mind. The audible resonance is consciousness itself, and internal repetition leads to resonant contact with the source of the vibrations itself in the frequency domain (Bohm's implicate order) of consciousness, allowing supersensible perception to arise. This is the state Patañjali calls *sabīja samādhi.*

The subject of mantra is an important one in India and Tibet and will be discussed more fully in a later chapter. The simplest mantra is a single "seed-syllable" which the practitioner utters either audibly or silently (internally, usually while focusing sensation upon one chakra, a specific spatial location with the body). It has long been considered to be a primary psychonautical exercise to focus awareness on such a single sound syllable or an entire prayer (or hymn) in order to develop the capability for supersensible awareness that is required for psychonautical exploration. Gonda writes, "*Mantra* are considered, not products of discursive thought, human wisdom or poetic phantasy, but flash-lights of the eternal truth, seen by those eminent men who have come into a supersensuous contact with the Unseen."[22]

In addition to focusing upon a mantra to bring about this initial *samādhi,* many adepts practice spiritual chants (*kirtan*), practice visualization of various symbolic drawings of chakra centers, visualize complex Tibetan *thangkas,* or focus upon internal psychic chakra centers. Specific techniques will be discussed in chapters 10 and 13.

---

*The Vedas are a collection of over 10,000 hymns that were composed in Sanskrit in northwestern India as early as 1700 BCE. The Vedas present liturgical ritual, meditation, philosophy, and spiritual knowledge that is traditionally memorized and chanted, much as the *Yoga Sūtras* were likely memorized and chanted when Patañjali compiled them around 400 CE.

Asamprajñāta Samādhi: Consciousness without an Object

A yet even more rarified state of *samādhi* is attainable through efforts to experience what has been called by some "consciousness without an object,"[23] and known in the *Yoga Sūtras* as *asamprajñāta samādhi* (also referred to as *nirbīja samādhi,* or "*samādhi* without seed"). This state is attained only when one learns how to completely let go or drop awareness of all seed objects in order to remain in a state that is fully detached from all objects of perceptual cognition and to maintain this formless awareness for some duration in time (ranging from several seconds for beginners to multiple hours for experienced practitioners). In many shamanistic and religious traditions this heightened state of awareness without an object is also known as the trance state.

The great philosopher of religion, Mircea Eliade (1907–1986) has characterized *asamprajñāta samādhi* as a state of "enstasis," a word which can be translated as "standing within."[24] In the ecstatic *samprajñāta samādhi* one is in a sense looking outward from the standpoint of the "seer," experiencing outward ecstasy, while by contrast in the enstatic *asamprajñāta samādhi* one is looking inward toward the center, the heart being, the deep Self so often described by Carl Jung.

It is logical to say that nothing can readily be said about this second category of *asamprajñāta samādhi,* since to arrive there we must go by way of silencing the normal mental memory-making-and-recording operations of the mind. I have always noticed how difficult it is to recall dream sequences or experiences undergone under the influence of entheogens such as LSD or mescaline, and my conclusion has been that the normal brain-mind memory-making systems have ceased (or have been highly attenuated) in order to even reach such states of awareness. One can experience these extreme states of awareness but later not be able to recall anything other than some vague feelings that something occurred within consciousness. This is not to say that there is no conscious experience associated with the state of *asamprajñāta samādhi,* but simply that in returning from the experience, as in returning from the state of dream sleep, no well-formed memories have been recorded and nothing saved, to the extent that the contemplative cannot even be sure he attained *asamprajñāta samādhi.*

How then does the practitioner know that *asamprajñāta samādhi* has been experienced? A scholar and practitioner of Patañjali's yoga, Ian Whicher, acknowledges this problem of memory:

> Upon returning from *asamprajñāta* to the waking state, the yogin observes the time that has elapsed and thereby infers that the state of nirodha has indeed occurred . . . there is no memory carried over from the "experience" in *asamprajñāta*.[25]

Certainly there is a paradox here, for we find that many, many words *have* been written over the centuries about these deepest regions explored by consciousness through means of *samādhi*. However, it is quite possible that the informative maps handed down by generations of psychonauts can be viewed as the cumulative efforts of many contemplatives over many lifetimes making repeated attempts to return from these supersensory dimensions of being with some kind of a map of the territories traversed as psychonauts. Such maps are to be found in the accounts recorded in the Vedas, Upanishads, and other texts and poems from many other cultures; all attempt to impart knowledge of a transcendent consciousness, experiences of the pure *Puruṣa,* the Absolute, *nirguṇa brahman,* or the Self.

Kaivalya itself is the focus of Patañjali's fourth section of the *Yoga Sūtras*. The term *kaivalya* describes a state of "consciousness without an object," a state of timeless, spaceless solitude, isolation, and detachment. The word *kaivalya* is derived from the Sanskrit *kevala,* meaning "alone" or "isolated." It is described by Patañjali as a separation of *puruṣa* (Self or Soul) from *prakṛti* (primal matter). The ability to enter the state of *kaivalya* is a primary goal of Patañjali's yoga (often referred to as *rāja yoga).* It is the goal of shifting one's center of consciousness from the limited space-time ego into the non-dual Self of Carl Jung or equivalently, the implicate order of David Bohm.

II. *SĀDHANA-PĀDA:* TUNING CONSCIOUSNESS TO ATTAIN *SAMĀDHI*

The next section of the *Yoga Sūtras,* chapter II, elaborates detailed instruction for methods aiding in quieting the *citta* noise fluctuations

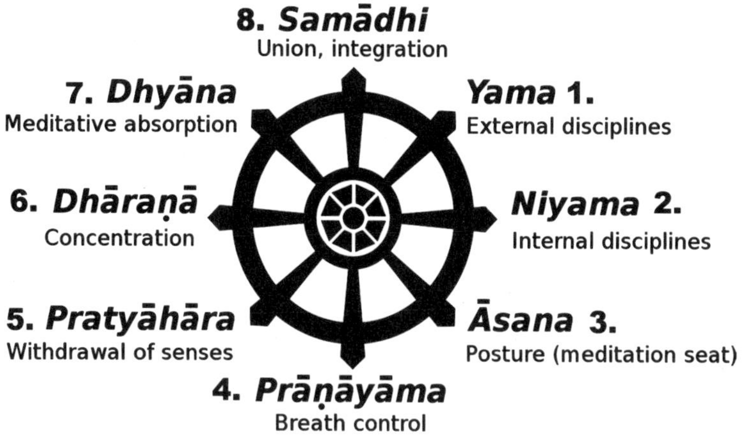

Fig. 8.4. Patañjali's *aṣṭāṅga yoga*.
Figure by Ian Alexander.

of the cognitive brain-mind. This quieting or attenuation of normal mind activity is essential in preparation for tuning consciousness into the more cosmic bandwidths of *samādhi*. The *sūtras* in this chapter describe in some detail the widely practiced *aṣṭāṅga yoga* or "eightfold-path" (fig. 8.4): *yama, niyama, āsana, prāṇāyāma, pratyāhāra, dhāraṇā, dhyāna, samādhi*. Note that there is a generally mistaken assumption in the modern public view of yoga, where even in yoga magazines there is a tacit assumption that *hatha yoga* (primarily instruction on *āsana* poses) is yoga itself, with disregard for the other seven approaches and of the primary objective, which is acquisition of supersensible perception that opens with the mastering of *samādhi*. Modern yoga studios teach *āsana* poses primarily for physical health and mental tranquility and are the primary objectives in the majority of Western yoga classes, which do not seem to teach those more contemplative practices described in the *aṣṭāṅga yoga*. The advanced contemplative exercises taught in *aṣṭāṅga yoga* are often referred to as *rāja yoga* or "royal yoga."

Yet according to Patañjali, anyone can eventually achieve mastery of the state of *samādhi* (which leads directly to *kaivalya* and wider psychonautical explorations) by practicing the eight principles of *aṣṭāṅga yoga* and working to apply them in one's daily life through sustained effort.

While it is generally thought that an individual must master each of the eight branches of yoga in sequence, beginning with *yamas,* this is not strictly required. Some individuals may be born with a proclivity for *dhāraṇā, dhyāna, samādhi* early in their life experience. However, there is a sound reason to consider mastering each "limb" of *aṣṭāṅga yoga* in sequence as follows:

1. *Yama:* Abstinences (nonviolence, refraining from lies, fasting, etc.)
2. *Niyama*: Observances (study, self-discipline, reflection "Who am I?")
3. *Āsana*: Physical exercises (yoga, postures for health and meditation)
4. *Prāṇāyāma*: Breath control (deep breathing, focus on breath movement)
5. *Pratyāhāra*: Withdrawal of external sensory input; internal silence
6. *Dhāraṇā*: Concentration (even if at first intermittently interrupted)
7. *Dhyāna*: Meditation (uninterrupted streaming of concentration)
8. *Samādhi*: Trance: perfect uninterrupted meditation at will.

And of course it should be noted that the final stage, *samādhi,* is just the beginning for the psychonaut. Before states of *samādhi* can be experienced on a regular basis, the individual must come to terms with numerous *kleśas,* variously called "afflictions," "habits," or "impediments." These *kleśas* tend to keep the mind jumping and noisy, unable to experience the subsidence of activity into the quiescence necessary for entering the various states of *samādhi* and the ultimate cosmic resonance, the congruent experiencing of *puruṣa* (small individual self) with Puruṣa (cosmic Self).

The most critical skill of yoga, attenuating the noise* fluctuations

*"Noise," from the physics standpoint, is any unwanted distracting or masking incidental frequency vibrations or stimulus that may interfere within an observing or receiving system.

of the mental subsystems (*Yogaś-citta-vṛtti-nirodhaḥ*), is required to attain the various dimensions of *samādhi* that were discussed at the very beginning of the *Yoga Sūtras.* The necessary states of sustained quiescence are far beyond any silence normally experienced in waking consciousness; they mandate practice that leads to mastery of skills generally undeveloped in human beings. Thus, this chapter describes in detail various exercises for reaching those realms of suspension in which *puruṣa* can be detected, contacted, and allowed to radiate. This second chapter of the *Yoga Sūtras* opens with a definition of *kriyā yoga,* and as elsewhere, the first *sūtra* is the most important *sūtra* in the chapter:

Sūtra II.1. Tapaḥ svādhyāy-eśvarapraṇidhānāni kriyā-yogaḥ
Practice, self-examination, and submission to a
higher Self is action (kriyā) *yoga.*

Patañjali here defines "action yoga" as consisting of the three most important elements of practice, self-knowledge (which reminds us of Plato's injunction, "to know thyself"), and developing a relationship with (acknowledging the existence of) a higher Self. The following *sūtras* in this chapter describe various aspects of yogic practices to bring peace to the personality in general and to gain control of various mental subsystems so that they will not interfere with deep contemplative experience. It is no good to learn to quiet the mind only to have addictive impulses, memories, and even creative thoughts continually arising to break the sought-after silence. Instructions in this chapter range from:

- encouraging *hatha yoga* to calm the body and thus make it easier to ignore bodily sensations that might distract during excursions into the deep psyche
- developing a personal entity-to-entity emotional relationship with the deeper Self, perhaps viewed as "God" through liturgical worship
- breathing exercises, all of which are meant to help the practitioner find the inner quiet and assurance that the silence will not be broken for the sustained period needed to bring about the experience

of a consciousness mode beyond the linear and temporal—the eternal effulgent radiance of *puruṣa* that flows outward from within our deepest sub-cellular selves.

III. *VIBHŪTI-PĀDA:* THE POWERS OF CONSCIOUSNESS

The next chapter of the *Yoga Sūtras,* chapter III, assumes that the material in the previous chapter, *pāda* II, has been mastered to the extent of ensuring that the next higher stages of contemplative practice will be minimally disturbed by physical, mental, or emotional distractions. In this third chapter, Patañjali begins with a focus upon the three specific instructions that facilitate entrance into *samādhi.* The rest of the chapter is an enumeration of various perceptual powers that may be acquired through the activation of various modes of supersensible perception.* Here again, the first *sūtra* is the most important in the chapter, describing a key skill that must be practiced in order to move into *samādhi.* This is the practice of *dhāraṇā,* the technique of holding the focus of consciousness steadily within a single localized region bounded by space and time:

Sūtra III.1. Deśa-bandhaḥ cittasya dhāraṇā
Focusing citta consciousness within a specific place is called dhāraṇā.

As John Lilly observed, *dhāraṇā* as a skill is currently highly developed in Western educational systems, though not frequently used in conjunction with yoga. *Dhāraṇā* is the skill of being able to focus consciousness as fully as possible in one specific region (*deśa*), the more focused the better, and to sustain that attention for some period of time, the longer the better. Accordingly, one would assume that in addition to academics, electronic "gamers" might also have such a skill through their long hours of intense concentration.

The next step is to "hold" that focus steadily without being diverted by distractions, and to learn to be able to sustain this laser-like focus

*See my earlier book, *Developing Supersensible Perception.*

unwaveringly for a protracted period of time, which is the subject of the next important *sūtra,* III.2., defining the fundamental practice of contemplation with the word *dhyāna,* which in later centuries, when Patañjali's teachings spread out from India, were translated into similar sounding words: in Chinese as *Chán* (禪) and in Japanese as Zen:

Sūtra III.2. Tatra pratyaya-ikatānatā dhyānam
Here the content of awareness held in a single stream is called dhyāna.

The "single stream" here is the unbroken sequence of time, and the practice of holding the *citta* consciousness steadily and continuously in the same place is here defined as *dhyāna.* The focus (*samādhi*-with-object) that is used to effect the transformational sequence from *dhāraṇā* to *dhyāna* can be various: a mantra (repetition of an audibly voiced or internally sensed *sūtra* or prayer), a yantra (usually a visual, painted diagram), a concept, an inner sensation, and so on. The key here is to be able to sustain this bounded focus of consciousness within such a particular region for a sufficient length of time and intensity of focus so as to ignite transition into the state called *samādhi,* which is the subject of the next *sūtra.* An analogy might be seen in using a magnifying glass to focus the rays of the sun on an object in order to set it aflame. When focusing rays of light through use of a glass lens, the object is a small visual object (e.g., a plant cell, amoeba, crystal, etc.) whereas in focusing consciousness with *dhyāna* the object might be a mantra, yantra (visual image), concept (such as love, death, detachment), an external point (tip of a candle flame, crystal ball), or an internal bodily location or sensation.

Success in this *dhāraṇā* to *dhyāna* sequence is obtained when the practitioner experiences a shift or threshold crossing of consciousness into a state of *samādhi* as described in the third *sūtra* of this chapter:

Sūtra III.3. Tadeva-artha-mātra-nirbhāsaṁ svarūpa-śūnyam-iva-samādhiḥ
Samādhi is when that same dhyāna *shines forth as*

the object alone and [the mind] is devoid of its own [reflective] nature.[26]

The rest of the third chapter describes numerous *siddhis* or "powers" that those contemplatives who have been able achieve *samādhi* have exercised and observed when exploring the domains of consciousness opened through entry into the ocean *puruṣa*, including such things as communication with other centers of consciousness (telepathy), becoming invisible to others, remote seeing, inner light, and other supersensible perceptual experiences.

IV. *KAIVALYA-PĀDA:* MULTIMIND AND ONENESS

The next chapter of the *Yoga Sūtras*, chapter IV, offers instructions for navigating the seas of consciousness into which *samādhi* has led the practitioner. The *sūtras* found in this chapter will not be readily understood by the pre-*samādhi* beginning practitioner of *kriyā yoga,* but as the adept progresses in mastery of the states of *samādhi* the meanings of the material in this chapter will become useful and more readily grasped.

Acquisition of Supersensible Perception

The chapter begins with *sūtra* IV.1, which describes five primary ways in which an individual finds his or her way into perception of states of higher awareness:

Sūtra IV.1. Janma-oṣadhi-mantra-tapas-samādhi-jāḥ siddhayaḥ
The supersensory powers of perception arise from birth, drugs, mantras, austerity, or samādhi.[27]

The presentation order is highly significant in the general construction of this type of teaching mnemonic, a *śloka* or verse line. Words introduced first in the *śloka* are given greater emphasis in the teaching, and carry more weight in the topic or statement being made. In this important *śloka* that opens the fourth and final chapter in Patañjali's

Yoga Sūtras, the five ways of acquiring *siddhis* (a word that can also be translated as "attainment," "accomplishment," or "success") are listed in order of efficacy:

1. By birth
2. By drugs
3. By mantra
4. By psychophysical effort
5. By contemplative meditation

Acquisition by Birth (Genetic)

A few rare saints and mystics are born with their minds already attuned to broader bandwidths or states of consciousness beyond the general experiences of contemporaries. These might include Tibetan *tulkus* such as the Dalai Lama and various saints, yogis, and shamans through the ages.

Acquisition by Drugs (Herbs/Mushrooms/Vines/Chemicals)

Others, according to Patañjali, are initially able to attain supersensory perception by ingestion of drugs (*oṣadhi*) such as the ancient soma described in the Vedas (believed by modern scholars to be either mushrooms or cannabis), the hallucinatory rye ergot of the Delphic oracle, or more modern entheogens such as *Psilocybe cubensis* mushrooms, ayahuasca vine, cannabis, peyote, synthetically manufactured psychotropics (e.g., LSD, DMT, MDMA), or other "designer drugs" of the twenty-first century.

Acquisition by Mantra (Verbal Prayer Repetition/Chanting)

Patañjali mentions that mantras, the repetition of short rhythmical prayers, are found to be efficacious in quieting the mind such that the Self or *puruṣa* can shine forth with a consciousness unimpeded by routine mental functioning. A currently accepted scholarly definition of mantra can be found in volume IV of the *History of Ancient Indian Religion* (1975):

> A mantra may, etymologically speaking and judging from the usage prevailing in the oldest texts, approximately be defined as follows: word(s) believed to be of "superhuman origin," received, fashioned and spoken by the "inspired" seers, poets and reciters in order to evoke divine power(s) and especially conceived as means of creating, conveying, concentrating and realizing intentional and efficient thought, and of coming into touch or identifying oneself with the essence of the divinity which is present in the mantra.[28]

This description of mantra may be understood as an important component of prayer. In Eastern Christianity, the widespread use of the "Jesus Prayer" used by monks and hermits for centuries falls under this definition. The importance of repetition of the mantra or prayer cannot be underestimated. With sufficient repetition, deep resonances build up between the psyche of the practitioner and the transcendental frequency domain (Bohm's implicate order), linking the consciousness of the contemplative with the consciousness of everyone who has previously (and may be currently) focusing upon the mantra/prayer.

Acquisition by *Tapas* (Psychophysical Effort)

A fourth way mentioned is *tapas* or austerities, which can include fasting, intense physical exercises, *hatha yoga,* or holotropic breathwork such as *prāṇāyāma*. These self-imposed physical austerities were found to develop the will and focus the consciousness; however, the reference also includes mental austerities and practices, such as gentleness, sincerity, honesty, humility, faith, and perhaps above all, patience.

Acquisition by *Samādhi* (Contemplative Meditation)

Finally, it is *samādhi,* the primary technique taught in the *Yoga Sūtras,* that is recommended as the most reliable, repeatable, and controllable technique for entering these wider realms of consciousness. This is the method found in the writings of Rudolf Steiner. We might imagine that Steiner encountered some of his ideas on this method from early interaction with the Theosophists and encounters with translations of

Indian philosophical texts in which Patañjali mentions the technique of *samādhi.*

The next five *sūtras* seem to have been widely mistranslated by many commentators early on, beginning with Vyāsa. An important misunderstanding must be clarified right away: the erroneous assumption, originated by Vyāsa and naively followed by virtually all subsequent exegetes and translators, that the initial aphorisms (1–6) treat a specific paranormal feat, namely, the ability to create "artificial" consciousnesses.[29]

The contemporary teacher Swami Hariharananda Aranya says the second *sūtra* in this final chapter is in reply to the following question: "When the *Yogin* constructs many bodies, have they only one mind or many minds?"[30] The contemporary Swami Satchidananda is closer to the mark in his translation: "A *Yogi's* egoity alone is the cause of [the other artificially] created minds."[31]

Similarly, we take the position that in this final chapter Patañjali is not suddenly explaining powers of magic (e.g., creating other bodies or other minds within other bodies). Patañjali already dealt with powers or *siddhis,* quite thoroughly enumerating them in the third chapter. Here, however, he is dealing specifically with the dynamics of consciousness as it affects and can be perceived, manipulated, and coaxingly controlled within the conscious field of the adept who has attained repeatable experiences within various states of *samādhi.* We thus assume the fourth chapter to be elaborating a map and handbook of the metaphysical dynamics of consciousness for the advanced *yogi.*

Developing Supersensible Perception

Having begun this fourth chapter of the *Yoga Sūtras* with the description of the five approaches to the acquisition of *siddhis* (supersensible perception in various dimensions), the following *sūtra,* IV.2, describes the process in which various distinct alternate centers of *citta* consciousness arise:

> ***Sūtra IV.2. Jāty-antara-pariṇāmaiḥ prakṛty-āpūrāt***
> *The birth of these new centers of consciousness*
> *results from an effulgent flow of radiation*
> *concrescing in space-time.*

These various new "centers of consciousness" (chakras) are the result of pure *puruṣa* transforming into centers of *prakṛti* in space-time. Each chakra acts somewhat as a separate brain, a sub-brain within human physiology, responsible for a specific subset of bodily and cognitive functions. Each can be viewed as a precipitating nexus of swirling effulgences of *puruṣa*-powered consciousness energy coalescing into variously involved centers of *citta,* their emanating resonances masking any perception of the initial source, *Puruṣa.* Each center is a unique frequency spectrum resonating in space-time, a stand-alone nexus of consciousness.

Following the model presented in *sūtra* IV.2, we can imagine the early cosmic universe coalescing its initial homogeneous unity into separate stellar formations until a threshold was crossed, ignition occurred, and light flared forth. But this model of the macrocosm applies equally well to the microcosm—as above, so below—and accordingly we can also imagine this process occurring within the domain of each single human being.

It is this energy resonating as new centers (stars of the universe, but also more specifically, of the adept) within the electrophysical mental structure, *citta,* that is mistakenly assumed to be the real center or "I" only because their source, *Puruṣa,* is masked by *citta-vṛtti.*

It may be helpful to visualize these centers as semi-independent personalities or sub-minds, each one having its own sense of "I-ness" for a limited period of time when activated. However, they mask the effulgent *Puruṣa* consciousness and are mistaken (in fact mistake themselves) for being the primary personality. These various centers wheel into the driver's seat of consciousness, often to the surprise of ourselves and our friends.

There is the self-depreciative center, the angry center, the alcoholic center, the food-addicted center, the lust-for-power center, the kind-to-animals center, the sexual center. The typical human being lives in what often seems to be a round-robin of these subpersonalities, a multi-mind or committee of centers of consciousness, each with its own nexus of memories and coping skills, and often exhibiting distinct personalities.

The third *sūtra,* IV.3, explains that these concrescing centers of consciousness arise and are activated through a characteristic property of matter (*prakṛti*): a tendency to gather in regions when obstructions are lowered (a process like that of a farmer removing obstacles to irrigation flows):

Sūtra IV.3. Nimittam-aprayojakaṁ prakṛtīnāṁvaraṇa-bhedastu tataḥ kṣetrikavat.
The process that results in an outflow into the centers of consciousness can be likened to a farmer removing a sluice gate so as to allow water to irrigate his rice field so rice can grow there.

In addition to being an observation adding a structural element to the model of consciousness, this *sūtra* clearly infers a method, a praxis, for attenuating many of these other centers simply by learning to modify, control, and possibly close the "sluice gates," thus withholding the waters of consciousness from irrigating those centers that form due to the various *saṃskāras* (thoughts, memories, impulses) that continually arise and normally make it difficult to enter the quiescence of *samādhi*. The word *saṃskāra* is found in the *Yoga Sutra*, where it indicates a kind of psychological imprint, predisposition, or subliminal trace memory that affects one's consciousness, one's proclivities, and thus one's actions. They are part of one's "memory," trace recordings of information deep within a human psyche, and they have tremendous influence on maintaining habitual habits of thought and of action. *Saṃskāras* can also be seen as innate dispositions one inherits from one's parents, ancestors, and culture, and they are constantly generated through one's own life experiences. They may be thought of as mental habits, some good, some not so good, but as they can arise and capture one's awareness, they are capable of distracting one's concentration during periods of deep contemplative practice.

The fourth *sūtra* describes how these newly emergent centers or vortexes of *citta* consciousness, sprouted and activated from *kleśa*-caused *saṃskāras,* are perceived as "standing alone," as newborn centers of infant separate selfhood due to *asmitā,* the quality of "I-am"-ness.

Sūtra IV.4. Nirmāṇa-cittānya-asmitā-mātrāt.
These multiple centers of consciousness spring from asmitā.

These distracting subpersonalities or centers of *citta* are caused by self-centered *asmitā* itself, a mistaken sense of "I-ness," and the yogic trick is to learn how to attenuate the operation of these subpersonalities for a sufficiently prolonged period of time in order for the *puruṣa* to begin to shine forth. It is only in the highest *asamprajñāta samādhi,* discussed near the end of this chapter, that such states (active multiple subcenters of consciousness) are not continually arising and wresting control over our primary consciousness, and thus making us believe they are our true Self when they are not.

Jumping ahead to *sūtra* IV.20, we find a statement of the problem of having multiple centers of consciousness active.

Sūtra IV.20. Eka samaye chobhayānavadhāraṇam
Radiant puruṣa *consciousness and* citta-vṛtti *centers of consciousness cannot be simultaneously tuned.*

Sūtra IV.25 describes how to overcome this problem and details the threshold across which the states of radiance in *samādhi* in which perception of *puruṣa* unfold.

Sūtra IV.25. Viśeṣa-darśinaḥ ātmabhāva-bhāvanā-nivṛttiḥ
Perceiving the distinction among the many centers of consciousness the attraction of the whirl of the vṛittis *comes to a complete cessation.*

Having gained the ability to "see" the distinction of the various centers of consciousness (chakras), at this point the adept enters the state of consciousness which is beyond words, certainly, but also "burns up" many of the sources (*saṃskāras*) of the subcenters of consciousness with their distracting activities, thus making it easier for an unbroken stream of consciousness to maintain a direct link and resonate only with the

Puruṣa. Experience of this new domain awareness leads eventually to the highest level of integration with the transcendent or what is called *dharma-megha samādhi* (literally "rain clouds of actuality" to indicate such a major transformation as when diffuse water vapor in rain clouds suddenly transforms into raindrops), as described in *sūtra* IV.29. This level of *samādhi* occurs at a stage of complete detachment in which there is no longer a sense of being a contemplative observer trying to observe something (which is essentially a dualistic state of awareness). Instead, in *dharma-megha samādhi* there is one unbroken non-dual awareness of "the One in the All" simultaneously in both explicate and implicate orders of being.

Sūtra IV.29. Prasaṁkhyāne-'py-akusīdasya sarvathā vivekakhyāteḥ darma-megha-samādhiḥ
Dharma-megha-samādhi *arises in one "who is able to maintain a constant state of detachment* (vairāgya) *even toward the most exalted state of enlightenment."*[32]

Professor of chemistry and yoga scholar I. K. Taimni here translates *vivekakhyate* as somewhat synonymous with *para vairāgya* (the highest detachment), while it also translates more as discriminatory discernment or the wisdom of identifying vision. This leads to victory over the *kleśa* afflictions of *saṃskāras* and *karma*, and to *sūtra* IV.31:

Sūtra IV.31 Tadā sarva-āvaraṇa-malāpetasya jñānasya-ānantyāt jñeyamalpam
Then with quiet mind and covers removed the infinities of knowledge shine forth.

This is reminiscent of a poem, "The Dark Night," by the sixteenth-century Spanish contemplative mystic Saint John of the Cross, which uses his "house" as a metaphor for his mind with all of its rooms and activities. The "dark night" indicates that the normal sensory input/activities of the brain-mind have been shut down ("my house being now all stilled"):

One dark night,
fired with love's urgent longings
—ah, the sheer grace!—
I went out unseen,
my house being now all stilled.[33]

And finally, at the very end of the *Yoga Sūtras*, we come to *sūtra* IV.34, which begins with the word *puruṣa*, and indicates the attainment of *kaivalya,* absolute liberation of *puruṣa,* independence—a state where *puruṣa* is finally established in its own nature, the influence of the *guṇas* having been reversed.

Sūtra IV.34 Puruṣa-artha-śūnyānāṁ
guṇānāṁ-pratiprasavaḥ kaivalyaṁ svarūpa-
pratiṣṭhā vā citiśaktiriti
Thus having been reversed, the freedom of the
pure consciousness power of puruṣa *is obtained*
and this is called kaivalya.

Even here words fail, and the experience itself cannot easily be expressed. In a commentary on this *sūtra* by Taimni:

> It should be noted that this is not a description of the content of consciousness in the state of *kaivalya.* As has been pointed out before, no one living in the world of the unreal can understand or describe the Reality of which the Yogi becomes aware on attaining *kaivalya.*[34]

PATAÑJALI'S YOGA AND MODERN SCIENCE

Having described in brief some of the more important *sūtras* and the most fundamental teachings in the model of contemplative yoga and *samādhi,* it is now time to articulate this model in the language of modern science.

We will not go further in this book into the wealth of additional details revealed by Patañjali concerning the practice and pitfalls of yogic technique that lead to the various *samādhis.* Nor will we discuss the elaborate structural theories of the *kleśas,* those afflictions or impediments to progress that spring up like weeds in our path, nor the *saṁskāras,* those leftover easily sprouted seed residues from previous struggles with *kleśas,* nor cultivation of the various *siddhis* with descriptions of the many "psychic powers." Instead, we will simply focus on the two states of consciousness thus far presented in the opening *sūtras* of *Samādhi-Pāda*:

1. The state of *citta-vṛtti,* in which all of the processing systems of the mind are switched on and processing full blast
2. The state of *samādhi,* wherein all of the mental processes have been attenuated, turned down as completely as possible, and the mind-in-the-brain computer-like biomaterial system is sufficiently silent to allow the radiant *puruṣa* to begin to increasingly glow into various stages of ecstasy/enstasy, the realms of the *samādhi* state

Two Beings in One Brain

The Stanford physicist Frank Heile[35] has proposed a theory that there are two streams of consciousness in our brain, one which he calls "Primary Consciousness" and the other "Symbolic Consciousness."* He says that "Humans have two different internal representations of the world," two conscious beings in the brain. Our hypothesis here is that one of these conscious beings can be seen to correspond to *puruṣa* and the other to *prakṛti,* in the form of *citta-vṛttis.*

Symbolic Consciousness is comprised of the verbal language that can be considered as a sequential time-based processing representational systems (memory, logic of comparison and choice, etc.) while the Primary Consciousness operates in a "massively parallel processing" mode perpendicular to time, the now.[36] A table of his comparisons is shown in figure 8.5 (p. 134).

I propose that we assume that the Heile model and the Patañjali model may be mapping the two domains of the same territory. In such a case, "Symbolic Consciousness" is equivalent to *citta-vṛtti,* while "Primary Consciousness" would be equivalent to *puruṣa.*

*See "Heile's Map: Bi-Modal Consciousness" in chapter 14 of this book.

Primary Consciousness	Symbolic Consciousness
Ancient (200,000 years old)	New (30,000 to 100,000 years old)
Primates and many other animals have this consciousness	This consciousness seems to be uniquely human
Massive parallel processing (sensory inputs)	Largely serial processing (a "voice" talking in your head)
High bandwidth	Low bandwidth
Intuitive, spatial, concrete thought, music, art, athletics	Language, logic, temporal sequences, abstract thought, science
Primary emotions sensed directly	Secondary sensory emotions evoked
Difficult to report the contents of consciousness without using the symbolic consciousness	Easily "reportable"; thus it is assumed to be *consciousness,* usually mistaken as the *only* consciousness
It is the entity that perceives the "blind sight" object	It is the entity that is blind to the "blind sight" object
Subconscious + Id	Ego
Does most of the work	Takes most of the credit

Fig. 8.5. Heile's two consciousness entities. From Heile, "Time, Nonduality and Symbolic versus Primary Consciousness."

We can construct these relationships into a bridge to a new model of consciousness by using the languages of science to more clearly articulate the introspective knowledge imparted in the *Yoga Sūtras* of Patañjali.

The Electromagnetic Field Theory of Consciousness

But what if it is the electromagnetic field that is the evolutionary driver, and the neurons and brain structures have arisen from and are continually maintained and operated by the electromagnetic field of consciousness itself? In the 2002 publication *The Nature of Consciousness: A Hypothesis,* the New Zealand neurophysiologist Susan Pockett states, "Consciousness is identical with certain spatiotemporal patterns in the electromagnetic field." That same year Johnjoe McFadden, a researcher in molecular genetics at the University of Surrey, published an article

"The Conscious Electromagnetic Information (CEMI) Field Theory" in which he states categorically:

> The brain's electromagnetic field represents an integrated electromagnetic field representation of distributed neuronal information and has dynamics that closely map to those expected for a correlate of consciousness. I propose that the brain's electromagnetic information field is the physical substrate of conscious awareness.[37]

Both McFadden and Pockett reveal what might be a shared tacit assumption due to their similar backgrounds in modern genetics and biological research in their common supposition that this electromagnetic component of consciousness is an epiphenomenon of neurons firing in the brain. This is a widespread, unchallenged assumption in the hard sciences—that physical neuron structures evolved first and were the forerunners out of which consciousness then arose, hence whenever we experience "consciousness," it is a direct result of the electrical firing of neurons in the brain.

THE SCIENCE OF YOGA: CONSCIOUS ENERGY FIELDS

But what if it is the electromagnetic field of consciousness itself that is the evolutionary driver, and it is the brain and the neurons that have risen from the electromagnetic field? Let us assume that (a) this field of consciousness may indeed be identified with Patañjali's *puruṣa*; (b) that it is out of *this* field that the neuronal and brain structures subsequently arise; and (c) that their activity generates what Patañjali calls the *vṛttis,* the myriad fluctuations of cortical brain subsystem programs in full operation, incessantly chattering, shielding, and masking the original *puruṣa* beneath.

As we have seen from the very first *sūtra,* it is learning to control these *vṛttis* in the Symbolic Consciousness that enables us to reach the powerful states of *samādhi* in the Symbolic Consciousness. This is the concern of the *Yoga Sūtras,* giving us a model and a range of techniques that allow us to grasp and manipulate the controls, operate inherited and newly programmed software, and upgrade our psychic software so that we can tune the mind to new dimensions beyond the limits of habitual, socially conditioned, and time-bound daily waking ranges of consciousness.

Puruṣa and Prakṛti: The Two Domains

Puruṣa and *prakṛti* in the *Yoga Sūtras* are the two poles of cosmic existence as described in the *Sāṃkhya* philosophy. In mathematics and in physics it has been established that pure energy also expresses itself between two states, the one state is the "solid object" configuration wherein energy is locked into lattice-like configurations of resonance (a "particle") and the other pole, and the other state a radiant mode of energy (a "wave"). These two states are associated with two dimensions or domains, the space-time domain and the frequency domain. Both of these domains have been firmly linked in the discovery of the Fourier transform, the mathematical relationship that is the basis of our twenty-first-century digital electromagnetic communication technology.

In radio engineering these two poles or two domains of energy, time (t_d) and frequency (f_d), are of essential importance in the fields of information theory and signal communication. On the first page of his standard textbook on electronic network information theory, Kuo states:

> In describing signals, we use the two universal languages of electrical engineering—*time* and *frequency*. Strictly speaking, a signal is a function of time. However, the signal can be described equally well in terms of *spectral* or *frequency* information. As between any two languages, such as French and German, translation is needed to render information given in one language comprehensible in the other. Between time and frequency, the translation is effected by the *Fourier series* and the *Fourier integral*.[38]

Using Fourier analysis and the Fourier transform, signals can not only be described either in the time domain or the frequency domain, they can also be converted between the two domains, and it can thus be said that they are two different aspects of one and the same thing—energy signals with information content—potentially existing in either one or both of two very different dimensions.

We will consider this third bridge of potentiality linking Patañjali's

Fourier's model	Heile's model	Patañjali's model
Time Domain (t_d)	Symbolic consciousness	*citta-vṛtti*
Frequency Domain (f_d)	Primary consciousness	*puruṣa*

Fig. 8.6. Mapping two domains of consciousness.

model into another language of modern science. The power inherent in the mathematical transforms of the Fourier* series cannot be underestimated, bridging as they do the space-time domain (t_d) and the frequency domain (f_d) repeatedly and reliably in our own hands every time we operate digital devices. Why would Nature not use these very same mathematical functions to process signals of consciousness and transformations of conscious energy in (and around) our human bodies? Accordingly, let us establish a new mapping of the two domains as shown in figure 8.6.

What would this new relationship imply for the tangential space-time domain of *prakṛti* and the radial indwelling of *puruṣa*? We discover here a purely mathematical model that may perfectly mirror the relationship between *puruṣa* and *prakṛti.*

At the one pole we have the *citta-vṛtti* of Symbolic Consciousness, seen as the otherwise radiant energy of *puruṣa* as it flows unaware, trapped, and captured within the many neuronal biomechanical cognitive systems of mind-in-the-brain. Its presence is masked and shielded by the combined noise of all the memory storage, search-and-retrieval activity, logic and associated subroutines, cognitive comparisons, sensory input processes, and more that are involved in *citta-vṛtti* processing of sequential information in a time-based domain (t_d).

By contrast, in the *puruṣa* we have Primary Consciousness, that which was before and that into which we return at the end of time. Here, we cross a threshold into the frequency domain (f_d), which is timeless and spaceless and therefore omnipresent, an ever-present origin that transcends both time and space.

*Jean-Baptiste Joseph Fourier, a French mathematical physicist, discovered these transform equations in 1799 while theorizing on the flow of heat.

In the mathematics of information theory the Fourier transform is the workhorse providing the direct connection interface between the time domain (t_d) and the frequency domain (f_d). For example, signal processing chips in cell phones are encoded with what are called fast Fourier transform algorithms, equations hard-coded in silicon, which transform audio voice speech-frequency patterns in the time-space domain into frequency-spectrum patterns that are then digitized and transmitted at the speed of light across the network. On the receiving end, another fast Fourier transform algorithm unpacks the frequency-domain spectrum into time-space frequency spectrums in low voltage circuits, which then drive the remote speaker allowing the remote human to "hear" the re-created audio time-space spectral energy.

PSYCHE AND THE CALCULUS OF REASONING

Norbert Wiener (1894–1964), who pioneered and coined the term "cybernetics" in his book *Cybernetics: Or Control and Communication in the Animal and the Machine*, uses the mathematics of Fourier to analyze and to model the activity of brain waves in both the time domain (t_d) and the frequency domain (f_d). The Fourier transform and inverse Fourier transform are shown in figure 8.7.

The preceding two Fourier transform expressions indicate that any arbitrary function (signal) in the time-space domain, *f*(t), can be transformed into and expressed by an infinite series of frequency spectra functions *dF*(F) in the imaginary frequency domain, and conversely, that any arbitrary function in the frequency domain, *f*(F), can be transformed into and expressed by an infinite series of time spectra functions *dt*(t).

Using the Fourier integral to analyze brain waves, Wiener describes how he has discovered that frequency centers within the brain tend to

$$f(t) = \int_{-\infty}^{+\infty} X(f)e^{j2\pi ft}\,df$$

Fourier integral transform of a continuous frequency function into the *time domain* (t_d).

$$f(f) = \int_{-\infty}^{+\infty} x(t)e^{-j2\pi ft}\,dt$$

Fourier integral transform of a continuous time function into the *frequency domain* (f_d).

Fig. 8.7. Fourier transform and inverse Fourier transform.

auto-correlate, attract one another, resonate and "self-tune" in the frequency domain. He concludes his book with an amazing conjecture:

> We thus see that a non-linear interaction causing the attraction of frequency can generate a self-organizing system, as it does in the case of the brain waves we have discussed. . . . This possibility of self-organization is by no means limited to the very low frequency of these two phenomena. Consider self-organizing systems at the frequency level, say, of infrared light or radar spectra.[39]

Wiener goes on to discuss these implications for biology, and in particular the problems of communication at the molecular and primitive cellular levels during which specific substances produce cancer by reproducing themselves to specifications in order to mimic preexisting normal local cells. Molecules do not simply pass yellow sticky notes to one another, so how do they communicate? Wiener conjectures:

> The usual explanation given is that one molecule of these substances acts as a template according to which the constituent's smaller molecules lay themselves down and unite into a similar macromolecule. However, an entirely possible way of describing such forces is that the active bearer of the specificity of a molecule may lie in the frequency pattern of its molecular radiation, an important part of which may lie in infra-red electromagnetic frequency or even lower. It is quite possible that this phenomenon may be regarded as a sort of attractive interaction of frequency.[40]

At the end of his paper, in a chapter titled "Brain Waves and Self-Organizing Systems," Wiener suggests further possible studies to "throw light on the validity of my hypothesis concerning brain waves."

He describes the widespread observations of seemingly simultaneous behavior of groups of living beings such as crickets or frogs that can only be attributable to simultaneous synchronization of a neuronal network through the frequency domain:

> It has often been supposed that the fireflies in a tree flash in unison. . . . I have heard it stated that in the case of some of the

> fireflies of Southeastern Asia this phenomenon is so marked that it can scarcely be put down to illusion. . . . Could not the same supposed phenomenon of the pulling together of frequencies take place? However this process occurs, it is a dynamic process and involves forces or their equivalent.[41]

YOGA AS REUNION WITH THE SELF

If we speculate that the Self is indeed the largest Self possible (inclusive of all dimensions both imminent and transcendent), then it would include *prakṛti,* the entire cosmic universe of space-time (t_d), as well as *puruṣa,* the nontemporal, nonspatial "eternal" frequency domain (f_d), the Absolute. We can only assume that the Self is in constant communication with itself and all its sub-selves, or (using Sanskrit terms from *yoga*), that *Puruṣa* is in constant communication with itself and all of the *puruṣas* in the cosmos (here we are accepting the theory of multiple *puruṣas,* subsets of the big *Puruṣa*). While a human being is awake, involved in space-time waking consciousness—"conscious personality in the normal waking mode"—there are billions of neurons firing and processing immediate and long-term memory, associations, comparisons, logical operations, projections, and perceptions. While a human being is sleeping, the quiescence of the enormous electrical noise allows the cosmic frequency dimension of the Primary Self to resonate with the Symbolic self in the ventricular cavities and toroidal body field, and dreams are generated during this period of communication of self with Self.

Thus the *Yoga Sūtras* can be seen as a manual of instruction meant to assist the human individual personality to free itself from having been hijacked by the hyperactivity of the cortical structures of *prakṛti,* the brain, with its multiple mechanical subprograms. Once freed by a relative quiescence, no longer hidden from itself, *puruṣa* becomes aware of itself and begins to resonate with an awareness that bridges the networks of space-time (t_d) brain and the nontemporal, nonspatial domain (f_d) of radiant electromagnetic fields. From this arises the state of *samādhi* that is the gateway to the activation of newly emergent senses and powers (*siddhis*) of consciousness, speeding the yogi toward the attainment of the ultimate experience of being, the oneness of *kaivalya.*

A model of human consciousness as an electromagnetic energy field extending outward from the human body provides a physical basis for validating the traditional south Asian belief in *darshan,* whereby proximity to the living body of a highly developed contemplative yogi can result in a resonance of energy that can be directly experienced. In support of this conjecture and in closing, I would like to quote the following firsthand description of a such an experience of *darshan* in 1948, brought about by entry into the proximity of the living presence of Sri Aurobindo, as recounted in the dissertation of doctoral student Rhoda Le Cocq.

> As I stepped into a radius of about four feet, there was the sensation of moving into some kind of a force field. Intuitively, I knew it was the force of Love, but not what ordinary humans usually mean by the term. These two were "geared straight up"; they were not paying attention to me as ordinary parents might have done; yet, this unattachment seemed just the thing that healed. Suddenly, I loved them both, as spiritual "parents."
>
> Then, all thought ceased, I was perfectly aware of where I was; it was not "hypnotism" as one Stanford friend later suggested. It was simply that during those few minutes, my mind became utterly still. It seemed that I stood there a very long, an uncounted time, for there *was* no time. Only many years later did I describe this experience as my having experienced the Timeless *in* Time. When there at the *darshan,* there was not the least doubt in my mind that I had met two people who had experienced what they claimed. They *were* Gnostic Beings. They had realized this new consciousness which Sri Aurobindo called the Supramental.[42]

The brilliant sage and mystic Sri Aurobindo may be definitely characterized as one of the preeminent psychonauts of the early twentieth century. An Oxford scholar, revolutionary leader, and ultimately a deep explorer of consciousness who was able to write profusely about his discoveries, Aurobindo produced over thirty books on consciousness and Indian philosophy. In order to obtain a deeper understanding of the concepts of integral Tantra mirrored in his writing, we will explore the rich arc of his life in the following chapter.

9

Sri Aurobindo

The Supermind

Tantric discipline is in its nature a synthesis. It has seized on the large universal truth that there are two poles of being whose essential unity is the secret of existence, Brahman and Shakti, Spirit and Nature, and that Nature is power of the spirit or rather is spirit as power. To raise nature in man into manifest power of spirit is its method and it is the whole nature that it gathers up for the spiritual conversion.

Sri Aurobindo, *The Synthesis of Yoga*

We now turn from Patañjali's yoga as our initial foray into the psychophysics of consciousness to a deeper exploration of Indian Tantric psychophysics as expressed in the written publications of Sri Aurobindo Ghose (1872–1950), who sheds light on the foundations upon which Patañjali's psychophysics stands. One of Aurobindo's deepest discussions of the philosophy of the Vedas is elaborated in his essay "The Philosophy of the Upanishads,"[1] an interpretation of the heart of Indian metaphysics as seen through the eyes of this twentieth-century scholar and mystic.

Aurobindo's writings, however, are in a rather high Victorian-Edwardian style of English (he entered Kings College in Cambridge University in 1900, where he studied Greek and Latin), which many modern readers, acclimated to sound bites in the media, texting devices, and Twitter, may find challenging at best, with sentences often stretching into entire paragraphs and pages containing subordinate clauses with the grammatical complexity of Latin. This and a sometimes richly archaic Edwardian vocabulary* present obstacles to many modern readers. It is hoped that the discussion here will help the reader overcome them and serve as an introduction to Aurobindo's deep thinking and style of articulation.

While the specific focus of this chapter will be to explore Aurobindo's articulation of the Tantric psychophysics as expressed in the Trinitarian terms of Indian philosophy, I will describe how one may also discern a universal trinitarian relationship mirrored in the mathematical language of physics and communication theory and will conclude by discussing how this might serve to begin constructing a much-needed bridge between consciousness and the sciences.

SANKARA'S VIEW OF REALITY

In India, the philosophy of Vedanta emerged as a philosophical system in its own right in the eighth century CE with the great sage Sankara's belief that the ultimate reality is perfect and without duality; the creating entity, Brahman, and the created universe of manifestation are not completely separate entities. Nor could they be, as one is the issue of and pervaded by the other.

Thus Sankara views the world not as unreal, but only "real in a certain sense." To Sankara the world is not the entire reality, in fact it is the issue, the creation, of an even more comprehensive reality, in Sanskrit called Brahman, which happens to have three hypostatic attributes or essences he called *sat, cit,* and *ānanda—saccidānanda*—which can be loosely translated being, consciousness, and bliss.

Let us now leap ahead 1,200 years from Sankara to the twentieth-century writer Sri Aurobindo. After exploring his life, we'll explore the nature of *saccidānanda* as developed in his essay "Philosophy of the Upanishads."

---

*In the first three pages of Aurobindo's essay here discussed the reader encounters words such as "gurges," "illation," and "irrefragable."

THE LIFE OF SRI AUROBINDO

Indian metaphysics tells us that beneath everything there must be, after all, only *one reality,* though it has been perceived and expressed in multiple ways by mystics and saints of widely different cultures. A particularly clear and insightful interpretation of Indian metaphysics can be found in a series of brilliant English language essays on classical Vedantic philosophy penned by the scholar and mystic Aravinda Ghose in the early part of the twentieth century. Much later in his life Aravinda was universally referred to as Sri Aurobindo. (*Sri* is a Sanskrit word denoting "that which glows with radiance," and is an honorific title often encountered within Indian culture, reserved for the most highly revered individuals, heavenly beings, or holy scriptures). Aurobindo's interpretation of Vedantic philosophy was expressed in detail over a seven-year period in a series of articles for *The Arya,* a monthly journal published between 1914 and 1921. The journal was meant to be "a review of pure philosophy" by its founder, the French theologian and lawyer Paul Richard, but for the forty-two-year-old Aurobindo, emerging from four years of intensive yoga and meditative withdrawal, writing for *The Arya* was "in its most fundamental sense, an effort or an uprising and overcoming" in the sense that he was forcing himself to move out of isolation into the public sphere of writing and publishing once more.

> I knew precious little about philosophy before I did the Yoga and came to Pondicherry—I was a poet and a politician, not a philosopher! How I managed to do it? First, because Richard proposed to me to co-operate in a philosophical review—and as my theory was that a Yogi ought to be able to turn his hand to anything, I could not very well refuse.[2]

Before exploring Aurobindo's rich metaphysical ideas, it is useful to review the intellectual foundation upon which he was able to draw in order to translate and to express clearly in English so many of the deep metaphysical ideas set forth in the ancient Sanskrit texts of the Vedas (Sanskrit for "knowledge," estimated to have emerged circa 1700 BCE) and the more recent Upanishads (700 to 600 BCE). Sri Aurobindo was one of those rare individuals who was a polyglot: "By the turn of the century he knew at least twelve languages: English, French, and Bengali to speak, read, and write; Latin, Greek, and Sanskrit to read and write; Gujarati, Marathi, and Hindi to speak and read; and Italian, German, and Spanish to read."[3]

This knowledge of twelve languages must certainly have aided Aurobindo in choosing the words to convey abstract metaphysical concepts based upon his deep introspective experiences. In addition, his Cambridge education exposed him not only to Greek and Latin classics and major European philosophers, but also to new theories of evolution being discussed by his contemporary, Charles Darwin.

In 1878 at the age of six, Aurobindo and his two brothers were taken to England by his pro-Raj and British-educated Indian father. When their parents returned to India, the brothers became part of the household of an Anglican minister in Manchester, the thirty-nine-year-old Reverend William Drewett. Nine years earlier, Sri Aurobindo's father had been trained in England as a surgeon and become an Anglican, and throughout his life he maintained an unquestioning admiration and respect for all things British, as did many British-educated Indians at the time, rejecting to a large extent his own cultural background and not wanting his three sons to be in any way influenced by their ancestral culture back in India, at least until they were fully educated in the classic British tradition.

Aurobindo and his brothers spent five years in Manchester with the Drewett family; however, the reverend had a calling to evangelism and made plans to move to Australia to teach the Aborigines. The three boys were left to continue their British education under the care of Drewett's elderly mother, who lived in London. Shortly after his twelfth birthday, Aurobindo and his two brothers left Manchester for London, where the boys were enrolled in the St. Paul's School for young men, a school founded by a friend of Thomas More in 1509 to help introduce the "new learning" of the Renaissance into England.[4] But after three years of relative stability, disaster struck in 1887 when their father suffered a serious financial setback in India. Soon after, the fifteen-year-old Aurobindo and his brothers were asked to leave Mrs. Drewett's house to find cheaper lodging, and thus began their most difficult year. As Aurobindo's biographer Peter Heehs described the situation:

> During a whole year [1888–1889] a slice or two of sandwich bread and butter and a cup of tea in the morning and in the evening a penny sausage formed the only food. . . . Aurobindo and his brother had no wood for the fire and no overcoats to wear in what turned out to be the coldest winter in memory. As time went by, the boys at St. Paul's noticed that Aurobindo's clothing "grew more and more dirty and unkempt" and that he himself "looked more and more unhealthy and neglected."[5]

Somehow the sixteen-year-old endured these stark and exceedingly difficult living conditions in London while at the same time diligently pursuing his studies at St. Paul's School, hoping to absorb enough additional knowledge and to develop his writing skills sufficiently to make possible his one dream, a scholarship to King's College in Cambridge. In spite of his poor diet and lack of heat in his living quarters, he undertook an unusually heavy load of study at St. Paul's School, and was not only able to improve his ability for ad hoc translation of classical Greek, but won a prize for "knowledge of English literature, especially Shakespeare."[6] Shortly after his seventeenth birthday, in December 1889, Aurobindo traveled to Cambridge to undertake the rigorous three-day scholarship examination given by King's College.

> Morning and evening he wrote translations from English into Latin and Greek and from Latin and Greek into English. There were also questions on classical grammar and history and an essay in English. On December 19, back in London, he learned that he had stood first. He later was told that he had "passed an extraordinarily high examination" with the best papers that the examiner had ever seen.[7]

During his two years at Cambridge, Aurobindo studied Western philosophy and Greek and Latin classics, usually read in the original languages. These included works by Homer, Plato, Epictetus, Aeschylus, Catullus, Virgil, and Dante, and as he had dreams of writing great

English poetry, he also read widely in Shakespeare and Milton.[8] But above all, he had a passion for English Romantic poetry, and read everything he could find published by William Wordsworth, Lord Byron, Shelley, and John Keats. According to one professor, Aurobindo possessed "a knowledge of English Literature far beyond the average of undergraduates" and "wrote a much better English style than most young Englishmen."[9]

When he was nineteen he left King's College and sat for a series of qualifying examinations for the Indian Civil Service, a goal that his father had set for him years earlier, even though Aurobindo himself had little interest in such a career. He passed most of the examinations but near the end of the process he continued to postpone the requisite equestrian test. Although his heart was not in returning to India, he departed England for India as a young man of twenty; sadly, while en route, his father died.

After several years as a college professor and administrator for the powerful maharaja of Baroda in the western state of Gujurat, Aurobindo became passionately involved with a small group of Bengalis intent on working to overthrow the British Raj and establish a free sovereign nation in India. In 1908 he and a friend began publishing a weekly newspaper in Calcutta called *Bande Mataram* or "Victory to the Mother [Mother India]" (fig. 9.1, p. 148).

Aurobindo was the primary editor of *Bande Mataram,* contributing numerous highly articulate but incendiary articles to the newspaper, however, he soon became caught up in the organizing and encouragement of several groups of young revolutionaries.

This ultimately led to an assassination attempt on a British chief magistrate, Douglas F. Kingsford, who was playing bridge at a British club in Calcutta. As luck would have it the two bombers ran up to the wrong carriage, which had left the club that night shortly before the one carrying Kingsford. Instead of killing the magistrate, the bomb landed in the carriage of a British mother and her daughter, killing both occupants. Although no evidence was discovered to directly implicate Aurobindo in the bombing, he was swept up by the police along with a dozen of his colleagues in the independence movement and sent to prison. He himself was put in isolation in a stone cell,

Bande Mataram

Weekly Edition.

PUBLISHED EVERY SUNDAY.

Price One Anna. Price One Anna.

VOL. I. CALCUTTA, SUNDAY, SEPTEMBER 29, 1907. NO. 18.

OUR PICTURE GALLERY.

SJT. AUROBINDO GHOSE.

Fig. 9.1. Aurobindo cover of *Bande Mataram,* 1907.

five feet wide by five feet long, in the Alipore jail (fig. 9.2) south of Calcutta.

Such enforced isolation of an individual is not always a setback in the life of a great spirit, however, and in Aurobindo's case we are reminded of the effect of enforced imprisonment upon the lives of such notables as Gandhi and Nelson Mandela.

During many months of isolation in his cell in Alipore, while awaiting trial, Aurobindo began a daily practice of meditation, contemplation, and fasting. Within several months he began to have what he thought to be direct experiences of what he later termed the "silent, spaceless, and timeless Brahman." He took up deep breathing exercises of *prāṇāyāma,* which he had learned earlier during his days as a professor in Baroda, but here he had adequate time to practice in a sustained manner. At one point after a prolonged fast, he experienced such a flood of inner energy that he felt no need to eat, which was convenient as the food was somewhat repulsive, and he "decided to throw it in his privy basket." During the same period

Fig. 9.2. Aurobindo mug shot at the Alipore jail 1909.

he did not require much sleep, and later told a friend that he only needed to sleep one night out of three. During the day he would often meditate while gazing at a large tree outside his jail cell window, and one day, to his astonishment, the tree assumed the spirit of Sri Krishna. Years later he wrote of his entry into confinement and its eventual result:

> Friday, May 1, 1908 . . . I did not know that day would mean an end of a chapter in my life, and that there stretched before me a year's imprisonment during which period all my human relations would cease, that for a whole year I would have to live, beyond the pale of society, like an animal in a cage. And when I would re-enter the world of activity, it would not be the old familiar Aurobindo Ghose. . . . I have spoken of a year's imprisonment. It would have been more appropriate to speak of a year's living in an ashram or a hermitage. . . . The only result of the wrath of the British Government was that I found God.[10]

After much delay and a long-drawn-out trial, Aurobindo was released from jail soon after his thirty-seventh birthday. Several of his co-conspirators had been banished to a brutal penal colony near Siam, but the court, presided over by a British judge who had been a classmate of Aurobindo's at Cambridge, ruled that there was insufficient evidence against the young professor, and charges were dropped. Immediately, Aurobindo began once more to write and to give public speeches to crowds of admirers. Now, however, his message was less political, and leaned more in the direction of promoting an ideal of cultural unity among all mankind, something far beyond the divisive nationalism that had formerly driven his thought and expression.

Unfortunately, the British authorities did not notice this change in Aurobindo's direction; they only saw that he continued to attract attention and a growing following. They decided that he was still a danger to British rule, and after what they saw as several months of stirring up the public, the local police made plans to arrest Aurobindo Ghose and to banish him to the British penal colony in the Andaman Islands, 800 miles to the west of India.

Up the Hooghly River to Freedom

Hearing that he was about to be jailed once more, Aurobindo and three friends fled at once by wooden boat up the Hooghly River to Chandernagore, a small town eighty miles north of Calcutta, where he all but vanished from view. There he spent long hours in silent yoga and meditation in the back room of a young revolutionary sympathizer's home. From this point forward he virtually abandoned politics in favor of exploring consciousness through reading, writing, and deep and prolonged periods of contemplative practice. However, he did manage to publish an amusing message to his followers in a regular column of his in the *Karmayogin,* a Calcutta newspaper, writing: "We are greatly astonished to learn from the local Press that Aurobindo Ghose has disappeared from Calcutta and is now interviewing the Mahatmas in Tibet. We are ourselves unaware of this mysterious disappearance."[11]

The following month, while still managing to elude the British, who wanted to arrest and banish him to the penal colony, Aurobindo managed to evade the authorities with the help of his close friends and travel surreptitiously by boat a thousand miles south of Bengal to the French port of Pondicherry on the Bay of Bengal.

When the French authorities in the sleepy town of Pondicherry were eventually informed by the British of Aurobindo's political nationalist background, they put him under surveillance. However, Aurobindo was no longer interested in external social or political activities, and instead he moved ever more deeply into an exploration of inner consciousness.

Eventually he began writing about his experiences in monthly publications of Richard's new journal *The Arya.* It was Richard's wife, Mirra Alfassa, who was soon to grow close to Aurobindo in his spiritual quest, and was to become known, many years later, as "The Mother" at Sri Aurobindo Ashram (fig. 9.4).

Mirra Alfassa (1878–1973)

Mirra Alfassa had an enormous influence on Sri Aurobindo and his followers. Born in Paris to Arabic-speaking parents who had emigrated from Turkey and Egypt, Mirra began her career as an artist, coming to know many of the early impressionists in Paris, and having her paintings selected for exhibition in the Paris Salons of 1903 and 1904.

Soon however, while in her mid twenties, she became fascinated with Buddhism and met Richard when they shared the same occult study group in Paris. The two married and moved to a small French colony in the southeast coast of India, where Richard, a political hopeful, believed he could be elected to the French senate to represent the colony at Pondicherry. Hoping to improve the chances of being elected, Richard soon met with Aurobindo Ghose, who had recently been a powerful political figure in northern India. Mirra was immediately struck with Aurobindo's presence, believing him to be the person she had often seen in vivid eidetic dreams. Richard lost the election in Pondicherry, and after working as a trade representative in Japan for several years, the two returned to Pondicherry and Richard soon divorced Mirra, who had taken an apartment close to Aurobindo's residence.

When Mirra was in her early forties an enormous cyclone swept across the Bay of Bengal, and Mirra was invited by Aurobindo to shelter with him and his followers in the same large house in Pondicherry. She continued to live close to Aurobindo for the next fifty years, falling into the role of shielding him from interruptions that might otherwise detract from his long periods of meditation and voluminous writing projects.

Mirra proved to be highly adept at administrative efforts and was instrumental in founding the Sri Aurobindo Ashram in Pondicherry as well as collaborating with the United Nations to establish the international "city of the future" known as Auroville. Nevertheless, there have been many who have criticized her for having created what they consider to be a cult-like atmosphere around Aurobindo's teachings and persona, believing that her work cast a negative light upon Aurobindo's life work that has impeded the spread of his central message. The formal "ashram" and large community of "devotees" that formed around Mirra Alfassa (and by association, Aurobindo himself) worked against any possibility that Aurobindo's work might be taken seriously (if even considered) by the global academic community. The label of "guru" that Aurobindo acquired thus reduced the chances that his extensive philosophical commentaries on the evolution of human consciousness would be seriously examined by a wider audience, and accordingly there have been few discussions or even acknowledgment of his well-articulated writings on the imminent emergence of what he experienced himself as the breakthrough of human awareness into "the Supermental" mode of human consciousness.

Fig. 9.3. Mirra Alfassa *(center, rear)* and Paul Richard. Tokyo, 1918.

AUROBINDO'S VEDANTIC MAP OF CONSCIOUSNESS

Sri Aurobindo's lucid interpretation of Vedanta, and in particular the trinitarian metaphysics of Saccidānanda is discussed in a long running series of articles (between 1914 and 1921) that were published in Richard's monthly journal, *The Arya*. A number of these articles, including Aurobindo's own translations from the Sanskrit, were collected and published later in *The Philosophy of the Upanishads*.[12]

Aurobindo's essays encapsulate a metaphysical system based upon his own immediate intuition of a metaphysical trinity acting to generate and sustain the universe and his own translation and interpretation of the Upanishads.

The Search for the Absolute

Sri Aurobindo wrote *The Philosophy of the Upanishads* at around age thirty, during his last year as a professor of philosophy at the University of Baroda. The book is a translation and interpretation of classical Indian ideas from the Vedantic Upanishads, originally written down at about the same time as Patañjali's *Yoga Sūtras* (circa fourth century CE). Aurobindo's lucid interpretation clarifies Vedantic ideas concerning consciousness, knowledge, and the cosmos. He begins with the earliest history of thought of the rishis* in India, who intuited the possibility of a unity and transcendental Oneness (or Absolute) behind the ever-shifting flux of change that manifests to human perception. He says that to discover this unity directly must have been the consummate goal of such early experiential exploration, and that one of the very first conclusions arrived at was that "the *sum* of all this change and motion is absolutely *stable, fixed* and *unvarying*,"[13] as must be the psychophysical relationships that operate at the most fundamental levels. While the goal of these ancient scientists of the introspective psyche was to determine these laws, their first conclusion was that "All this heterogeneous

*"According to post-Vedic tradition, the rishi is a 'seer' to whom the Vedas were 'originally revealed' through states of higher consciousness. The rishis were prominent when Vedic Hinduism took shape, as far back as three thousand years ago." See Wikipedia, s.v. "Rishi."

multitude of animate and inanimate things are fundamentally homogeneous and one."[14]

Aurobindo comments that while modern materialist science is realizing this same fact about the universe "slowly but surely," the rishis began exploring the vast domain of consciousness over two millennia ago, using tools and techniques developed out of and from within their own consciousness. Their collective discoveries were handed down and refined over numerous generations, reaching at last the following conclusion:

> Within the flux of things and concealed by it is an indefinable, immutable Something, at once the substratum and sum of all, which Time cannot touch, motion perturb, nor variation increase or diminish, and that this substratum and sum has been from all eternity and will be for all eternity.[15]

With regard to humanity and life itself, the rishis discovered not just that "death itself is not a reality but a seeming, for what appears to be destruction, is merely transformation," but also that "life itself is a seeming," for beyond life and death there lies a condition which is "more permanent than either."[16]

These ancient explorers of mind eventually found ways to connect with a Oneness to which they could then focus their attention. As they explored, further questions arose. Was the Oneness intelligent or was it non-intelligent? Was it a God or was it a mechanical, insentient nature? Endless exploration and speculation by these early Aryan rishis as to what was experienced resulted eventually in the following six divergent questions regarding the nature of this Oneness:

1. Is this Oneness simply the thing we call "time" that underlies all and everything?
2. Or is it *svabhāva,* an archetypal "essential nature" of things, taking various forms?
3. Or is it chance, blind mechanical interaction producing things by infinite permutation?
4. Or is it fate, predestined causative formation, fixed laws by

which this world evolves itself in a preordained procession of phenomena and from which it cannot deviate?

5. Or is it a mother matrix that molded the original elements of the universe, the womb of the universe?
6. Or is it simply pure illusion projected by myriad separate "Egos?"

To make sense of all these speculations the sages tried the method of enumeration, called *Sāṃkhya,* developed by the early sage Kapila (sixth century BCE). Their work led them to conclude that this Oneness about which sages had been speculating "was the great principle of *prakṛti,* the single eternal indestructible principle and origin of Matter which by perpetual evolution rolls out through aeons and aeons the unending panorama of things."[17] And yet *behind* this *prakṛti,* or *before* this manifestation of material things in space-time, is its other half, which they labeled *puruṣa,* loosely translated as "spirit."* *Prakṛ ti* and *puruṣa* can be seen as a duality within the trinity, while the third element or hypostasis, that which unites and transcends both of them, is consciousness, designated by the word *cit* (pronounced "chit") in Sanskrit. Thus the Egos, beings made of matter, exhibit *consciousness* both in their on-going activity and in the very act of their creation. Aurobindo here paraphrases Kapila to answer the question of just why these seemingly separate egos of consciousness have been created:

> Those conscious, thinking and knowing *Egos* of living beings, of whom knowledge and thought seem to be the essential selves and without whom this world of perceivable and knowable things could not be perceived and known, and if not perceived and known, might it not be that without them it could not even exist?[18]

*That the universe is divided into *prakṛti* and *puruṣa* clearly aligns with David Bohm's quantum map of the universe as consisting of an *explicate order* and an *implicate order*. In this sense *prakṛti* can be seen as material in space-time (the explicate order) and *puruṣa* can be viewed as the timeless, spaceless dimension of the implicate order.

But why? And for whose benefit? Aurobindo answers: "Surely for those conscious, knowing, and perceiving Egos, the army of witnesses, who, each in his private space of reasoning and perceiving Mind partitioned off by an enveloping medium of gross matter, sit for ever as spectators in the theatre of the Universe!"[19]

It must be remembered that Kapila's cosmological model of the Whole was published three hundred years before the birth of Socrates, and over the intervening centuries between Kapila and Aurobindo other major philosophical streams have branched from the initial *Sāṃkhya* structure:

1. Some saw that the army of Ego witnesses must be resolved into an ultimate single pre-existing and post-existing Witness, and thus arrived at various conceptions of Duality:
   a. God vs. Nature
   b. *Puruṣa* vs. *Prakṛiti*
   c. Spirit vs. Matter
   d. Ego vs. Non-Ego
2. Others, more radical, perceived *prakṛti* as the "shadow creation" of *puruṣa,* so that "God alone remained" as the Real.
3. Still others believed that each ego is "only a series of successive shocks of consciousness and that the persistent sense of identity is no more than an illusion due to the unbroken continuity of the shocks."[20]

According to this last viewpoint, consciousness is only a subset of *prakṛti,* merely an illusion or at best one of its many sub-aspects, "so that *Prakriti* alone remains as the one reality, the material or real factor eliminating by inclusion the spiritual or ideal."[21] We can see in this argument a parallel to the modern widespread materialist paradigm held by the majority of neuroscientists that consciousness is a derivative, emergent *byproduct* of the firing of neurons in the brain. If this were true, it would preclude the notion that consciousness might be co-extensive with a panpsychic universe of *prakṛti.*

But, Aurobindo points out, it is by this denial that *prakṛti* is seen as an "ultimate part of reality apart from the perceptions of *Purushas.*"

This leads to "the position of the old Indian Nihilists" which led directly to Buddhism, often accused of having a goal of trying to escape from pleasure and pain into a void of nothingness.[22] However, Aurobindo tells us that they were only trying to escape from a "limited pleasure which involves pain," and to escape from "pain which is nothing but the limitation of pleasure."[23] In actuality, he says, both approaches are really seeking an *absolute absence of limitation,* which is not a negative condition, but a positive infinity. Their so-called escape from individuality does not lead them into a void of nothingness at all, but into a state of experienced infinite existence, absolute consciousness, a transcendental awareness not necessarily limited by space or time.

In addition to such numerous interpretations of experiential reality by these sages, passed down through history in their attempts to articulate verbal, rational understanding to the results of their yogic explorations of consciousness, there remains another view that led "to the very threshold of Vedanta." This view was the "speculation that *Prakṛti* and *Puruṣa* might **both** be quite real, and yet not ultimately different aspects, or sides, of each other and so, after all, of a Oneness higher than either."[24] *Prakṛti* was seen to be real by close analysis of the phenomenal world, and *Puruṣa* was acknowledged to be real "by the necessity of a perceiving cause for the activity of *Prakriti.*"[25] In light of this dawning Vedantic view, the rishis held that they themselves must be real, and that "they were the receptive and contemplative Egos" viewing *prakṛti* itself from outside *prakṛti*, as observers viewing space-time from a region outside of space-time.[26] It was as if each one of us were a single unique "small *puruṣa*," an avatar of the one single *Puruṣa* peering out into space-time from out of a single transcendent center.*

Over many generations of searching, investigating, and experiencing, the seers of India developed a toolkit of incisive techniques required for any serious introspective first-person participatory inves-

*Note that when begun with a capital letter, *Puruṣa* indicates the unitary "big Self" much as Jung writes about the transcendent, singular Self that underlies the entire space-time universe of "little selves." When begun with a lowercase letter, the terms *puruṣa* and *self* indicate one of the many "small selves" that populate and exist within space-time. However, in his writings (as quoted in this book), Aurobindo often capitalizes both *puruṣa* and *prakṛti* to indicate the larger concept.

tigation of the realities behind being, consciousness, and causality. These tools are the methods of yoga, codified in writing by Patañjali as early as the fourth century CE. Through exploring consciousness with the tools of yoga they discovered three "crowning realizations" in their search:

1. *Being* was determined to be real; Absolute Brahman; the true Self; absolute and transcendent, out of time; it must transcend time and space; *nityo-nityānām.*
2. *Puruṣa* was determined to be real; "This then was the second realization through Yoga, *cetana-ścetanānām,* the One Consciousness in many Consciousnesses."[27]
3. Finally, the all-important realization was that the Transcendent Self, the *puruṣa* in individual man, is not separate from the Transcendent Self, the *Puruṣa* of the Universe, that they are contiguous in being and share the same essence.

But here is the paradox. The customary non-yogic sense of separate individuality is absolutely required by and is the key to the creation and maintenance of the universe itself. It is this illusory sense of separate individuality, which is, as Aurobindo says, "one of the fundamental *seemings* on which the manifestation of phenomenal existence perpetually depends." It is through this third realization that "the Absolute which would otherwise be beyond knowledge, becomes knowable."[28] The connection between *puruṣa* and *Puruṣa* (much as in the case of Jung's theory of individuation where one works to unite the self with the Self) will be seen as the key to accessing the riches of participation in Saccidānanda.

In actuality, Aurobindo tells us, the entire metaphysics of the Upanishads rests upon the four *Mahāvākyas* ("Great Sayings") presented in figure 9.4 on page 160.

> Based upon these four grand truths, *Nityo-nityānām, Cetana-ścetanānām, So'ham,* and *Aham brahma asmi,* as upon four mighty pillars the lofty philosophy of the Upanishads raised its front among the distant stars.[29]

Sanskrit from the Upanishads	Sri Aurobindo's Translation
Nityo nityānām	The One eternal in many transient.
Cetana ścetanānām	The One Consciousness within many consciousnesses.
So 'ham	I am He/She/That.
Aham Brahma asmi	I am Brahma, the Eternal.

Fig. 9.4. The four Great Sayings of the Upanishads.

The Nature of the Absolute Brahman

The Upanishads can be viewed as a great collection of metaphysical data, of "observations and spiritual experiences with conclusions and generalizations from those observations and experiences," and, as Aurobindo states, "they have a scientific rather than a logical consistency."[30]

However if the Upanishads are critiqued primarily for logical inconsistency, an approach European scholars have often taken, their coherency seems to fall apart. They are seen to base themselves on an initial fundamental inconsistency, for in the Upanishads "it is distinctly stated that neither mind nor senses can reach the Brahman and that words return baffled from the attempt to describe It."[31]

Here we note the irony of the situation, that Brahman, while clearly not definable, and not intellectually knowable, remains yet the one true object of knowledge. In fact, the Upanishads seems to be, paradoxically, an attempt to describe Brahman with great detail.

Aurobindo addresses this irony by pointing out that Brahman as ultimate reality is transcendent, absolute, and infinite, whereas the human senses and intellect are definitely finite. Thus, the absolute reality of Brahman is unknowable to and uncontainable by the intellect and the senses. This is perhaps due to their limited range, and perhaps because they are focused in the wrong direction, looking outward rather than inward. It is accordingly beyond the powers of speech to describe Brahman because experience of Brahman lies outside of the ranges of speech as we know it.

Nevertheless, aspects of Brahman in its manifesting "shadows of light" in time, space, causality, and consciousness can indeed by perceived by mystics, shamans, yogis, and psychonauts through the means of *yoga vidya,* the science of "knowledge of union." While modern scientists only reluctantly admit that there may be some great ultimate reality "unknown and probably unknowable" to humanity, the Upanishads assert on the contrary that the ultimate Brahman does indeed exist in an absolutely real sense.

Although such existence is inexpressible in terms of any delimiting finite verbal expression or syntax, it is *immediately realizable* and attainable through special modes of direct experience. How this occurs is explained by the various yogic and contemplative means that have been discovered by noetic explorers and handed down through the ages in texts such as the Upanishads, first recorded in the early part of the Axial Age, sometime between 800 to 500 BCE.

But while the material scientist searches for knowledge only in the limited measurable and recordable phenomena of gross matter in space and in time, the Vedantic scientist has not limited himself to the field of space-time but has ranged farther and farther into dimensions not even considered by the scientist of physical matter. In numerous instances these psychonauts have brought back reports that they have "discovered a universe of subtle matter penetrating and surrounding the gross." It is into this dimension of "subtle matter" that the spirit moves during normal human sleep. In fact, says Aurobindo, this universe of subtle matter "is the source whence all psychic processes draw their origin."[32]

But even beyond these two dimensions—the *gross* and the *subtle*—experienced and named by Vedantic explorers, Aurobindo describes their discovery of an additional domain, the *causal*:

> There is yet a third universe of *causal matter* penetrating and surrounding both the *subtle* and the *gross*, and that this universe to which the spirit withdraws in the deepest and most abysmal states of sleep and trance and also in a remote condition beyond the state of man after death, is the source whence all phenomena take their rise.[33]

Domains of Brahman	Sri Aurobindo's Characterizations of These Domains
Causal Domain	**"Absolute Self"** > Prajña, The Wise One
Subtle Domain	**"The Creator"** > Golden Embryo birthing life and form
Gross Domain	**"Cosmic Ruler"** > Helper, The Shining One (Deva)

Fig. 9.5. Sri Aurobindo's three domains of Brahman.

Aurobindo says that it is upon this trinitarian scheme (of *gross, subtle,* and *causal*) that the whole structure of the Vedanta is built. Brahman manifests in each of three domains as shown in figure 9.5.

He then goes on to declare an amazing possibility, that in each of these three manifestations, "He (Brahman) can be known and realized by the spirit of man."[34] Here by "spirit of man" Aurobindo is referring to the individual self, *puruṣa* (with a small *p*), only one of trillions upon trillions of the metaphorically tiny droplets of self that make up the vast ocean of the big Self, *Puruṣa* (with a capital *P*), named in the Upanishads as the Parabrahman, Absolute Brahman, the great Self, or God.

> The position has already been quite definitely taken that the transcendent Self in man is identically the same as the transcendent Self in the Universe and that this identity is the one great key to the knowledge of the Absolute Brahman.[35]

Because of this ultimate identity of the individual, seemingly separate *puruṣa* from Brahman (the "big *Puruṣa*"), human knowledge of Brahman is possible, "for this identity is a fact in the reality of things" states Aurobindo.[36] Thus, all phenomena are nothing but "seemings" which only *appear to be* differences between the individual and Brahman, but the illusion is so convincing and pervasive "that it is almost always impossible for the material sensual being to conceive of the Supreme Soul as having any point of contact with his own soul, and *it is only by a long process of evolution* that an individual finally arrives at the illumination in which some kind of identity becomes to him conceivable."[37]

Knowledge of Brahman in the Gross Domain

We have seen how Vedanta arrives at the conclusion that Brahman can be known and realized, perhaps separately, in *each* of the gross, subtle, and causal domains (as described by Theosophists). Accordingly, while it seems a remote possibility to the vast majority of humans, Aurobindo assures us that Brahman *can be known directly* in our everyday material encounter in the gross domain of material existence in space-time.

But how is it possible for us to know Brahman in the gross material realm? How do we recognize such daily intimate contact, can it be felt, and if so, how? Aurobindo says "it can be felt, by the supreme sympathy of *love* and *faith,* either through love of humanity and of all other fellow-beings, or directly through the love of God."[38]

But Aurobindo cautions that these feelings alone are not the fullest knowledge of Brahman. Each of the religions that stress love and faith alone are seen also to experience only a limited, perhaps one-sided, knowledge of the Absolute. It is only knowledge of all three hypostases of the trinity that offers the possibility of the complete experience of God. Thus, it is imminently practical to acquire knowledge of the trinity in every domain, and it is our contention that this is mirrored in the approach to the Vedantic knowledge of Brahman.

Knowledge of Brahman in the Subtle Domain

Those who are able to move beyond the gross material phenomenal dimension through discovery and practice of various psychophysical techniques such as found in yoga, drugs, shamanism, contemplative prayer, and so forth, find themselves beyond the gross domain, and discover "an entry into the universe of *subtle* phenomena."[39]

The subtle domain is the domain of energy, of radiant plasmoids, electromagnetic energy fields experienced in Christianity as a "descent of the flames of the Holy Spirit" upon the apostles. This experience is that of the very radiance of the oceans of electromagnetic fields filling an otherwise dark empty shadow of empty space, a flickering awareness, lightning flashes at the boundaries of dark energy.

Knowledge of Brahman in the Causal Domain

Knowledge of the subtle domain of energy in space-time is only the beginning for the psychonautic explorer sailing toward Brahman. "From the subtle Universe the individual rises in its evolution until it is able to enter the universe of *causal* matter, where it stands near to the fountain-head."[40] This is the "causal universe," an equivalent to the pure transcendent eternal atemporal nonspatial domain in which the multiple *puruṣas* resonate with the One *Puruṣa*:

> [In this state] the difference between the individual and the Supreme Self is greatly attenuated. . . . He is moreover, on the other side of phenomena and can see the Universe at will without him or within him; but he has still not necessarily realized the supreme as utterly himself, although this perfect realization is now for the first time in his grasp.[41]

This, says Aurobindo, is "Monism with a difference," but also a monism* that can be ultimately grasped by the formerly separate *puruṣa*, and the question then becomes, what then happens to the individual Self, to the separate, unique yet isolated *puruṣa?* His answer is clear:

> Then the individual Self entering into full realization, ceases in any sense to be the individual Self, but merges into and becomes again the eternal and absolute Brahman, without parts, unbeginning, undecaying, unchanging.[42]

The problem for the rishis, and for us today, is that normal human senses and memory were evolved in order to sense, reflect, and remember external phenomena. Any experience of this Brahman, of God, the "big *Puruṣa*" is not fully registered by normal human biosensory

*Monism holds that the universe is ultimately one, rather than ultimately dualistic or pluralistic.

qualia systems (eye, ear, taste, touch), nor can the experience be clearly recorded and stored in human memory because, in part, it is definitely outside of both time and space.

Aurobindo qualifies the term "Nirvana" by pointing out that while Buddhists might interpret this "lack of recording of experience" as a "Void" during this highest experience, another way of describing the beyond-visual experience is to say that it leads to a "luminous ecstasy" of infinite light, as Aurobindo says here:

> The culmination of knowledge by the superseding of our divided and fallible intellect with something greater must lead not to utter darkness and blank vacuity but to the luminous ecstasy of an infinite Consciousness. Not the annihilation of Being, but utter fullness of Being is our Nirvana.[43]

Thus we see that human rational knowledge really cannot begin to penetrate or accompany the serious seeker into this experience of a new kind of knowledge, the knowledge of God, the direct knowledge of Brahman, the Absolute Self, the *big Puruṣa.* Here indeed the word *knowledge* itself becomes a problem for us.

According to Aurobindo's discussion of Vedanta, there are at least three different types of knowledge: knowledge by experience, knowledge by hearing (or reading), and knowledge by *becoming one with* the object of knowledge. The one-dimensional human intellect, fed by sequential word tokens, is superseded when encountering deeper levels of transcendent experience. Verbal knowledge becomes obsolete and shuts down "at a point where the Knower, Knowledge and the Known become one."[44]

Knowledge of Brahman beyond All Domains

In the ultimate state of union, the "knowledge of Brahman beyond all domains," the Upanishads tell us that the individual *puruṣa* has realized the Supreme Being as himself as Aurobindo here explains:

> To realize and unite onself with the active Brahman is to exchange, perfectly or imperfectly according as the union is partial or complete,

> the individual for the cosmic consciousness. . . . By detaching himself from all identification with mind, life and body, he can get back from his ego to the consciousness of the true Individual, who is the real possessor of mind, life, and body.[45]

This state of being, he says, is called *laya,* the highest state of knowledge-being-bliss, extinction from separation, beyond phenomena. He goes on to say that it is obvious that here words and even memories cease to have meaning and are not needed. It is a condition that is perfectly pure and absolutely infinite in all dimensions. He comments that an approach to this state often creates anxiety and fear if approached by the average "undisciplined imagination" of present-day humanity, by those who are uncomfortable even in brief moments of silence, let alone in the more rarified psychotropic contemplative states attainable through advanced psychodynamic practices.

> The normal human senses never glimpse this state because they have evolved over many millions of years to sense externalities in the world of gross, material, relatively large-scale objects, and to filter out and hide a myriad of finer, higher bandwidth activities of consciousness. Such is the power of *Māya* working through *avidya.** But there is a mistaken assumption that this state of *Laya,* of "consciousness without an object," is a state of dark emptiness. On the contrary, says Aurobindo of the experience, the state is not a blank empty vacuum but (with a slight dig at Buddhism): "this experience is the luminous ecstasy of an infinite Consciousness, not the annihilation of Being, but utter fullness of Being is our Nirvana."[46]

And it is here that Aurobindo gives a description, which later in *The Life Divine* he will call the "method of Vedantic knowledge:"

*The Sanskrit word *vidya* means "to know," "to perceive," "to see," "to understand," however the prefix *a* in word *avidya* is a negation; accordingly *avidya* connotes "ignorance," "lack of understanding."

> For the final absolution of the intellect can only be at a point where the Knower, Knowledge and the Known become one, Knowledge being there infinite, direct and without media. And where there is this infinite and flawless knowledge, there must be, one thinks, infinite and flawless existence and bliss.[47]

Metaphor of the Porch

But even here, in this last (the fourth) state of the Self there are *stages* and *degrees* by which experience can vary. To describe these stages, Aurobindo here chooses a visual metaphor. He asks us to visualize different viewpoints as seen from an individual standing on a porch. He describes the various ways a person might see things while standing on the porch near the entrance (here the entrance between space-time and the eternal, between little self and big Self).

For practical purposes we may speak of three stages—the *first* when we stand at the entrance of the porch and look within; the *second* when we stand at the inner extremity of the porch and are really face to face with the Eternal; and the *third* when we enter into the Holy of Holies, as described here by Sri Aurobindo:

> The first stage, when we stand at the entrance of the porch and look within, is attainable through yoga, and the person who attains this stage returns a *Jivanmukta,* "one who lives and is yet internally released from the bondage of phenomenal existence." The person who reaches the second stage, standing at the inner extremity of the porch and face to face with the Absolute Eternal, we call a *Buddha* or Avatar. But here, entering into the Holy of Holies, says Aurobindo, "From the third stage none returns, nor is it attainable in the body."[48]

The Five Levels of Brahman

Before beginning detailed discussion of the mysterious trinity of Saccidānanda, Aurobindo describes what he has perceived to be the full range of Brahman's manifest reality, derived from the psychonautical discoveries of the ancient Indian sages and verified in his own experiences. The early explorers of the transcendental psyche came to the consensus that when these deeper dimensions of reality are experienced by an individual human, there are five levels or operational modes that can be navigated, as shown in figure 9.6.

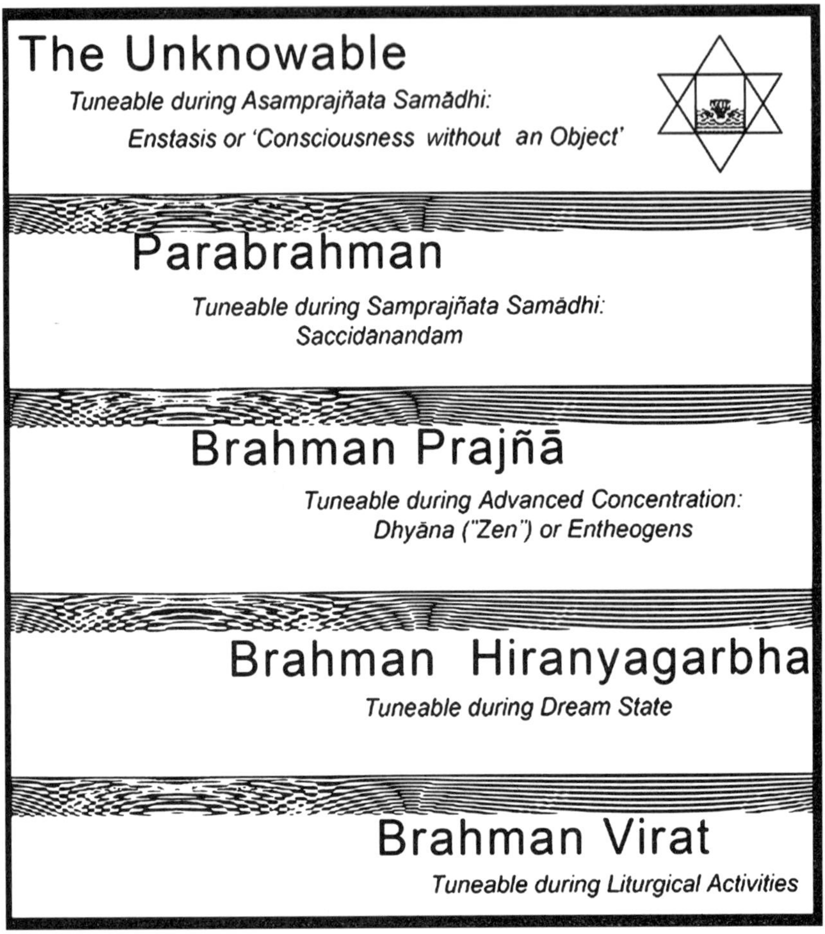

Fig. 9.6. Five levels of absolute Brahman.

The objective of these early contemplative Vedic forefathers in articulating this five-level map was solely to help other psychonauts to navigate the wide oceans of consciousness by identifying and articulating distinct regions for future explorers.

It is worth describing these five levels in some detail.

Level 1 "The Unknowable"

At the top of the diagram, the most exalted or deepest level of Brahman is "The Unknowable," congruent with what David Bohm refers to as the "implicate order," and Teilhard de Chardin's "Omega Point."

Thus Level 1, "The Unknowable," is *outside of* space-time and thus beyond relative consciousness. The nontemporal state of Brahman can only be reached by the human soul during the deepest stages of contemplative, entheogenic, or shamanic trance wherein the seer has been able to *completely detach* from the suspended ego. Here mind fluctuations and memory have come to a halt, and limited self-identification vanishes in an ultimate communion with transcendent non-duality, what Bohm calls "the Whole." To reach this absolute mode of being requires arriving at a state of what has been called elsewhere *enstasis*, or by one mathematician, "consciousness without an object."[49] But for explorers attempting to map the navigation of consciousness, this state is far too deep, as nothing conceptual can be brought back as food for thought. The poet T. S. Eliot expresses the problem clearly:

> *I can only say, there we have been: but I cannot say where*
> *And I cannot say, how long, for that is to place it in time.*[50]

Level 2 "The Parabrahman"

Just before the entrance to "The Unknowable" Brahman lies the realm or state of "Parabrahman." Here the prefix *param* in Sanskrit may be translated as the word "different," and thus Parabrahman signifies a state of consciousness/being that is slightly "different" than the pure unknowable Brahman.

It is this difference in the Parabrahman level that provides the contemplative the ability to maintain awareness of *both* the transcendent non-dual domain *and* the immediate, imminent domain of space-time simultaneously, as if having one foot in each realm. Referring back to the metaphor of the porch, one could say that here the psychonaut is standing in the doorway, neither totally within Brahman, nor totally external to Brahman.

It is useful to note that this level of experiencing Brahman is what is meant by "an experience of God" in many religions, as it is reachable to a limited extent by human beings through various means of communion. Sages and seers have been able to experience Parabrahman through yogic techniques, ritual, ingestion of plant entheogens, or through falling into this extraordinary psychophysiological state through intense mental or physical activity.

The experience of Parabrahman, though transcending space-time, allows some vestigial co-reflecting focus of awareness to remain in time, during which memory functions sufficiently such that when returning to normal consciousness, something can be said about the experience. It is primarily from encounters within this state that we have received the most significant written and verbal accounts of God handed down to us by mystics and saints throughout the ages.

Aurobindo says, with a bit of Edwardian-phrased humor, that *something* can be understood of Parabrahman because "always if *the liberal use of loose metaphors* is not denied, it can be practically brought within the domain of speech."[51] Due to the almost inexpressible impact of the effulgent Brahman state, normal human language cannot begin to describe the experience, and it is poetry with its "loose metaphors" that comes closest to capturing the phenomenon in words.

Level 3 "Brahman Prajñā"

At this level the experience of Brahman is fully within space-time, though beyond the normal ranges of ego consciousness. The contemplative psychonaut is able to tune in to the radiant cosmos, to resonate with the Whole within all of the regions of space-time, and through such resonance to "bring back" knowledge and wisdom through the immediate experience of the Whole, free of normal local mental limitations. This reminds us of the myth of Prometheus who was able to "steal fire" from Mount Olympus and bring it back to mankind.

This is the region explored by psychonauts through ingestion of psychotropic substances or psychophysical exercises. It is within the *prajñā* level of consciousness that individual humans are able to encounter beings in other levels of space-time, ancestors, alien entities and civilizations so well described in Olaf Stapledon's novel *The Star Maker,* and in books by the writer and psychonaut Terence McKenna such as *True Hallucinations.* The "Brahman Prajñā" is also the domain discussed by occultists in the nineteenth and twentieth centuries, and one currently being explored by parapsychologists.

Level 4 "Brahman Hiranyagarbha"

It is this level that is experienced nightly during the human "dream state," though it can also be reached through various contemplative practices; it is the stage that must be passed through before reaching "Brahman Prajñā." According to the rishis it is possible to navigate within this dream state, which is a repository of myriad levels of consciousness entered into by all sentient beings in the space-time region of existence. It is often experienced as an intersection between higher levels of Brahman and the individual human consciousness, and though memory and normal ego operation function at a reduced level, it is often possible to recall experiences within this realm after resuming normal operations of awareness.

Level 5 "Brahman Virat"

Also known as "Master of the Waking Universe," it is here that God is approachable through liturgical activities during which, through repetition and concentrated emotional effort, the normal waking ego can be fairly easily transcended to reach the immediacy of the "Brahman Virat" stage of consciousness. When this state is entered into by the practitioner through prayer, meditation, or music, there is a strong taste or hint of the subtle feelings of the joy, consciousness, and bliss that can be experienced with entrance into the higher levels, and in particular it is an adumbration of the full experience of the Parabrahamn, the mysterious trinity of Saccidānanda.

PARABRAHMAN: BRAHMAN OF THE IMPLICATE ORDER

After describing these five levels of Brahman, Sri Aurobindo now turns to focus more specifically upon the Parabrahman (*para* translates as "highest"), in which the trinity fully manifests in its active form outside of space-time. This is the *nirguṇa* Brahman filling Bohm's implicate order. Aurobindo tells us that Vedanta describes Parabrahman "in two great trilogies, subjective and objective," the first trilogy being of course *sat*, *cit*, and *ānanda* (fig. 9.7). Here it is important to note that this trinitarian structure of the Parabrahman can be found underlying a multitude of relationships in the world of space-time, and as such has been revered for many centuries by Indian mystics with the term *saccidānanda*.

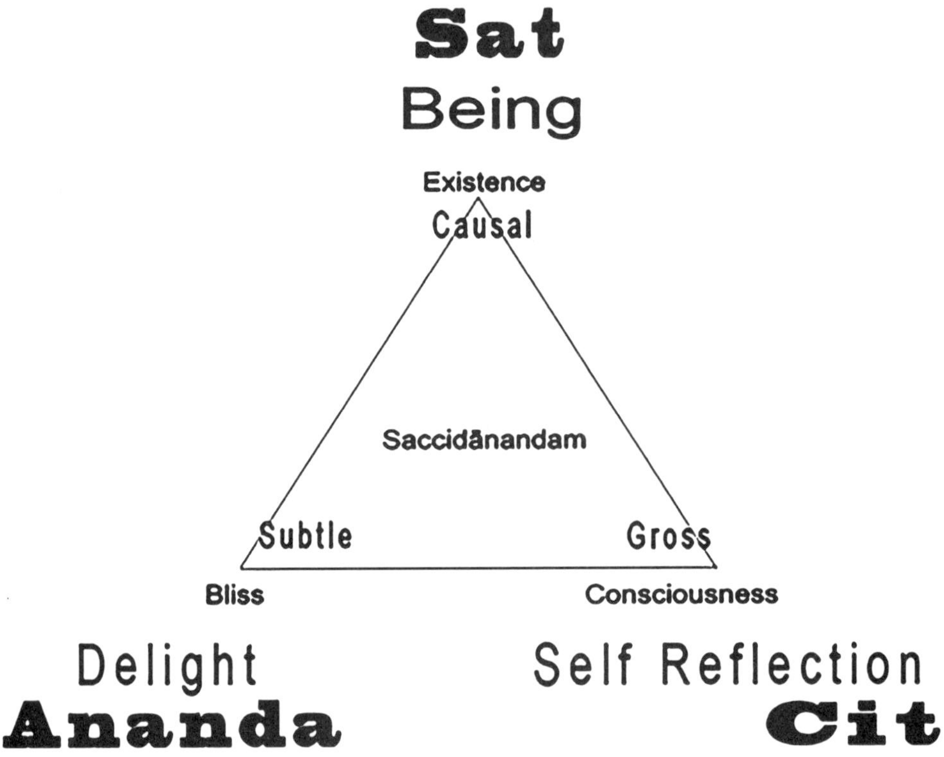

Fig. 9.7. Hypostases of Saccidānanda.

"*Sat* and *cit* are really the same" writes Aurobindo, yet they are both also seen as *ānanda,* or delight. Here we "equate Being (*ananda*) with the pleasure of self-reflection or Conscious Existence." Saccidānanda is Parabrahman and has three attributes or hypostases, as shown in the diagram:

1. Absolute Existence, Being, sat, but also
2. Pure Awareness, Absolute Consciousness, cit, and finally
3. Pure Ecstasy, Absolute Bliss, ānanda.

This is the great teaching of Vedanta, and in this sense Parabrahman as Saccidānanda can be regarded fundamentally as a three-component hypostasis similar to the Christian Trinity.

But these three hypostases are *not completely immanent* in our material universe of space and time. They are a sort of triadic interface that reside, exist, or take their being in the intermediate realm or dimension that lies between the inexpressible infinities of Brahman and the quite expressible limitations of the material, time-bound world of galaxies, stars, and zebras. They function as a bridge for human consciousness between the immanent and the transcendent, between the non-dual implicate order and the space-time explicate order. Parabrahman or *sat-cit-ānanda* (grammatically elided into the single Sanskrit word *saccidānanda*) has both a subjective, inward-turning side (fig. 9.8), and an objective, outward-turning side (fig. 9.9).

Subjectively, Saccidānanda is a self-contained hypostasis of Existence-Consciousness-Bliss, approachable and able to be resonantly experienced (if not completely "knowable" by the mental rational

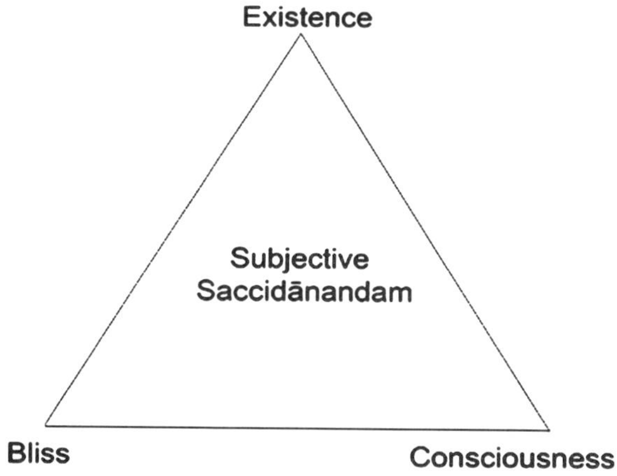

Fig. 9.8. Subjective (inward-turning) Saccidānanda.

human mind) by human sages, shamans, and rishis, and modern psychonauts.

Objectively, however, Saccidānanda can also be understood, Aurobindo tells us, by use of the three Sanskrit terms *satyam, jñāna, anāntam*. Brahman is *satyam,* or Reality, and is a term encountered widely in Indian philosophy and metaphysics; the word *satyam* itself defines Reality or Truth in these discussions. *Jñāna* on the other hand is Brahman's objective Knowledge hypostasis. "Brahman is absolute *jñānam,* direct and self-existent, without beginning, middle or end, in which the Knower is also the Knowledge and the Known."[52] Finally, he tells us, "Brahman is *anāntam,* Endlessness, including all kinds of Infinity."

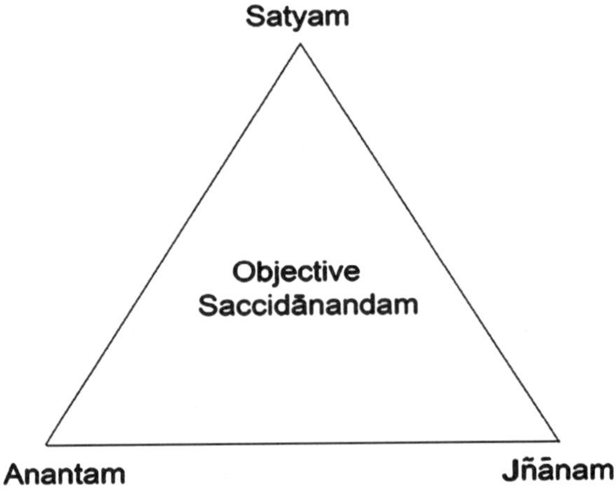

Fig. 9.9. Objective (outward-turning) Saccidānanda.

The Vedantic Theory of Maya, Energy of the Absolute

Brahman projects a luminous shadow of itself that is called the Parabrahman. Under the play of Maya, the One becomes the Many. "But why? To what purpose?" asks Aurobindo, and he immediately gives one possible philosophical explanation:

> Absolute One, it is argued, passes through the cycle of manifestation, because He then returns to His original unity enriched with a new store of experiences and impressions, richer in love, richer in knowledge, richer in deed.[53]

The questions then arose of how and why the One became the Many. "Why did the Absolute turn His face toward Evolution?" asks Aurobindo. Why did that which is beyond Causality "need to act on a purpose," and "what was the nature of the process"? The answer, it was discovered, lies in a power or force they named Maya.

What is Maya and how and where might it have come into existence? The term *maya* is commonly interpreted as indicating illusory appearance that makes the phenomenal world seem "real" to us. But according to Aurobindo, the Upanishads tells us that Maya, a function of the Parabrahman, precedes phenomena and is a force that is outside of space-time.

> The birth of Maya, if it had any birth, took place on the other side of phenomena, before the origin of time, space and causality; and is therefore not cognizable by the intellect which can only think in terms of time, space, and causality.[54]

Maya must then be an objective action, a function of Parabrahman turning outwardly. The action of Maya is analogous to the working of a prism at the very source of creation. Through Maya Brahman is refracted into the three rays, the emerging primary spectrum called Saccidānanda. Brahman finds itself split by Maya into a diffraction pattern of existence, consciousness, and delight, releasing the powers of *sat, cit,* and *ānanda* to create the universe. Brahman morphs into Saccidānanda, and the one becomes many.

And though they remain One in origin, the many now awaken to the transformations of Maya. They discover the endless possibilities in relating with one another in an evolving, spiraling, reciprocal fashion. Accordingly, we may say that with Maya's transformation, Brahman finds delight in existence and discovers delight in consciousness. Likewise, it can be said that Brahman is now enjoying awareness of the consciousness of existence, consciousness of delight and the delight of existence. Brahman has discovered joy, the exuberance of creation, the discovery of infinite delight in being, the exuberant thrills of consciousness in an infinite universe.

As this flowing transformation into phenomena deepens, the single *Puruṣa* differentiates into an infinity of separate *puruṣa* beings. Parabrahman is the luminous shadow of the Absolute projected in itself by itself, and Maya is similarly the dark shadow projected by the Absolute in Parabrahman.[55] Seen from the viewpoint of *ānanda,* it is the Will of Parabrahman that is dividing itself into innumerable forms, each of which represents itself "as individual selves solely for the pleasure of existence or Will to live."[56]

The Function of Vidyā and Avidyā

But still not answered is why the Parabrahman, who is absolute knowledge, should limit himself. Why should "the pure ultra-Spiritual *unrefine* Itself into the mental and material"?[57] Sri Aurobindo's answer is that this is necessary for free creativity to commence in the form of imagination. He tells us that the Vedantic sages had identified the two polar functions that power creative action as it blossoms in the universe; these are expressed in the Sanskrit terms *vidyā* and *avidyā*, roughly translated as "knowledge" and "ignorance." It is this dynamic duo, *vidyā* and *avidyā*, knowledge and ignorance, working as a tag team similar to the popular "good cop/bad cop" paradigm, through which Parabrahman is able to discover the delight of consciousness as it transforms through exercises of imagination and pure creativity.

Aurobindo gives several examples of the necessity of *avidyā.* Without *avidyā* we might see before us a complex conglomeration of whirling energy vortexes of different frequency, atomic nuclear patternings of holographic vibration. But through the power of *avidyā* we are able to ignore this and focus instead upon what we see to be a brown stone; thus, *avidyā* acts as a filter. Again, without *avidyā,* when we go for what otherwise would seem to be a casual walk down a path in the woods, we might instead perceive that we were walking upside down on the spherical body of the planet, our actual motion on an ellipse about the sun at 70,000 miles per hour combined with our circular motion about the planetary axis at 1,000 miles per hour.

Avidyā is thus required for filter, focus, imagination, and creation, and must be present in every operation of normal human consciousness. *Avidyā* allows the human to co-create the universe through the arts, sciences, and through sheer consciousness. Aurobindo talks about Shakespeare's imaginations and the origin of his creative images:

> These mighty images live immortally in our minds because Parabrahman in Shakespeare is the same as Parabrahman in ourselves; thought, in fact, is one, although to be revealed to us, it has to be bodied forth and take separate shapes in sound forms which we are accustomed to perceive and understand.[58]

We see also that *avidyā* is also inherent in engendering the delight that arises in approaching *ānanda,* the bliss of existence, and we see in nature a "fundamental impulse toward phenomenal existence, consciousness, and the pleasure of conscious existence, though the deepest bliss is after all that which she left and to which she will return."[59]

A summarizing diagram relating the arc of Brahman is presented in figure 9.10, where our everyday space-time of butterflies and zebras (on the right) is symbolized as a projection by Maya refracted into the three beams of *sat-cit-ānanda* feeding a Taoist yin-yang symbol. According to Sri Aurobindo, the non-dual, unmanifest (*avyakta*) and indescribable Level 1 Brahma (the "Unknowable God the Father" on the left) resides in a non-dual, nonspatial, nontemporal condition called *avyakta,* or "unmanifest." Another way to interpret the diagram would be to see

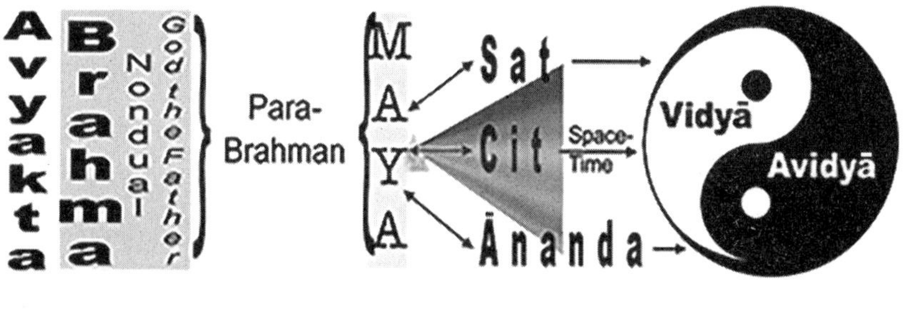

Fig. 9.10. Vedantic relationships from *avyakta* to *avidyā.*

Fig. 9.11. Vishnu dreaming the Universe.
Image of Vishnu by Arnold Betten.

that God the Father on the left is connected to God the Son (space-time) on the right, through the transformational bridge of the Holy Spirit, Parabrahman.

We are reminded of the image of Vishnu (fig. 9.11) sleeping on the cosmic ocean of *avyakta* and dreaming the universe. It is Parabrahman (in the center of fig. 9.10) that bridges *avyakta* and Maya linking the non-dual eternal on the left with space-time on the right, and within space-time we see the *vidyā-avidyā* duo, "me and my shadow," interlocked and spinning in the yin-yang symbol, exhibiting an unending cyclical flow of the energies of creation and destruction, light and darkness.

Avyakta as Concealed *Puruṣa*

Avyakta is a Sanskrit term that indicates a state prior to manifestation in space, time, or causality. *Avyakta,* as observed by Vedantic seers, is said to be that state of nontemporal, nonspatial manifestation of Brahman, which is not prior to time but outside of time, not outside of space but having neither outside nor inside, non-dual and nonlocal everywhere and everywhen. According to sages who wrote the seventh-century Avyakta Upanishad, this *avyakta* is of an intelligent and joyful nature, consisting of a superpositioning of all of the three elementals of the Parabrahman: *sat, cit,* and *ānanda.*

Spirit and matter, *puruṣa* and *prakṛti,* are indissolubly welded together simply because they are "the one thing viewed from two sides." Spirit takes the shape and appearance of matter through the powers of *avidyā* (ignorance, obscuration) and *vidyā* (clarity, knowledge) and the gross material universe is rendered forth from the Parabrahman which, in the course of evolving phenomena, enters into three states or conditions, *sat, cit, and ānanda,* which are called in one passage "His three habitations" and in another, "his three states of dream."[60]

Words fail here, of course, and at this point Sri Aurobindo recalls an image of *avyakta* to describe these ethereal relationships in the form of a mythical image of the Golden Egg (fig. 9.12), related in the

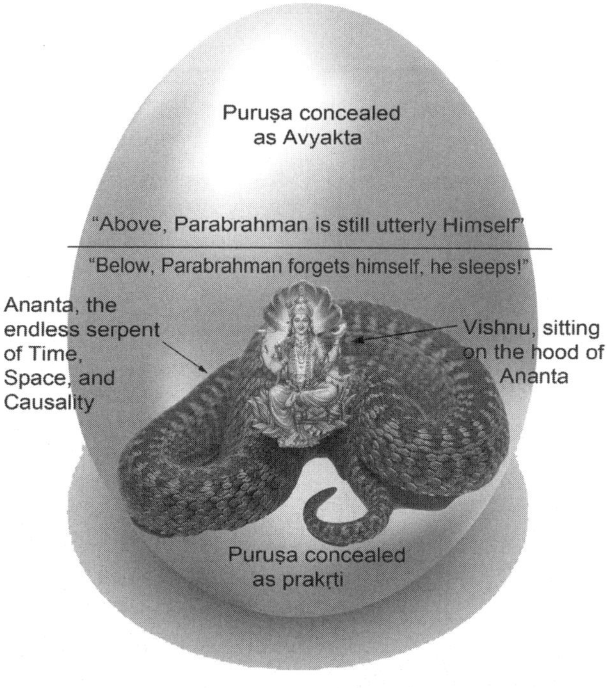

Fig. 9.12. Avyakta as the Golden Egg of the Purāṇas.
Diagram by author.

Purāṇas (literally the "ancient or old" folk tales of India, recorded circa 200 CE).[61]

> Let us then imagine Avyakta as an egg, the golden egg of the Purāṇas full of the waters of undifferentiated existence and divided into two halves, the upper or luminous half filled with the upper waters of subjective ideation, the lower or tenebrous half with the lower waters of objective ideation. In the upper half Purusha is concealed as the final cause of things, in the lower half he is concealed as Prakriti, the material cause of things.[62]

If we rotate the Golden Egg ninety degrees counterclockwise, a similar cosmological relationship can be seen in figure 9.13, where "*Puruṣa* concealed as *Avyakta*" is now seen as "Nonlocal *Puruṣa* > Implicate Order" and "*Puruṣa* concealed as *Prakṛti*" now becomes "Local *Puruṣa* > Explicate Order," on either side of a continuous Fourier transform process bridging the two regions in an endless feedback loop (discussed more fully in chapter 3 and my previous book *The Electromagnetic Brain*).[63]

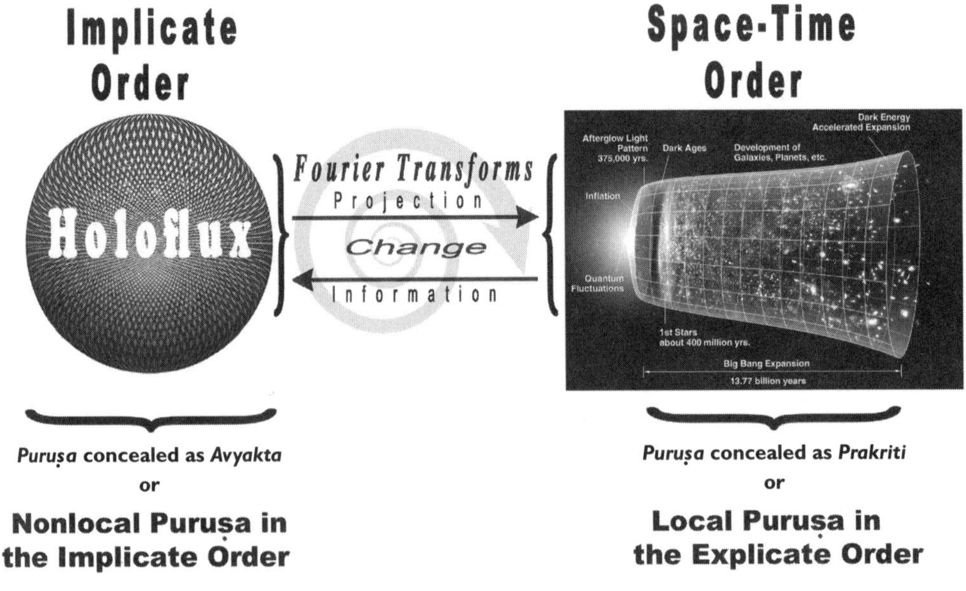

Fig. 9.13. The two regions of Puruṣa consciousness.

Thus the Whole, both seen and unseen, space-time as well as other dimensions enfolded within the implicate order, can be seen as a process consisting of three parts or movements, mirrored in description from the Christian tradition as "the Father, the Son, the Holy Spirit," and which the ancient Vedic seers described by combining the three hypostases into one—Saccidānanda.[64]

Implicate Father and Explicate Son

The diagram implies that one way to see the Christian relationship presented by the Holy Trinity might be two distinct domains bridged by a third domain of pure energy flux:

Region 1	"God the Father"	The Implicate Order
Region 2	"The Holy Spirit"	Energy
Region 3	"God the Son"	Space-Time Order

In the diagram we see the transforming flux ("spirit" or "consciousness") processing between two orders of being in "an undivided flowing movement without borders."[65] The consciousness identity at the left in the diagram can be expressed as a *spectrum of holoflux energy* in Bohm's "implicate order" (as previously discussed in chapter 3 In the conceptual map of Vedanta, this is termed the single all-seeing *Puruṣa,* while Christians use the phrase "God the Father."

A continuous energy transformation (the Spirit) between left and right regions (i.e., between "God the Father" and "God the Son") is depicted as a prism at the center of the diagram. To the right of the diagram our space-time local region might be called "the Son" by Christian theologians. In fact, there has been much controversy over the publications of Matthew Fox, a former Dominican priest (now Anglican) with a Ph.D. in medieval theology, for his conception of the "Cosmic Christ" in what he called "Creation Spirituality."[66]

When gender is considered and overlaid upon the configuration (fig. 9.14, p. 182), it can be seen that the trinitarian relationship of *sat-cit-ānanda* is reflected in the universal human conditions of consciousness, mind, and love. The feminine aspect *(ānanda)* corresponds more with empathic love, touch, and creation while the male (*cit*) equates

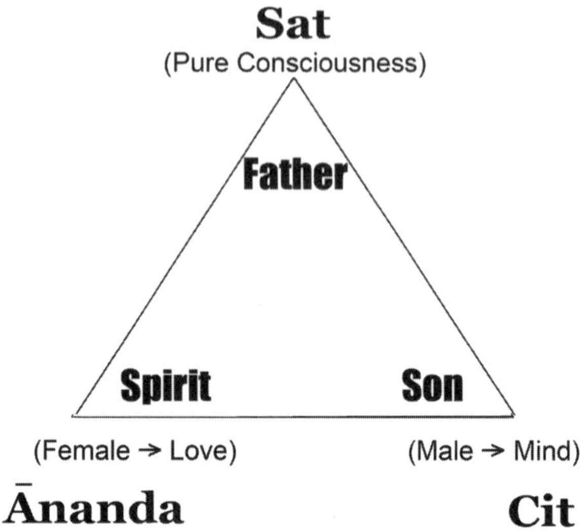

Fig. 9.14. *Sat-Cit-Ānanda* as consciousness (bi-gendered)-Love (female)-Mind (male).

more with the clarity of logic and cognitive processing. Pure consciousness itself combines both genders as represented in *sat*.

Aurobindo's Trinity and the Supermind

Aurobindo's experiential understanding of the Trinity largely agrees with that of the Christian tradition, as can be seen here from Aurobindo's thousand-page opus, *The Life Divine*:

> The Trinity is the source and basis of all existence and play of existence, and all cosmos must be an expression and action of its essential reality.[67]

Aurobindo's understanding of the Trinity is a modern one, though in full agreement with the concepts of the Vedantic Trinity as they are expressed by Saccidānanda. Aurobindo frequently uses the term Saccidānanda in his writing, telling us that an experience of Saccidānanda is possible through a state of consciousness which he calls "the Supermind," a term that appears to be identical to one of Teilhard de Chardin's terms, "noosphere," which refers to the same intermediary link. It is access to Saccidānanda, through networking with the Supermind (or the noosphere), that will afford the individual human psyche the full experience and knowledge of the Holy Trinity during contemplative prayer.

During my retreat with Father Bede Griffiths in South India, not far from the town of Pondicherry where Sri Aurobindo had lived his final fifty years, I recall singing local hymns at the end of each mass, using words both from English as well as the Tamil language. I noticed in particular the many refrains offering up praise and thanks to the Holy Trinity that ended with the word *saccidānanda,* a term I had first heard years earlier when studying Aurobindo's *Life Divine.*

Practically speaking, the Supermind designates a configuration of consciousness toward which each individual human psyche has the potential to grow and eventually to access, assuming sufficient sustained effort and will have been applied. Metaphysically, Aurobindo uses the term Supermind to designate the bridge, link, or interface between our normal everyday consciousness (our "thinking meat" mind) and that region of pure non-dual infinite Being termed Saccidānanda, outside of space-time. We suggest that Aurobindo's Supermind is congruent with Teilhard de Chardin's noosphere and with the Christian notion of an experience of "the Spirit."

According to this hypothesis, when the individual human psyche resonates with, links, or communes with the Supermind, it knows itself to be One by immediacy, having reached the rarified condition of non-duality. It has at this stage reached the integral mode of consciousness or awareness. At this moment, there arises an omni-dimensional mode of non-dual awareness beyond that of normal space-time observations, which rely upon the exterior human sensory systems. Aurobindo tells us that we (or "I" or "we") then see "without any process of construction . . . the totality."

> The Supermind distinguishes by a direct seeing without any mental process of taking to pieces the peculiarities of the thing, form, energy, action, quality, mind, soul that it has in view, and it sees

> too with an equal directness and without any process of construction the significant totality of which these peculiarities are the incidents.[68]

According to Aurobindo the knowledge of Supermind can eventually be reached through accumulated experience and evolutionary growth which, according to many schools of Indian philosophy, is the goal of each soul, although it may take multiple incarnations. A similar belief can be found in Christianity in the belief that eventually the individual soul will find God and link, through the Holy Spirit, with God the Father (Bohm's implicate order), and with God the Son (Bohm's explicate order, also called the "Cosmic Christ" by the former Catholic priest and mystic Matthew Fox), or both simultaneously.[69] In bridging the two, the three become one, even within what was formerly believed to be an individually separate soul.

It is our contention, as previously discussed in this book and more fully developed elsewhere,[70] that the Parabrahman can also be effectively identified as a concept that can be readily mapped within the domains of mathematics and quantum physics, in particularly it can be related to the frequency domain or Bohm's implicate order, both transcendent and outside of space and time. However abstract this concept is, it is possible for a human being to learn to experience this Parabrahman as many saints, mystics, and shamans have reported in various cultural-specific terms.

Having spent much of this chapter in developing the outlines of this rather abstract metaphysical map, we can now turn to exploring practical techniques for approaching the experience of the Parabrahman through advanced contemplative praxis as developed within Hindu culture.

10

Further Techniques of Hindu Psychophysics

This chapter highlights both the technique and psychophysics (i.e., practice and theory) of highly effective contemplative exercises that have been developed and used by generations of psychonauts in Tibet and India. It should be noted that all of these techniques involve the phenomenon of communication and control through energized frequency resonances that link space-time (Bohm's explicate order) with numerous other dimensional realities that exist (within Bohm's transcendent implicate order). Every vibrating packet of electromagnetic energy flux can be seen as a uniquely patterned "signature" that, through direct resonance, links (via the Fourier Transform) to corresponding frequency entities within the implicate order.

MANTRA (AUDIBLE RESONANCE)

Mantra is a highly developed technique practiced in Tantra. M. P. Pandit (1918–1994), a Sanskrit scholar, philosopher, and contemplative who wrote over 150 books and articles on yoga describes the repetition of mantra as the second of four stages of practice:

> The *Tantra* provides for a graded system of *sādhana* according to the competence of the seeker. *Puja,* external worship with flowers, incense, offerings, etc., is a first stage; next comes *Jāpa,* repetition of *Mantra* according to prescribed procedure; then *Dhyāna,* mental contemplation, adoration; the last and highest is the Brahmabhava

> or Brahmasadhana, attainment of the knowledge and feeling that one *is* Brahman and All is pervaded by Brahman.[1]

The audible resonance of sound vibration is powered by consciousness itself, and internal repetition leads to contact with the source of the vibrations in the implicate order, the frequency domain of consciousness, allowing supersensuous perception to arise.

> Mantra are considered, not products of discursive thought, human wisdom or poetic phantasy, but flash-lights of the eternal truth, seen by those eminent men who have come into a supersensuous contact with the Unseen.[2]

Mantra can be seen as much more than words, even sacred words, though all prayer can be mantra. Even single words or sounds, repeated over and over, are mantra when practiced with as continuous a focus of awareness as possible, and, of course, the mantra, the repetition, does not have to be audible, it can be a silent repetition, which is internally audible. As the scientist and Indian philosopher I. K. Taimni (who obtained his Ph.D. in inorganic chemistry from London University in 1928, and later became the president of the Theosophical Society in Adyar) writes:

> The aim of all mantra, in short, is to purify and harmonise the vehicles of the seeker so that they become increasingly sensitive to the subtler layers of his own spiritual consciousness. As he comes into contact with these he becomes increasingly aware of that Reality of which his own consciousness is a partial expression.[3]

Rephrasing this statement in psychophysical terms, we would say that the aim of mantra is to tune into or resonate with a particular bandwidth of energy frequencies, a spectrum of energy accessible to our own consciousness that can be contacted through mantric vibration resonating in a bandwidth of atemporal conscious energy.

Within this bandwidth or region of atemporal consciousness (which cannot even really be called a region as it is both atemporal and aspatial, i.e., outside of time and space), or what is called the frequency domain in the electromagnetic field theory of consciousness, can be found all of the vibrations that have ever been generated, interpenetrating in all of their complexities. In many Indian schools of thought this is called the *ākāśa,* or *alaya-vijñana,* the "storehouse of all consciousness"; and it is this domain that is "touched" by the contemplative Tantric yogi during sessions reaching *asamprajñāta samādhi,* when the various separate cognitive systems of thought and perception have been attenuated and the deepest silence has been entered.

It is ironic that in order to reach this state of *asamprajñāta samādhi* and touch the Akashic records short-term and long-term memory must be "silenced," detached, attenuated, or deactivated. Hence the difficulty, back in the world of time and space, of communicating the "experience" or of describing this state, and thus the resulting myriad metaphors and symbols throughout cultures and religions serving as substitutes for the authentic experience.

YANTRA (VISUAL RESONANCE)

The Sanskrit word *yantra* derives etymologically from the root *yam,* which is translated "to sustain," "hold or support" and in some contexts as "a tool." In common usage it can be used to refer to any physical structure or instrument that may be used to assist in furthering the transformation of consciousness. Thus the scholar Madhu Khanna characterizes yantras as "aids to and the chief instruments of meditative discipline . . . a yantra used in this context and for this purpose is an abstract geometrical design intended as a 'tool' for meditation and increased awareness."[4]

Among yantras the Sri Yantra is highly revered as an advanced contemplative instrument. Every yantra has a vibratory mantra (recited aloud or silently) associated with it. The mantra that is associated with the Sri Yantra (which resonates with the yantra when recited and invokes the energy deities associated with the yantra) can be seen in Devanagari script in a circle just within the inner surrounding row of petals in the yantra (see fig. 10.1).

The Sri Yantra is also used as mnemonic tool to help the practitioner recall a variety of attributes and issues that should be made consciously explicit in the psychophysical practices leading to the transformative experiential dimensions associated with the Yantra.

For example, in the image of the Sri Yantra in figure 10.1 the outer linear shape conveys the idea of fortress walls facing in the four cardinal directions. In order for the contemplative to move psychophysically toward the center of the Yantra (the central dot is called the *bindu*), all of these external attributes must be dealt with and harmonized in the life of the practitioner. Generally, what exists outside the gates of the Yantra are what we experience of the world through sense-activity and cravings of our ego constructs. Before gaining entrance to richer psychophysical experience, the one who begins to use the Yantra must work on dealing with and transforming such things as worldly desire, anger, avarice and greed, infatuation, obstinance, hubris, jealousy, and desire for earthly rewards and self-recognition. In order that all of these issues be systematically approached and focused upon during the beginning of each meditation period, the Yantra has these issues associated with different specific parts of the surrounding shape of the Yantra,[5] as can be seen in figure 10.1.

CHAKRA AND PHYSIOLOGICAL RESONANCE

The chakra is experienced as a psychophysical matrix with a definite spatial location within the human body. M. P. Pandit here describes the chakras:

> In the system of the Tantras there are recognised in the human body certain centres of consciousness, along the spinal column, with their respective spheres of activity. They are six, beginning from the lower end of the spine called the *Mūlādhara* (foundational support) with an additional seventh at the crown of the head—the *Sahasrāra*.[6]

Within the human body there are areas of particular psychophysical significance. During the practices of *samādhi,* contemplatives have discovered loci which are particularly sensitive for tuning in to resonance both the explicate order (space-time) and the implicate order (frequency domain). A sixteenth-century chakra diagram circulated in Nepal can be seen in figure 10.2 on page 190. Diagrams of chakras are

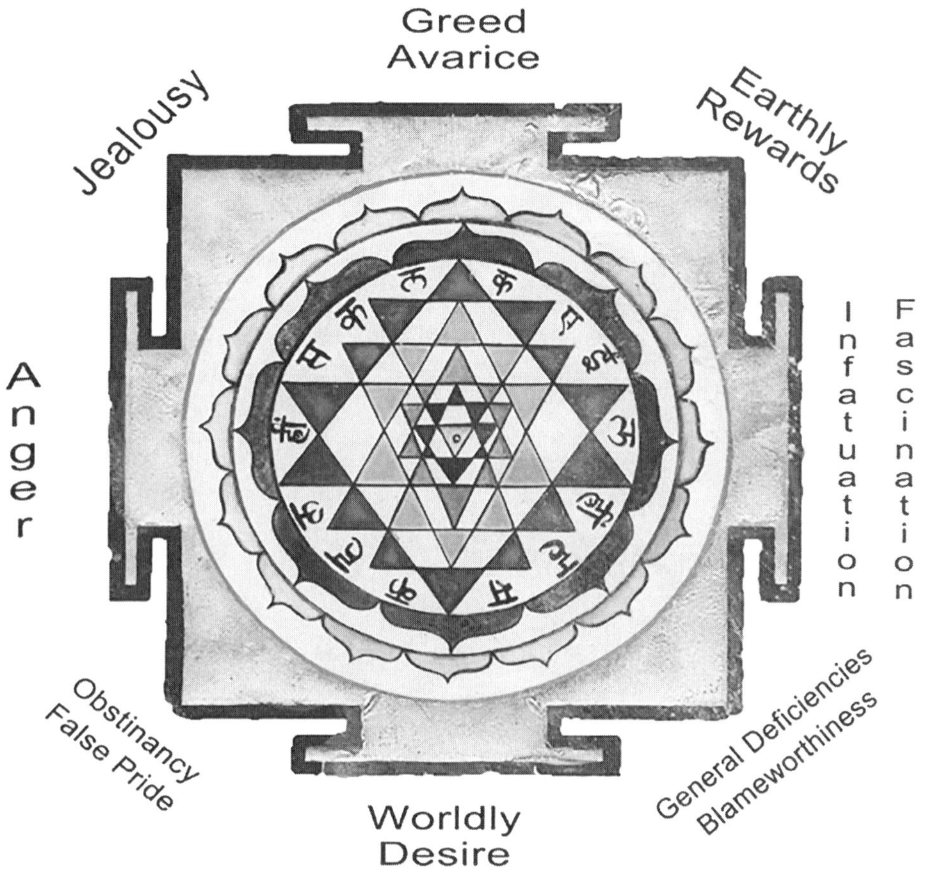

Fig. 10.1. Sri Yantra as mnemonic diagram for contemplation.

used as mnemonic tools to assist the practitioner in recalling the various locations within which to focus consciousness during periods of contemplative practice. A more Western, medical description of these areas was presented before the Bombay Medical Union in 1926 by Dr. V. G. Rele, a well-known surgeon who presented a paper for other physicians who might be interested in "a science of Yoga." For example, Rele describes here the *Ājñā* chakra, located behind the forehead in the cranium:

> This *chakra* is the naso-ciliary extension of the cavernous plexus of the sympathetic through the ophthalmic division of the fifth

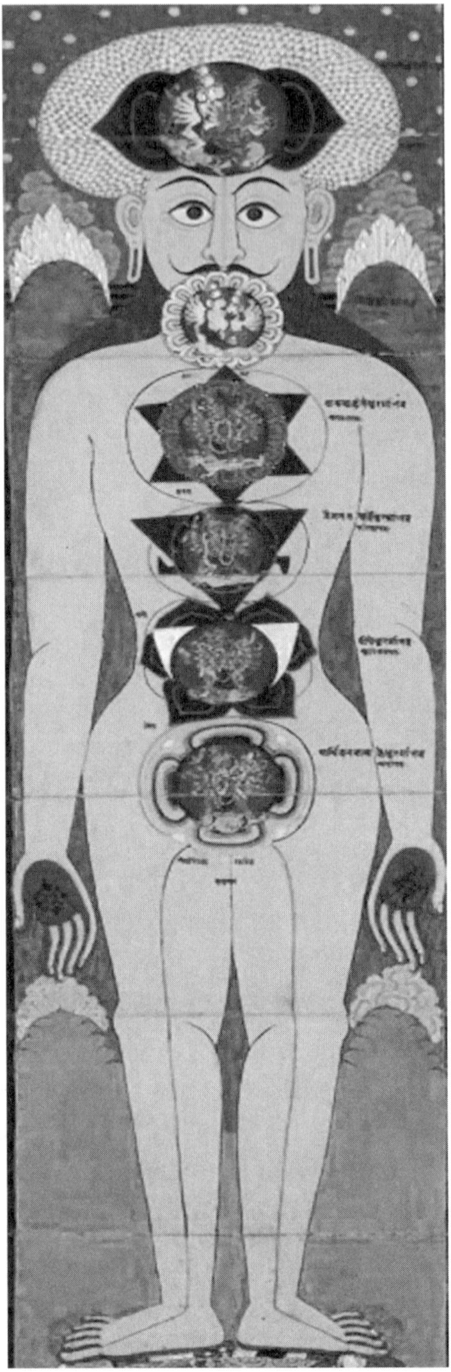

Fig. 10.2. Chakra diagram, Nepal, sixteenth century CE.

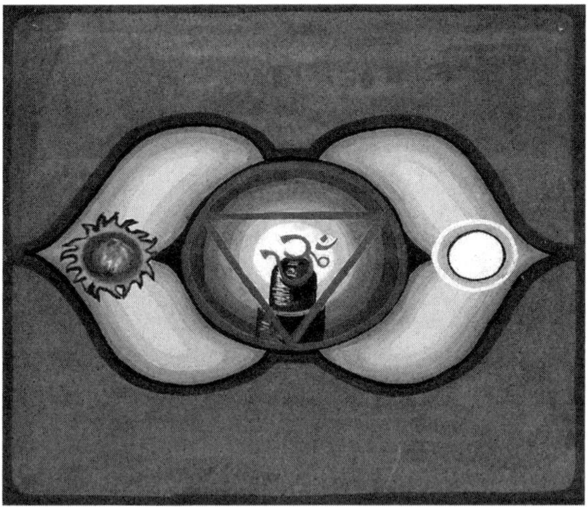

Fig. 10.3. *Ājñā chakra.* Also known as the third eye. Illustration from *The Serpent Power* (1918) by Sir John Woodroffe.

cranial nerve, ending in the ciliary muscles of the iris and at the root of the nose, through the supra-orbital foramen. It has two petals or branches and is situated between the eye-brows. It is the spot which is contemplated while undergoing the process of *prāṇāyāma*.[7]

"THE SERPENT POWER" > CIRCULATION OF LIGHT

Dr. Rele presented a theoretical psychophysical explanation for some of the experiential changes in consciousness described by yogis as a result of Tantric practices—in particular, the activation of the Kundalini, the "Serpent Power," a phenomenon that appears identical to the Chinese Taoist term "circulation of light" throughout the body of the contemplative. Dr. Rele also happened to be a close friend and associate of Sir John Woodroffe, known also by his pen name "Sir Arthur Avalon," under which he had published numerous books and translations of Tantric material.

Rele, whose lecture series was later published as *The Mysterious Kundalini: The Physical Basis of the "Kundalini Yoga"*[8] asserts that the Kundalini corresponds to energy flowing in the right vagus nerve. He says that a yogi, through the vagus nerve, "establishes a complete control over the unconscious automatic action of the involuntary muscular fibres."[9] This accords well with the *Hatha Yoga Pradīpikā,* in which the Kundalini is said "to be lying dormant guarding the opening of the passage that leads to the seat of Brahma." Rele goes on to describe the very physiological substrate of yogic processes when he says that:

> This seat is said to be *Brahma-randhra* (cave of Brahma), that is, the ventricular cavity in the brain. . . . Unless she (*Kundalini*) is awakened, or made consciously active, one cannot send one's embodied soul (*Jivātma*), which is supposed to reside in the heart (*Hridaya*), along the *Sushumṇā nāḍī* to the *Brahma-randhra* nor is he able to assist the soul captured in the *Randhra,* to be freed to join the Universal Soul (*Paramātmā*) outside."[10]

Here Rele is careful to explain that his understanding of the English translation of the Sanskrit word *randhra* is definitely "cavity," and should not be translated as "hole" as is found in numerous other English translations. He states that this *randhra* is "the inter-communicating cavity of the four ventricles of the brain and is continuous with the central canal (*chitra*) of the spinal cord (*sushumṇā nāḍī*). Figure 10.4 is a physiologically accurate sketch of the contiguous ventricular cavity within the brain.

Thus, the experience called by yogis the movement or flow of Kundalini energy might also be understood as the phenomenon of a magnetic plasma field being tuned and resonating within the ventricular "cave of Brahma."

THE MYSTERIOUS KUNDALINI

Dr. V. G. Rele's presentation before the Bombay Medical Union was so well received that he was encouraged to publish it in long form for those interested in "the science of Yoga."[11] In the resulting book, the author attempts to give a physiological explanation of the powers which the yogis attain by their methods.

The book, ninety-two pages long, contains many clear diagrams and photographs, as well as a fascinating three-page foreword written by

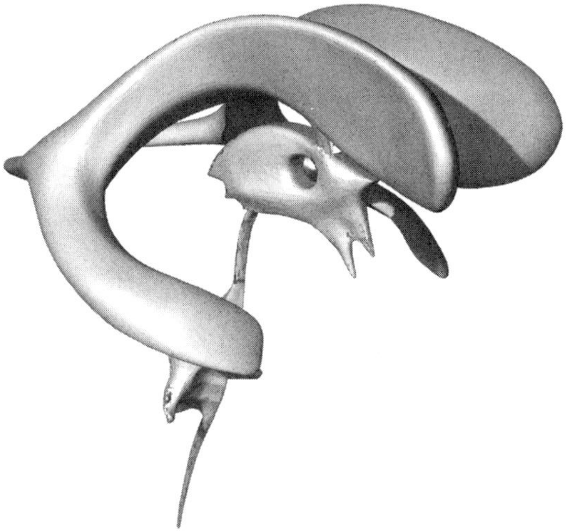

Fig. 10.4. Sketch of ventricular cavity.
Illustration by BodyParts3D by DBCLS.

his friend, Sir John Woodfroffe (1865–1936), who was both a Tantric scholar and chief justice on the Supreme Court of the British government of India.

My own interest in Rele's *The Mysterious Kundalini* stems from having acquired it forty years ago, prior to leaving New York to begin graduate studies in Indian philosophy in 1974 at the California Institute of Asian Studies in San Francisco. Having completed an undergraduate engineering program, I was impressed by the fact that Rele had the scientific training of a physician, and even more so by the carefully detailed pen-and-ink diagrams with which he backed up his theory of a physiological basis of the phenomena associated with Kundalini yoga. This encouraged me to include visualization of anatomically correct internal components during meditation on the various chakra loci within my own body, which I believe has greatly enhanced my own experience of yogic contemplation over the intervening years.

Woodroffe explains in his foreword to Rele's book how Rele's view on the perceived physiology of the powers which yogis attain by their methods "has much to be said for it," and that it is a scientific approach to a description of *Laya* or Kundalini yoga. He mentions, however, that Rele's theory of Kundalini being the right vagus nerve differs from Woodroffe's own view that Kundalini is "the Grand Potential" and cannot, in his view, "be identified with any of the products which she becomes."

Regardless of the credibility assigned to this type of yoga, Woodroffe affirms it as an area of investigation by saying "that it has a parapsychic interest is very clear." He goes on to summarize:

> That such Yoga has been practised with some result I believe, not because I have personal experience in the matter but because it is an ancient Yoga and *a priori* it is not credible that men should continue to practice anything without attainment of any result. . . . Kundalini Yoga is of great scientific, parapsychic, and metaphysical interest and I am glad to provide an introduction to the present conscientious and valuable enquiry. . . . I am glad then to know that a man of the scientific attainments of the Author has taken the matter in hand and has thus encouraged others to follow or to criticize him. . . . From the friction of the mental Arani, the Fire of Knowledge is kindled.[12]

Woodroffe explains that taken as a whole, the Tantras have a significance that is twofold:

1. *Upāsanā,* or "by way of worship"
2. *Siddhi,* or by "extension of natural powers"[13]

The first part of Woodroffe's observation, focused upon the fact that all of the Tantras reserve significant focus upon liturgical "worship" might be readily dismissed by many contemporary agnostics, atheists, and those with only a casual acquaintance with the liturgical rites of any particular faith. Yet perhaps the richest liturgical complex, "by way of worship," of any sect in the world can be seen in Tibetan Vajrayāna rituals, discussed in the following part.

In *The Mysterious Kundalini* Rele goes on to describe numerous astounding feats he has witnessed firsthand in India by practitioners of Kundalini yoga. These observations led him to an in-depth study of the practice, and it was during these years of inquiry and self-experimentation that he had developed a scientific basis for the experiences of Kundalini yoga development, firmly based upon and integrated with his own knowledge as a trained British physician. Here the author says:

> I think, medical men, knowing as they do both anatomy and physiology of human body, ought to be able to explain these rare phenomena, and nevertheless even to them, it is a very difficult matter. Perhaps what is abnormal to men living on a lower plane of vibrations, is normal to those who live on a slightly higher plane of vibrations.[14]

Rele describes several philosophical approaches to yoga, mentions Patañjali's aphorism as "suppression of thought," and seems to focus on *prāṇāyāma* as yoga. Dr. Rele summarizes with his own definition of yoga:

> Yoga is the science, which raises the capacity of the human mind to respond to higher vibrations, and to perceive, catch and assimilate the infinite conscious movements going on around us in the universe. In fact it makes one a transmitting as well as receiving station of radio activity with the mind as the aerial.[15]

In this first chapter, Rele introduces his theory of the vagus nerve, describing its relation to *prāṇāyāma* practice and experience.

> We know that the respiratory act is under the control of the Vagus nerve, which has two sets of fibres afferent and efferent; *Prānāyāma,* then, is in effect a process of bringing under control the Vagus nerve, over which, normally, we have no control. Thus we see that *Prānāyāma* really signifies the controlling of energy.[16]

Rele then goes through the three major stages of praxis in Patañjali's approach to Yoga: *dhāraṇā, dhyāna, samādhi.* Rele says "*Dhāraṇā* and *dhyāna* naturally lead to *samādhi,* which is the state of superconsciousness."[17] Of these steps, it is *dhāraṇā,* says Rele, that from the medical point of view allows a practitioner of yoga, when he has attained to the *dhāraṇā* state, to develop "an internal vision, and is able to see what is going on in his body or in nature not perceived ordinarily."[18] One of my mentors, John Lilly, often commented that *dhāraṇā* is a skill that is developed by students as they learn to focus without distraction on a narrow subject area in order grasp abstract material. He felt that such training is creating a large population of adults with the potential to quickly move on into the higher practice of *dhyāna,* which then leads to *samādhi.*

In a chapter on practice, Rele draws upon medical physiological terminology, relating it to inner yogic experiences, and while sometimes obscure to the nonphysician, some of the descriptions are intriguing: for example, "it may be that the corroboration of the spinal nerves and the sympathetic nerves are both consequences of a formation of new organs and structure in the splanchnic area."[19]

Rele describes the vagus nerve itself as located within the spinal cord. He explains how the sympathetic nerve fibers and the parasympathetic nerve fibers are complementary. The purpose of the sympathetic nerve fiber is to prepare the body for quick reaction to its environment, causing an acceleration of heartbeat, dilation of pupils, dilation of sphincter and bladder, and inhibiting the secretion of the salivary glands.

The parasympathetic nerve fibers, on the other hand, reside in a bulbar portion of the spinal cord, and their purpose is to slow the action of the heart, increase the activity of the digestive tract, and stimulate salivary and digestive secretions. One of the goals of yoga practice, suggests Rele, is to bring both of these nerve systems (the sympathetic and the parasympathetic) under conscious control to interact simultaneously in a feedback loop through the practice of contemplative meditation.

TANTRIC ANATOMY: NADIS AND CHAKRAS

Rele wonders as to how the ancients might have come upon their knowledge of the internal anatomy of the body; did they dissect human bodies, or did they gain their knowledge by some sort of mystic vision?

Rele concludes, "Whatever it may be, the fact remains that the anatomy of nerves given in the Tantric manuals can stand comparison with our present knowledge.[20]

According to yoga, says Rele, there are ten important *vāyu-nāḍīs,* or nerve-impulse pathways, without a knowledge of which the process and technique of *prāṇāyāma* is not possible. He includes *iḍā* (on the left side of the body), *pīṇgalā* (on the left), *sushumṇā* in the center, piercing the skull and joining the cerebrum (*Brahma-chakra*), and numerous other nerve-shakti pathways. Of these all he says that *sushumṇā* is the most important, and this importance lies in the fact that by certain practices one can "put a stop to the flight of time" by drawing *prāṇā* from the *iḍā* and *pīṇgalā nāḍīs,* or as Rele says, "by consciously controlling the incessant working of these sympathetic cords, it is possible to put a stop to the katabolic activity of the body."[21] In fact, says Rele, when these *nāḍīs* are controlled by and made inert by the conscious exercise of the *sushumṇā nāḍīs* "there is said to exist no night or day for a Yogi, as *sushumṇā* is said 'to devour time.'"[22]

Rele goes on to describe the chakras and says that in the Tantric literature there are primarily six chakras, independent units, each having a *shakti* controlling its own type of energy. However, in addition to these six independent shakti-controlled chakras, there is a "universal Shakti" which has the power to energize and/or control the other six chakras. This mistress shakti is called the Kundalini, and Rele says that in "the physical form she is lying dormant and coiled up like a serpent in an individual, but when awakened by Yoga practices the individual gains for himself the power of performing miracles."[23]

Chapter 13 describes the major chakras in detail, including a description of their appearance to the yogi and also a medical physiological description.

Rele spends some time extolling the virtues of internal meditation on the thalamus, due to its being a central hub or nexus for myriad sympathetic and parasympathetic nerve systems from throughout the body. He states that a "yogi, by a conscious control over the *udana-prāṇā* (thalamus), suppresses all incoming and outgoing sensations in it, and the suppression is necessary to prevent that distraction of the mind which he is anxious to control."[24]

RESULTS OF AWAKENING OF KUNDALINI

Rele states that a perfect adept in Kundalini yoga should be able to move the focus of consciousness out from the captivity of the *Brahmarandhra* and out of the brain into the "bigger cavity surrounding the brain and the spinal-cord, known as *ākāsha*." In this state there will arise awareness of a much wider field of perception, and the yogi "becomes absorbed in the Infinite Intelligence from which it emanated."[25]

The benefits, Rele goes on to say, include that he "begins to function through his Astral body, even at points in space far removed from his physical body."[26] In all of this, he says that Kundalini itself does not take part directly, but that "it does prepare the ground for the soul to vibrate through another channel than the nerves."

At the conclusion of his book, Dr. Rele discusses the difficulties of obtaining such progress in Kundalini yoga. Though the various practices appear simple, they may not be effective for all people:

> All are not equally fitted to receive instruction; man inherits at birth his mental and physical capital according to his actions in previous births and has to increase them by manipulation, but even among such, there are different grades.[27]

The knowledge of the chakras and Kundalini are intimately involved in the Vedic theories of vibration (*vak* and *shabda*) and accordingly it should be possible to find parallels and congruent explanations from the modern understanding of human physiology and frequency vibrations as studied in physics and engineering.

THEORIES OF VIBRATION IN INDIAN THOUGHT

Theories of vibration are widespread throughout written Indian traditions, and as far back as the Vedic period many references to vibrational energy, or *vak,* can be found. Around the middle of the ninth century CE, one of the most comprehensive early texts on vibration was produced in Kashmir, a fertile valley kingdom in northwest India. The *Spandakārika* (Stanzas on Vibration) is thought to have been compiled by Kallatabhatta. Inhabitants of Kashmir at the time enjoyed widespread religious tolerance, and for centuries the region experienced a rich confluence of Hindu, Buddhist, and Tantric practice and thought.

Almost two centuries later, Abhinavagupta wrote the *Tantrāloka,* a detailed commentary on the *Spandakārika*. In these works on the doctrine of vibration, stress is laid on the importance of experiencing *spanda,* the vibrating energy of consciousness, in various ways through different methods and techniques, in order to cultivate a growing interconnection with the primal vibrating energy of the universe itself. Much of ninth-century Kashmir practice "deals with how to lay hold of this inner power and identify with it."[28]

Other movements that center on vibration have arisen in more recent centuries. One example is *surat shabd yoga,* which arose from north Indian origins as early as the thirteenth century. In this context *shabd* means "audible sound current," or "soundstream," and the objective of this approach is for the individual to fuse with the essence of the absolute supreme being in a yoga of the sound current.

In books on Tantra, we find innumerable references to vibration, as in the following paragraph from *Japasutram: The Science of Creative Sound*:

> Everything vibrates. The resting atom has within it the perpetually vibrating atomic solar systems. It is emanating cosmic radiations all the time. . . . Sound is deathless. It is preserved forever in the matrix. It is the claim of the Indian metaphysics of sound that you can fashion and refashion your needle of awareness by "Mantram" and "Japam," the subject of this book.[29]

The author of the book, Swami Saraswati, was the principal collaborator with Sir John Woodroffe in the preparation of numerous published works expounding in great detail the fundamentals of Tantra (e.g., *The Garland of Letters, The World as Power* series, *The Serpent Power*).

THEORIES OF VIBRATION IN WESTERN THOUGHT

In Western Greek culture we find in Plato's *Timaeus* a systematic discussion of vibration. Plato writes that sound is the perception of a systematic vibration propagated through air. And, of course, the opening line of Saint John's Gospel reads in translation, "In the beginning was the Word, and the Word was with God."

In the biological sciences new evidence is coming to light to support the theory that sensory information is communicated via vibrations alone, not through chemical-reaction mechanisms.[30] In 2013, findings were announced that indicate the sense of smell appears to be the direct sensing of vibrations, rather than some byproduct of chemical-bonding mechanisms.[31]

Vibrating Electromagnetic Energy

Electromagnetic energy is the vibrating radiant energy known to the modern material sciences, and while this energy has been thoroughly studied and modeled mathematically—and harnessed within ingenious circuitry to produce our modern technologies—its nature as a potential locus of consciousness is tacitly dismissed in favor of the synaptic sparking of the neuronal system.

To understand, psychophysically, the major modes of human consciousness we must first examine the basic structure of the electromagnetic field and electromagnetic energy itself. Electromagnetic energy is observed to consist of three components, termed "domains" in electrical engineering. The electric field and the magnetic field are always at ninety-degree angles to one another as energy flows through space-time (fig.10.5).

All radiant energy is electromagnetic energy, and it is described mathematically and in communication-signal processing as having a time domain (t_d) and a frequency domain (f_d), also mathematically perpendicular to one another. A special mathematical function has been developed that can transform an energy pattern or signal in the time-space domain into the frequency domain (f_d) and vice versa. Called the "Fourier transform," this mathematical tool is so widely used in digital communications that it might be viewed as essential to our digital technology. For example,

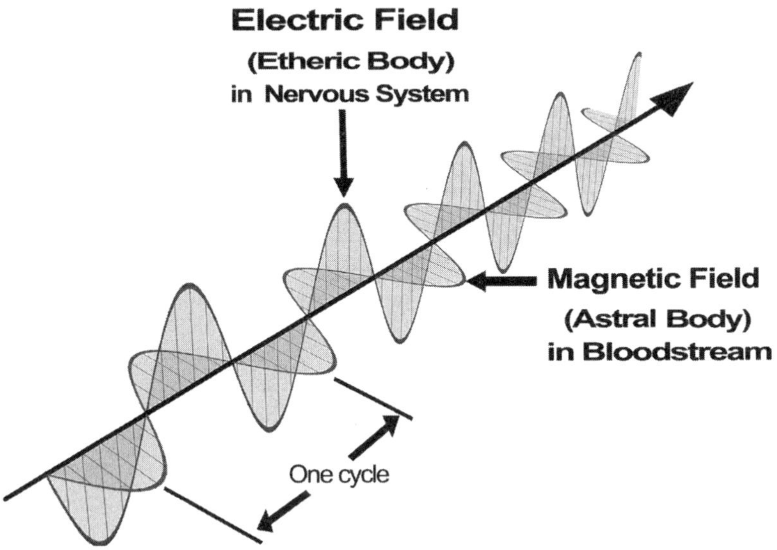

Fig. 10.5. Structure of the electromagnetic field.

video images in time and space are converted into frequency patterns using a Fourier transform algorithm that has been encoded in silicon chips, which are then transmitted via digital internet and reassembled at the receiving end using a "fast Fourier transform" to unpack the frequency information and transform it into time-space images on a video monitor.

Where then might we see planetary geophysical features corresponding with vibration? Like the invisible water in which all fish swim we emerge into and throughout our lives within the vibrating geomagnetic field of the earth. Constantly bathed by this swirling vortex of geomagnetic radiation, we never see nor seldom think of the fact that directly below us, occupying half of the diameter of the planet, is a glowing vibrating source of geomagnetic radiant flux emanating from an enormous crystalline iron-nickel* core of glowing energy.

*"On August 30, 2011, Professor Kei Hirose . . . became the first person to re-create conditions found at the earth's core under laboratory conditions, subjecting a sample of iron nickel alloy to the same type of pressure by gripping it in a vice between 2 diamond tips, and then heating the sample to approximately 4000 Kelvins with a laser. The sample was observed with x-rays, and strongly supported the theory that the earth's inner core was made of giant crystals running north to south." See Fandom's Geography Wiki page, "Structure of the Earth," "Core," par. 3.

Yet we have all seen magnetic compass needles line up with the magnetosphere and for centuries have relied upon that field to chart a course on land, sea, and air. And this field is far from static, as we can see in the swirling glow of the aurora borealis when the geomagnetic fields are lit up with ionized gasses in far latitudes.

What is less commonly realized is that what we call "heat" is an epiphenomenon of radiant energy vibrating in the infrared band of the electromagnetic energy spectrum of the cosmos. What we call "light" is the same kind of energy though of a higher frequency, a smaller wavelength, but a vibration nonetheless—a vibration of pure energy that we happen to call "electromagnetic."

Consciousness as Vibrating Electromagnetic Information Fields

Earlier we discussed the contemporary hypothesis that consciousness may be seen to be identical with vibrating spatiotemporal patterns that are being generated within the brain's electromagnetic field.[32] The primary proponents of this view, Susan Pockett and Johnjoe McFadden, working independently, assume that consciousness is an epiphenomenon, something new and unique in nature. Their opinion is that these electromagnetic fields of consciousness are novel byproducts that have arisen either from (1) the sparking of neurons in the brain, or (2) through some type of quantum resonance occurring within the structural building material for human cells (called microtubules), or both.

Tantra would take the converse view, that consciousness is the underlying primary *first cause* of the entire universe and that consciousness is *not* some new epiphenomenon. Tantrics hold that it is the Shakti, the electromagnetic energy matrix of consciousness and the bioelectromagnetic field matrix of earth itself, out of which arises life, the neuron, and brain structures. According to this perspective it is the electromagnetic field of the cosmos that is the "horse before the cart" in the evolutionary sequence: radiant energy came first and out of this field arose matter and eventually neurons and the brain.

Radiant Energy and Resonance

The phenomenon of resonance was first recognized by Galileo Galilei during his experiments with pendulums and musical strings, when he noticed that tuning a vibrating string to the same frequency as a nearby vibrating string caused a strong and obvious interaction of the two. The initial string seemed to vibrate more strongly and grow louder. He called this phenomenon "resonance" (from the Latin *resonate* "it echoes," or *resonare* "to resound"). As the phenomenon is not fully understood, there can be found various definitions[34] for "resonance," which include:

- the condition in which an electric circuit or device produces the largest possible response to an applied oscillating signal
- the condition in which an object or system is subjected to an oscillating force having a frequency close to its own natural frequency
- the state attributed to certain molecules of having a structure that cannot adequately be represented by a single structural formula but is a composite of two or more structures of higher energy
- a short-lived subatomic particle that is an excited state of a more stable particle

To understand resonance more clearly in terms of consciousness in general and Tantric practices in particular, we focus on the definition of resonance as "the condition in which an electric circuit or device produces the largest possible response to an applied oscillating signal."

In terms of contemplative Tantric practices, resonance can be seen as the condition in which the practitioner's effort to focus consciousness upon an internal region (a chakra) or on a particular sound vibration (a mantra), or both simultaneously, results in a corresponding increase in awareness of and sensitivity to the object that is the focus of attention. Resonance is a "feedback" phenomenon where the amplitude of the interaction between the *perceiver* and the *perceived* increases, usually exponentially, through a sustained co-reflection or "feedback" condition as awareness oscillates between the two. The power of resonance can be seen in the resonant response of a green plant leaf to incoming specific frequencies of the radiant light of the sun. In Tantric psychophysical terms, the resonance effect of sustained and regular attention through meditation on a chakra eventually results in a two-way flow of energies between the consciousness of the meditator and the resonant system that is the chakra itself. In both of these examples (plant leaf and chakra) there is a transfer of energy that results in the accumulation of new energy and the growth of the focal object. In the case of a plant, the leaf grows, and likewise the focus of awareness upon the chakra provides new energy for development of the "psychic center" and its eventual activation as a new center or organ of perception.

DOMAINS OF CONSCIOUSNESS

Tantra's conceptual framework is founded in a view that each human can be seen as functioning simultaneously through multiple bodily systems or levels of operation, each operating within a categorically distinct region, mode, or spectrum of conscious energy. At the same time, it is a fundamental principle of Tantra that holds the human to be a microcosm, that whatever exists in the outer universe exists also within, resonant in many various levels of the human being. Thus, these multiple dimensions of a human being are reflections of or in resonance with corresponding dimensions of the cosmos.

Three Vedic Domains

From the Taittiriya Upanishad (2:11.1–8),[33] compiled 3,000 to 3,500 years ago, we find an injunction that the opening formula for recitation of any Vedic chant *must* be the "great utterance," which is, first, the syllable *Oṃ,* followed by the three syllables *bhūr bhuvaḥ svaḥ* emerging from the initial *Oṃ*. These three syllables signify an understanding that the world (of consciousness, of energy, of the human being) must be viewed as consisting of three distinctions. Various interpretive translations of these Sanskrit terms can be seen in figure 10.6.

bhūr	bhuvaḥ	svaḥ
Physical	Mental, Cognitive	Transcendental

Fig. 10.6. Three syllables signifying the three dimensions of the human being.

Theosophical Domains

In the nineteenth and twentieth centuries, a movement called Theosophy gained prominence in Europe, India, and America, based upon rich encounters with Hindu and Buddhist thought and increasingly available translations of the *Yoga Sūtras,* the Upanishads, the Agamas, and other important Indian texts that included a wealth of Tantric material. Several prominent academics became deeply involved in the Theosophical movement and published their own versions of the structure of consciousness, synthesized from various traditions and their own experiential perception. We will present the structural charts given by two of these authors: I. K. Taimni and Curuppumullage Jinarajadasa.

Early in the twentieth century an Indian scientist, I. K. Taimni, a chemistry professor at Allahabad University, worked to clarify traditional Indian models of consciousness and psychophysics for a Western audience by presenting these teachings in a Theosophical framework. The chart in figure 10.7 is from his book *Self-Culture: The Problem*

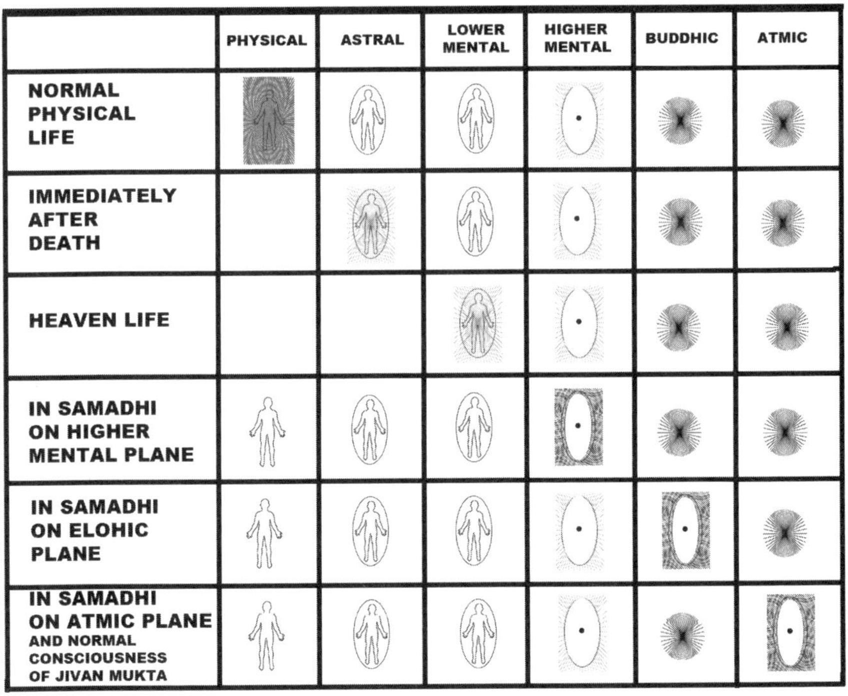

Fig. 10.7. Six dimensions of the human being.

of Self-Discovery and Self-Realization in the Light of Occultism; it illustrates a six-dimensional diagrammatic structure of the human being.[34]

Linear rays surrounding the image indicate the locus of consciousness in each of the six levels of consciousness (rows), while circles indicate the possible ranges within a given plane.

Curuppumullage Jinarajadasa was a Sri Lankan professor closely associated with J. Krishnamurti and Annie Besant. He was fluent in Portuguese, Italian, Spanish, French, Sinhala, Tamil, Pali, and Sanskrit. As president of the Theosophical Society in Adyar in 1945, he published a four-level diagram of human consciousness that he called "The Vehicles of the Soul (fig. 10.8)."[35]

The Three Domains of *Samādhi*

Three levels or domains of *samādhi* are indicated in Taimni's table. Simply attaining an initial *samādhi* experience is not the final goal, as the practitioner is taught that there are more than one major categories of *samādhi*. And, in general, there is a certain sequence in which each successive *samādhi* develops. These are typically experienced in the unfolding of contemplative experience prior to full knowledge by identity of "little" *puruṣa* by "big" *Puruṣa*.

The initial *samādhi* experience is typically *samprajñāta samādhi*, or *samādhi* with object, shown in the chart to be "*Samādhi* on higher mental plane," as well as "*Samādhi* on Buddhic plane." The highest level or more rarified domain is attained only with *asamprajñāta samādhi*, or without object. In the chart this domain is described as "*Samādhi* on Atmic Plane and Normal Consciousness of a Jivan Mukta." It is in the eternal, beyond (or outside of) time and space, in what might be called the frequency domain in electromagnetic quantum brain mechanics.

Here perhaps is what might be seen as the key to understanding how human consciousness can possibly shift into the implicate order (frequency domain) from out of the ordinary stream of perceptions. This is done, at least conceptually, by adjusting one's focus in time to seek for a target that is "in between" perceptions:

<table>
<tr><th colspan="5">THE VEHICLES OF THE SOUL</th></tr>
<tr><td rowspan="2">MENTAL PLANE</td><td>HIGHER MENTAL</td><td>CAUSAL BODY</td><td>To Evolve With</td><td>IDEALS
—
ABSTRACT THOUGHTS</td></tr>
<tr><td>LOWER MENTAL</td><td>MENTAL BODY</td><td>To Evolve With</td><td>IDEAS
—
CONRETE THOUGHTS</td></tr>
<tr><td colspan="2">ASTRAL PLANE</td><td>ASTRAL BODY</td><td>To Feel With</td><td>EMOTIONS
—
DESIRES</td></tr>
<tr><td colspan="2">PHYSICAL PLANE</td><td>PHYSICAL BODY</td><td>To Act With</td><td>SENSORIAL REACTIONS
—
ACTIONS</td></tr>
</table>

Fig. 10.8. Jinarajadasa's four dimensions of the human being.

In the center *between perceptions* the attentive soul can experience the pure indeterminate awareness (*nirvikalpa*) that serves as the basis of determinate perception as its source, resting place, and end. In the center abides what Vamanadatta calls "pure experience," that is, the fundamental self-awareness through which consciousness is perceived and is the basis of all knowledge which Kashmiri Saivites identify with absolute "I" consciousness.[36]

SYNTHESIS OF INDIAN PSYCHOPHYSICS

In this part of the book we have reviewed elements of the classic teaching handbook of Patañjali's *Yoga Sūtras* and have also explored the metaphysics of Vedanta as expressed in the articulate English publications of Aurobindo Ghose in the early twentieth century. The contemplative tradition of India thus provides unique structural maps for contemplatives at all stages of practice and reveals a cosmology that is seen to be congruent with modern science. These ideas, formed more than a millennium ago, found their way north into the high Tibetan plateau to nourish new generations of contemplatives in the Buddhist tradition. Through the efforts of countless monks and meditation masters in Tibet these maps of consciousness were expanded and refined in the Vajrayāna tradition of Tantric Buddhism that will be explored in the following part.

PART FOUR

Tibetan Tantric Psychophysics

11

Foundations of Tibetan Tantric Psychophysics

Given its vast empty regions of windswept valleys and snow-covered peaks, the isolation afforded Tibet has long been fertile ground for the growth of deep contemplative practice. Living on windswept plateaus with sudden thunderstorms and driving hail, the isolated human inhabitants (first appearing 38,000 years ago) developed a rich culture that perceived nature as manifesting living demons of tumultuous energy.

In Tibetan history, the Bön religion, with its animal sacrifice and multitudinous nature spirits, dates as far back as 3,800 years, when it is thought to have been brought into the region from ancient Persia. A recent Chinese census suggests that approximately 10 percent of Tibetans continue to practice the Bön religion, and there are almost 300 Bön monasteries that continue to be active. Ordinary Tibetans clearly differentiate between Böns and Buddhists, with members of Tibetan Buddhist sects (Nyingma, Sakya, Kagyu, and Gelug) often being referred to as *nangpa* ("insiders"), while practitioners of the Bön religion are often referred to as *chipa* ("outsiders").

Buddhism itself was introduced into Tibet 1,400 years ago from northern India in its *Mahāyāna** form, a movement that had become

---

**Mahāyāna* Buddhism developed in India from the first century BCE onwards. Vajrayāna is thought to be a "subset" of *Mahāyāna* and makes use of numerous Tantric methods that are considered to be faster and more powerful than the mindfulness contemplative techniques taught in the earlier *Theravāda* Buddhist schools of Sri Lanka and Tamil Nadu (South India).

noted for its ability to readily adapt to indigenous cultures. This effort to introject the element of nonexclusiveness into the more rigid ("purer") *Theravāda* Buddhism (traditionally taught in southern India) is definitely in line with the Tantric characteristics of openness to women, lower castes, and indigenous cults. Certainly, in Tibet, the success of the early Buddhist "missionaries" (such as Nāropā, Padmasambhava, and so on) appears to be due in large part to the eagerness of the previously autonomous Bön culture to learn and adopt the myriad highly developed and refined Tantric practices at which these early Indian Buddhist teachers were also known to be great adepts.

> The Buddhist Tantras came into existence, according to the Tibetan evidence, after the time of Dharmakīrti (c. 600–660 CE). Their origin as a distinct class of literature and a mode of sadhana may be placed in the seventh century, and they underwent great development during the three succeeding centuries.[1]

Buddhism in Tibet quickly evolved into a form that is now known as Vajrayāna. Some scholars hold that Tantric Buddhism is simply a relatively recent offshoot of a more ancient Hindu Tantra in India. However, archaeologists have strongly disagreed, pointing out that written records of Buddhist Tantra have been found dating back to 300 CE, centuries prior to the creation of any known Hindu Tantric texts in India.

This chapter will not go deeply into the vast range of Tantric techniques developed by Tibetan psychonauts, but will instead focus upon a clear articulation of a major map of conscious states pioneered by Tibetans that they have discovered. Many Tibetan techniques go beyond Patañjali's Yoga Sūtra.

Common to both Patañjali's yoga and Tibetan *Vajrayāna* is the observation that the path to enlightenment consists of three fundamental training categories:

- *Sīla* (ethical training)
- *Samādhi* (meditative absorption or trance)
- *Prajñā* (effulgent wisdom-knowledge of reality)

Ethical training, covered extensively in the second chapter of Patañjali's *Yoga Sūtras,* is required in every school of Buddhism and Hinduism (and in every religious tradition) in order to facilitate the ability of the human brain-mind to master the state of calm detachment that is a precursor to the attainment of *samādhi.* The practice and mastery of the various "virtues" as described in the second chapter of the *Yoga Sūtras* (including actions to avoid such as lying or killing, and practices to cultivate such as nonviolence, truthfulness, kindness, generosity) leaves the psychonaut untroubled by conscious or subconscious conflicts that would otherwise be sure to arise during attempts to reach and to maintain the state of *samādhi* due to distractions caused by various emotional afflictions (guilt, fear, anger, jealousy, hatred, impatience, and so on).

Samādhi itself, and in particular *asamprajñāta samādhi,* is the primary tool that has been found necessary, both in Tibet as well as India, for entering the "higher worlds" of contemplative exploration and is the eighth and final "limb" in Patañjali's *aṣṭāṅga-yoga** set forth in great detail within the *Yoga Sūtras.*

We begin first with a brief history of the Vajrayāna schools in Tibet. Over the centuries, four distinct orders or schools of Buddhism have emerged in Tibet, somewhat distinguishable by the color of ceremonial hats, which is either red or yellow. Some Tibetans consider only the Nyingma sect to be authentic "Red Hats."

Tantric Buddhism primarily emphasizes *method* as opposed to piety or scholarship, and the very root of the word *tantra,* suggesting as it does "to weave," implies an activity of integrating multiple threads of practical activity from which a whole pattern will eventually emerge into the awareness of the contemplative practitioner. To aid in this endeavor, Tibetans have developed an entire "contemplative technology" to assist aspirants in their development of new powers of supersensible perception, and one might even liken their approach to that of

*The eight limbs according to Patañjali are *yama* (abstinences), *niyama* (observances), *āsana* (yoga postures), *prāṇāyāma* (breathing meditations), *pratyāhāra* (withdrawal of the external senses), *dhāraṇā* (concentration, introspective focus), *dhyāna* (uninterrupted contemplation) and *samādhi* (trance absorption).

Name	Order	Founders/ Teachers	Approximate Date Founded	Nickname and Attributes
Nyingma 2nd largest	"Red Hats"	• Padma-sambhava	8th century CE	"Ancient ones" – oldest; focus on mantra
Kagyu 3rd in size	"Red Hats"	• Milarepa • Naropa • Marpa	11th century CE	"Ear Whispered" – strict practice; similar to Zen
Sakya Smallest	"Red Hats"	• Atisa	10th century CE	"Pale earth" – focus on the path and its fruit
Gelug Largest	"Yellow Hats"	• Tsong Kapa (the Dali Lama)	15th century CE	Newest sect – monastic focus on discipline and scholastic learning

Fig. 11.1. Schools of Tibetan Buddhism.

engineers developing practical applications based upon the principles of a "spiritual science."

Vajrayāna, often called the "Thunderbolt Vehicle," "Diamond Vehicle," or "Indestructible Vehicle," refers to the *vajra* (fig 11.2, p. 214), a ritual implement widely used along with the ritual bell in Tibetan Tantric meditations and ceremonies. The *vajra* as a symbolic instrument emerged in India during Vedic times and was said to be the weapon used by the king of the gods to dispel ignorance and fear. It was thought to be adamantine hard, stronger than a diamond, and able to generate immense lightning bolts and thunder, revealing the absolute truth of reality in a flash of insight.

The ritual *vajra* instrument is typically two or three inches long and cast in bronze, silver, or gold and originally taken to be the weapon (and symbol) of the Vedic deity Indra, chief of the gods. The shape of the *vajra* symbolizes the fusion of duality in the balance of the non-dual center. The *vajra* is often held in the right hand of the contemplative at the beginning of a meditation session, during which a mantra is recited, usually the traditional *Om mani padme hum.* The *vajra* represents the male energy of the universe that bursts into

Fig. 11.2. Tibetan ritual bell and *vajra* by Jean-Pierre Dalbéra, courtesy of the British Museum.

existence (space-time) from within the transcendent Void (implicate order).

The ritual bell is held in the left hand of the contemplative and is rung at the beginning and end of a meditation period. It symbolizes the female energy that projects and sustains the universe through pure vibration of sound waves and energy frequencies.

THREE STAGES OF VAJRAYĀNA PRACTICE

Contemplative practices in Vajrayāna are used as the means to attain three different skills that are generally thought to be acquired sequentially within the lifetime of the contemplative. They are used

1. For stilling the active cognitive ego-mind with its monkey-like leaping of thoughts
2. For the development and activation of latent powers of consciousness called *siddhis* in Sanskrit (e.g. supersensory perception, precognition, telepathy, knowledge of higher worlds, etc.)
3. For attaining the goal of complete suspension of the normal cognitive activity of the ego-mind (thinking, remembering, conceptualizing) which then triggers a radical shift into nondual awareness, perceptual integration with the source of consciousness and an accompanying sensation of being flooded by an infinity of dazzling lights of pure wisdom understanding

The teachings of the nineteenth-century psychonaut Düdjom Lingpa (1835–1907) go far beyond Patañjali's *Yoga Sūtras* to reveal a landscape that opens up to those psychonauts who are able to use *samādhi* to reach unimaginable states and stages of awareness lying far beyond everyday normal human brain-mind consciousness. Lingpa's teachings will be explored in the next chapter.

12

The Teachings of Düdjom Lingpa

Tibetan Vajrayāna

One of the great Tantric meditation teachers of recent times was the nineteenth-century contemplative master Düdjom Lingpa (1835–1904), born 16,000 feet above sea level in the Lower Ser Valley of eastern Tibet. Unlike many other meditation masters who have left written guidance for student contemplatives, Düdjom Lingpa did not belong to any established Buddhist school or tradition for most of his life, nor was he known to have had any sort of formal education. Yet it was Düdjom Lingpa's contention that he was directly "self-taught" from an early age by various entities from within his own consciousness that appeared to him throughout his lifetime, beginning with his first inner vision-dialogue when only three years old.

During his lifetime Düdjom Lingpa produced five major written works that elaborate with unusual clarity major aspects of contemplative practice. Presented in the form of dialogues between himself and his "inner guides," these texts describe detailed techniques and experiences that offer a clear map and lucid description of the various states and stages of consciousness that will be entered into and experienced by any serious practitioner who seeks to access new dimensions of perceptual awareness. Düdjom Lingpa's detailed question-and-answer texts show how to use one's growing new powers of supersensible perception to safely navigate the vast, numerous, and often dangerous domains of the universe (cosmic reality) itself.

An ancient tradition in Tibet, begun during the earlier Bön religion, encouraged highly revered shamans and meditation masters to hide written texts and spiritually empowered implements in remote locations for eventual discovery by future generations of contemplatives. Buddhism arrived in Tibet as early as the sixth century CE. The great Padmasambhava (b. 717 CE), founder of the Nyingma school of Tibetan Buddhism, traveled around Tibet to conceal copies of important written "secret teachings" as well as other ritual objects and relics, hiding them in extremely remote caves, forests, fields, and even lakes throughout the Himalayan region. Padmasambhava told his followers that these treasures would be reclaimed by future contemplative seekers when the time was right. These hidden objects were called *terma,* or "treasure," and those who were able to find a terma cache became known as a *tertön,* or "treasure revealer."

In 838 CE, under the reign of the conservative king Langdarma, the earlier Bön religion once again rose into power, and Buddhism was ruthlessly suppressed, many monasteries closed, and monks disrobed. At the close of King Langdarma's reign Buddhist practices once more were resumed, monasteries were rebuilt, and monk-scholars made a concerted effort to seek out the precious spiritual tools and spiritual texts that had been hidden, scattered throughout the vast Tibetan landscape. One well-known example of a terma recovered long after Padmasambhava's era is *The Tibetan Book of the Dead* (*Bardo Thodol*).

However, not all texts were considered to be physically written or existing in any particular spatial location. In many instances these treasure-teachings were said to exist only within the transcendental mode of the ākāśa, a region of consciousness beyond time and space. In such cases the *tertön* would be able to perceive them during deep contemplative connection with the higher realm or dimension in which they are stored and be able to recite them word for word or write them directly.*

*This is much in accord with the tradition in Islam during which the Prophet Mohammad, while in a deep dark cave to practice prayer and contemplation when the angel (Gabriel) dictated the text of the Holy Qur'an. The founder of the Mormons, John Smith, might also be considered a sort of *tertön* as he also encountered a rich spiritual treasure when he was alone, deep in the forests, and discovered the Book of Mormon.

A similar idea can be found in many other religious traditions where a highly evolved spiritual being, perhaps a god or an angel, dictates the words of an important spiritual teaching to an isolated contemplative. One example can be found in the early seventh century CE in the story of the Prophet Mohammad who, praying alone in a dark cave near Mecca, suddenly began to hear the words of the Angel Jibrīl (Gabriel in English) revealing the words of the Holy Qur'an. A similar tradition was held among yogis in India where it was thought that all teachings are stored eternally in the Akashic records that such teachings can be retrieved during dream periods or advanced states of contemplation.

Over a thousand years after Padmasambhava, the young Düdjom Lingpa was able to locate, with the help of visions revealed to him by his invisible mentors, innumerable caches of written texts and spiritual implements left by earlier generations of contemplatives. Accordingly, Düdjom Lingpa is regarded by Tibetans as a major treasure revealer, both in the sense of having discovered caches of precious ritual objects, but also for having received treasures of teaching-wisdom in both written form and through Akashic dialogue with his numerous spirit teachers.

It is ironic that Düdjom Lingpa, the now-revered teacher, was once reviled. His teachings were initially met with great skepticism by many of his contemporaries due to the fact that despite not studying under any established Buddhist teachers of his time (and thus having no lineage) he claimed to have received his own teachings on meditation and spiritual practice directly from transcendental sources of wisdom-knowledge. Düdjom claimed to have received guidance over many years from at least fourteen transcendent sources who transmitted to him a wide range of practical knowledge that he was able to translate into written texts to bequeath to his students. He himself and his many students have found these texts, written in dialogue form, to be of great use for attaining the ultimate goal, the direct experience of the underlying reality of the cosmos.

This chapter will discuss one such teaching-wisdom text, Düdjom Lingpa's *Vajra Essence,* purported to have been revealed to him when he was twenty-seven during what has been called a *pure vision.*[1] In the *Vajra Essence* we find practical instructions and guidance for all contemplatives presented in a dialogue explaining what is known as the Dzogchen* path, a major practice that had been developed and refined in Tibet since the tenth century CE. (Elsewhere in this book, in terms of psychophysics, this same "ultimate goal" is mapped to David Bohm's implicate order, a concept developed in modern quantum physics to denote the ground of reality, a nonspatial, non-temporal domain of absolute consciousness beyond space-time out of which everything we take as physically existing in the cosmos unfolds into our space and time.)

Slowly over many years it was seen that many of his direct students clearly exhibited signs of profound spiritual advancement, and Düdjom's status rose considerably. Late in his life, after being welcomed into the Nyingma sect, he founded the Dartsang Kelzang Monastery in eastern Tibet where he continued to teach and meditate while also raising a family of eight sons, seven of whom became teachers in their own right and all of whom lived well into the twentieth century.

The dialogue presented by Düdjom Lingpa in the *Vajra Essence* explains in great detail the various states and stages of Dzogchen contemplative practice known as the "Great Perfection" that begins with a human individual working to purify body and mind in preparation for the practice of higher stages of contemplation that lead directly to increasingly powerful experiences of integrated consciousness.

The author's direct experience as well as conceptual material from both Patanjali's *Yoga Sūtras* and Düdjom Lingpa's *Vajra Essence* have been woven together in this chapter to support a seven-stage map of psychonautic development that is set forth in the following section in an image called "The Ladder of Psychonautics" (fig. 12.1, p. 221).

---

*Dzogchen (known as the "Great Perfection" or the "Great Completion") arose in the tenth century in Tibet as a Tantric goal in the Nyingma tradition. Also known as *atiyoga* ("utmost yoga") this teaching tradition has continued to evolve as a guide to developing knowledge (*rigpa*) of the higher worlds and especially the direct, non-dual experience of reaching the underlying omnipresent ground of absolute Being (comparable to Jung's "Self," Brahma, God, the Void).

STAGES OF PSYCHONAUTIC DEVELOPMENT

The "ladder" diagram integrates terms contributed from both Indian (Patañjali's *Yoga Sūtras*) and Tibetan (Düdjom Lingpa's *Vajra Essence*) teaching texts to map seven progressive stages that are open to the experience of contemplatives seeking to explore higher dimensions of consciousness. Beginning with Stage 1 (bottom of figure), the inquiring psychonaut practices various well-known yoga techniques to tame the ordinary "monkey mind" of the human ego and train it to be able to move into a more calm, centered, and receptive state of awareness, detaching from the normal activities of the brain-mind, and preparing it for the possibility of attaining and mastering the powerful contemplative mental psychophysical tool that is known as the primary objective of Patañjali's *Yoga Sūtras,* the psychophysical state of *samādhi,* also referred to as *vipaśyanā* (वपिश्यना in Sanskrit, pronounced "vi-puh-shyu-nah") among Tantric Vajrayāna practitioners in Tibet.

At the highest level, shown in the diagram as Stage 7, the contemplative has sailed completely out of the space-time consciousness into union (communion) with what has variously been called the One Self, the implicate order, Brahman, Yahweh, or what is called in many religions, God. The diagram can be viewed as laying out seven stages or states indicating the major stages of a path. This has been mapped effectively through the contemplative explorations of many generations of Indian and Tibetan seekers during the more than a thousand years that elapsed since Patañjali wrote the *Yoga Sūtras.* Each of the seven stages shown in the figure will now be discussed in detail, beginning with the bottom stage, "Yoga," or what Patañjali termed *aṣṭāṅga yoga.*

The Ladder—Stage 1

Aṣṭāṅga Yoga

Beginning at "Stage 1" at the bottom of the diagram, a prospective psychonaut begins with the practice of *aṣṭāṅga yoga* or "the eight branches of yoga" enumerated in Patañjali's *Yoga Sūtras.* The eight different branches of yoga are shown in figure 12.2 (p. 222). Unfortunately, the word *yoga* is now misunderstood to indicate *only* a regime of physical exercises or poses. This single branch, currently considered to be yoga

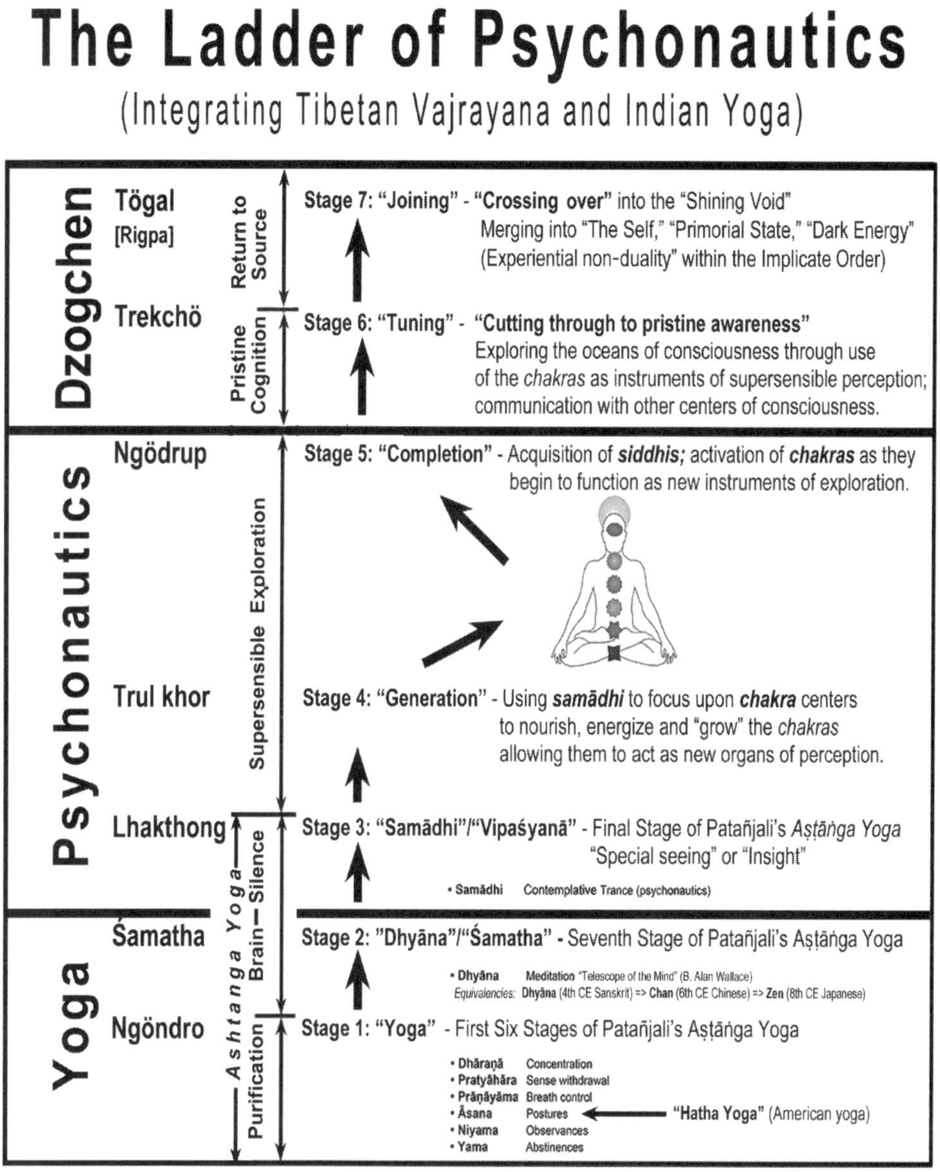

Fig. 12.1. The ladder of psychonautics.

by the general public (and most of the world's estimated 300 million yoga practitioners), can be seen in the lower right quadrant of the figure as *āsana,* meaning "posture," "meditation seat." Thus yoga has become misconstrued in the popular press as simply a sport or physical exercise,

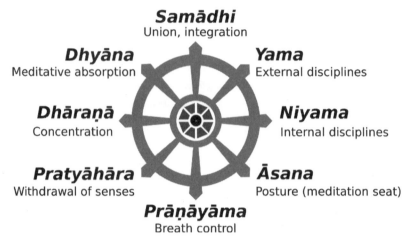

Fig. 12.2. Aṣṭāṅga yoga. The eight branches of yoga.
Image created by Ian Alexander.

whereas in actuality *āsana,* also known as *hatha yoga,* is only one of the seven preparatory practices that facilitate entry into the eighth branch of Patañjali's yoga, the state of *samādhi.* It is *samādhi* itself, the eighth branch of yoga, that is the primary tool or gateway used to advance psychonautic exploration into higher modes of conscious awareness.

The primary objective of practicing *āsana* poses is to prepare the body for sitting meditation. *Āsana* poses condition the joints and musculature system of human physiology to be flexible, healthy, and free of pain, thus reducing sensory distractions during the subsequent deeper yogic contemplative practices that lead to *samādhi* and beyond.

Patañjali recommends that the initial five branches of *aṣṭāṅga yoga* (fig. 12.3) should be practiced consistently in order to attain facility in the skill of entering the state of *dhāraṇā* (pronounced "dhah-ruh-nuh"), the sixth stage, which can be defined simply as "steady, uninterrupted concentration" focused upon (or within) one single region or locus of awareness without allowing one's consciousness to be interrupted by various bodily pain or sensation distractions, unwanted trains of mental thought, or rising memories. The idea is similar to that of focusing the rays of the sun by holding a magnifying glass steadily without interruption, focused steadily upon a small single region of straw in order to cause combustion of the straw into flame.

Practices leading to Dhāraṇā ↑

Dhāraṇā:	**Concentration** (even if at first intermittently interrupted)
Pratyāhāra:	**Withdrawal of external sensory input**; internal silence
Prāṇāyāma:	**Breath mindfullness** (deep breathing, focus on breath movement)
Āsana:	**Physical exercises** (yoga, postures for health and meditation)
Niyama:	**Observances** (study, self-discipline, reflection "Who am I?")
Yama:	**Abstinences** (nonviolence, refraining from lies, fasting, etc.)

Fig. 12.3. First five branches of Patanjali's *aṣṭāṅga yoga* practice.

It might be said that the entire eight steps of *aṣṭāṅga yoga* elaborated by Patañjali are efforts that are undertaken in the four dimensions of space-time in order to shift consciousness into and through the state of *samādhi,* which is a portal for *transcending* space-time into one (or all) of the additional seven dimensions predicted to exist according to modern quantum physics.*

Aṣṭāṅga Yoga 1 and 2: *Yama* and *Niyama*

The first two branches of yoga described by Patañjali are *yama* and *niyama,* which can be colloquially translated simply as "dos" and "don'ts." Such practices are generally found in all religious teachings, and together they include ethical and physical practices and restraints that develop self-discipline, nonviolence, patience, refraining from lies, fasting, studying skills, and various physical exercises (the *āsanas* of *hatha yoga*), all of which work to facilitate periods of regular sitting in silent, undistracted meditation.

The first branch in Patañjali's *aṣṭāṅga yoga* is *yama,* or abstinences (things one ought *not* to do). One practices abstaining from telling lies—even the most simple—and from becoming angry or violent. More advanced practices under the topic of *yama* include many types of fasting, usually from food, but often practicing fasting from habitual activities that waste one's time and energy.

The second branch is *niyama* (things one *ought* to do), the opposite

*Modern physics, in particular "M-theory," recognizes eleven distinct dimensions. Four are space (three dimensions) and time (one dimension), and seven dimensions manifest in Bohm's implicate order, beyond space-time.

of *yama* in that these *niyama* practices are positive rather than negative. For example *niyama* would include studying material to improve one's mind and understanding as well as practicing kindness, generosity, optimism, and cleanliness of mind, speech, and body, in addition to reciting prayers and practicing *āsanas*. All virtuous habits, behaviors, and observances fall under this branch of yoga.

Aṣṭāṅga Yoga 3: Āsana (Haṭha Yoga)

Patañjali's third step or limb is *āsana,* known today more commonly as *hatha yoga,* or simply "yoga" to the wider public. In the Western world the term *yoga* currently denotes the practice of physical exercises that focus upon static poses of the body, many of which require considerable flexibility. While regular practice of these poses is considered to contribute to stress relief, exemplary good health, and a sense of well-being, it is surprising that in this modern approach to yoga, little interest is given to meditation, which is actually the primary objective of Patañjali's yoga. Thus yoga is now seen as simply one of numerous physical sports.

Haṭha yoga has developed into a growing industry in the twenty-first century with over 300 million practitioners and a recent market research report indicates that the "yoga market" size was valued at $37.5 billion in 2019, and is projected to reach $66.5 billion by 2027.[2] Yet *hatha yoga,* having its origin in *āsana* or posture, is only the third of the eight "limbs" of *aṣṭāṅga yoga*. What has happened to the other seven limbs of yoga, and why does there seem to be so little interest in the rest of Patañjali's teaching? That is, why is there so little focus on the traditional practices that lead to deep contemplation and the eventual attainment of the state of *samādhi*?

In fact it seems that *hatha yoga* itself was not yet a "thing" in Patañjali's time. Though the word *yoga* has become synonymous with the term *hatha yoga* in the public mind, no discussion of *hatha yoga* appears in Sanskrit texts until six or seven hundred years after Patañjali's *Yoga Sūtras* was first written. Perhaps it is a reflection of the pervasive materialistic approach that the modern era takes not only to science but to every aspect of daily life. Religious attendance is on the decline as modern secular society scoffs at the invisible, unknown domains of reality that have been reported by saints and mystics throughout the centuries.

Yet *hatha yoga* or *āsana* is an important part of *aṣṭāṅga yoga* as it prepares the body for long periods of quiet sustained relaxation during the higher contemplative yogic practices. Again, the idea is that the human body should be flexible and without pain or discomfort that might distract from the mental exercises of contemplation leading to *samādhi* and higher states of conscious awareness. Modern schools of *hatha yoga* also include instruction for the practice of breathing exercises or *prāṇāyāma*, which is known to have a great beneficial effect on the physical body as well as charge the body with energy. After *āsana*, it is *prāṇāyāma* that happens to be the next subsequent step, the fourth stage or branch in Patañjali's eight-limbed system, and this focus upon the breath also happens to be a major practice taught in Tibet among Vajrayāna practitioners as a primary intermediate stage as one moves from sitting in *āsana* to entry into the deeper states of contemplation.

Aṣṭāṅga Yoga 4: Prāṇāyāma

Patañjali's fourth step (*prāṇāyāma*) is a focus of consciousness upon the process of breathing itself. Contemplatives both in Tibet and India had discovered that watching (focusing awareness upon) one's breath as it moves in and out of the body is an extremely effective practice for quieting the brain-mind activities. Focusing upon the movement of air as it enters and leaves the body gives the mind time to settle down and detach from other thoughts, helping one to shift awareness into deeper states of quiescence. Attempts to practice mentally silent meditation are frequently derailed due to numerous cognitive interruptions as "trains of thought" arise unbidden, much like irritating messages and advertisements that pop up on a computer screen when one is trying to read material on a web page with sustained attention.

There are numerous *prāṇāyāma* exercises taught by various schools of yoga. Some approaches focus on watching the breath as it flows into and out from the nose and sinus areas; others include watching one's breath as it slowly expands within the chest cavity. Various *prāṇāyāma* exercises are given such names as "bellows breath," "victorious breath," "skull-shining breath," and so on. The exercises included in *prāṇāyāma* allow the user to build up the "psychic muscle" (or neuroplastic subroutines) to be able to ignore and detach from cognitive interruptions in the flow of simple awareness. A basic approach to *prāṇāyāma* can be seen in the breathing cycle diagram of *kumbhaka prāṇāyāma* shown in figure 12.4.

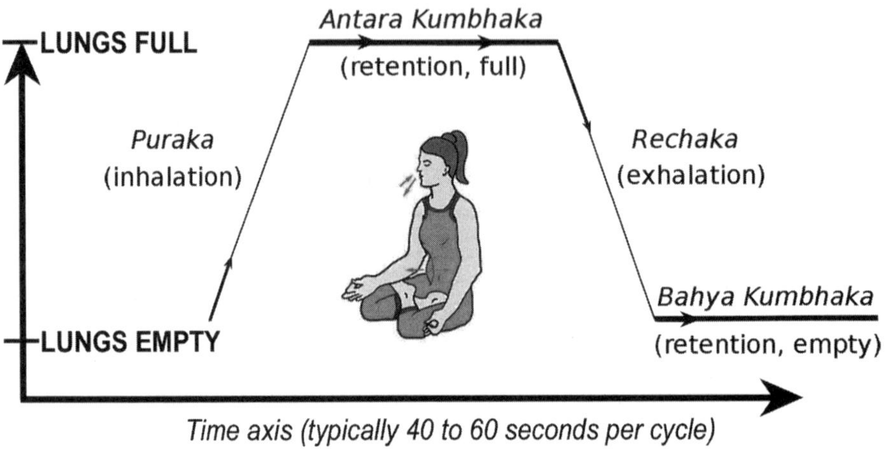

Fig. 12.4. Breathing cycle during *kumbhaka prāṇāyāma*.
Modified image created by Ian Alexander

As indicated in the figure, one begins by emptying the lungs as much as possible, then breathing in slowly, focusing attention on the incoming air moving through the nose. When no more air can be taken in, there is a period of retention during which the lungs do not move (and the mind remains empty of thought). After the short period of retention (the length depends upon the skill of the practitioner), the breath is slowly let out while one's awareness follows the movement of the exhalation through the nose. When the lungful of air has been exhaled as fully as reasonably possible, there is another period of sustained quiescence during which the lungs remain relatively empty for a sustained period. After a short period of physical (and mental) quiescence, inbreathing commences once more as another complete cycle is begun. Many experienced psychonauts use their fingers to count off ten of these sequences just prior to moving into the next level and subsequent deeper states of contemplation.

Numerous additional breathing exercises are often practiced, including breathing in and out through alternate nostrils (while holding one nostril shut with one hand), or undertaking a series of very rapid breaths in and out (hyperventilating) in order to increase one's metabolic rate, warm the body, and charge one's system with *prāṇā* (the Sanskrit word for life force or living energy).

Aṣṭāṅga Yoga 5: Pratyāhāra

The next (or fifth) level of practice in Patanjali's *aṣṭāṅga yoga* is *pratyāhāra,* or detachment. The idea is that, through exercise and practice, one can eventually build up the power to quickly detach from thoughts and sensory inputs *as they arise.* This is a basic practice in modern schools of "mindfulness" meditation. The previous practice of *prāṇāyāma* aids in the effort of *pratyāhāra* by holding awareness focused upon breath and breathing. By focusing awareness on breathing, the tendency for the mind to be caught up by incoming interruptions is reduced, and it becomes easier to drop mental and sensory images close to the moment they begin to arise into awareness. Such interruptions might come in the forms of memories, hearing, smell, touch, and verbal thoughts, but the practice of *pratyāhāra* eventually gives the psychonaut the ability to consistently ignore all such interruptions and to maintain focus of awareness in a single steady state (which will initially be the physiological process of breathing during the *prāṇāyāma* exercises that immediately precede moving into the deeper stages of focus that lead to *samādhi*).

Aṣṭāṅga Yoga 6, 7, and 8: Dhāraṇā, Dhyāna, and Samādhi

While these three important concepts have been discussed in the previous chapter, it is important to review them here in the context of Patañjali's yoga and Tibetan Vajrayāna as the three taken together (termed *saṃyama*) open the gateway to all of the higher domains of supersensory perception.

The sixth limb of Patañjali's *aṣṭāṅga yoga* is *dhāraṇā* or concentration, the initial focus of awareness within a specific limited region of reality. When one is able to hold this concentration steadily for a "thread" of time, even a short duration, one enters what is called *dhyāna,* and this, Patañjali tells us, is the prerequisite to entering the state of *samādhi.* As Patañjali's teachings spread north and east into other regions of Asia, the Sanskrit terms received local translations. (The Sanskrit term *dhyāna* in India became *śamatha* in Tibet, while in China the term became *chan,* and in twelfth-century Japan it was called *zen.* The Sanskrit term *samādhi* in India became *vipaśyanā* in Tibet, while in China it is *wushin,* and in Japan the term is *mushin.*)

These three final "limbs" of Patañjali's eight-limbed yoga are practiced simultaneously, or at least sequentially bound together in one effort, and together called by Patañjali *saṃyama*:

> ***III.4. Trayam ekatra saṃyama***
> These three taken as one [*dhāraṇā, dhyāna and samādhi*] are *saṃyama.*

- *Dhāraṇā* is the binding of conscious awareness within a specific region (for example, within the psychophysical body it might be placing the focus of awareness within the heart center, or cranial center, or perineum; alternately it could be the focus of perception on a *thangka* painting or on a yantra drawing, or on a visible Sanskrit syllable like the *om*).
- *Dhyāna* is the sustaining of that conscious awareness for an unbroken, continuous length of time. Much as the rays of the sun that are focused by a lens on a block of ice will soon melt the ice, this *dhyāna* effort will soon lead to a transformation of conscious awareness into the state that is termed *samādhi.*
- *Samādhi* can be seen as the doorway, portal, or key to the exploration of higher stages of consciousness. It is a state uninterrupted (unencumbered) by the activity of the brain-mind's sensory input or cognitive gyrations or memory interruptions; at the point at which one is able to enter the state of *samādhi,* the individual's conscious awareness suddenly opens more fully to a vastly wider range of effulgent information that is constantly flowing throughout the universe, somewhat like turning on a radio receiver or

transmitter. Attaining *samādhi* has the same effect on the flow of consciousness within the body that opening wide an outdoor water faucet has on water in a system of pipes and hoses used to nourish plants in the garden. In the case of *samādhi,* the water in our garden example is considered to be what is called *prāna* in Sanskrit and *chi* by Chinese Taoist contemplatives. In electrophysiological terms it might be called *holoflux* or *electromagnetic plasma* that streams through the circulatory system and beyond. These energies of consciousness sustain and nourish the various complex nerve-plexus regions identified by generations of mystics and saints as centers or organs of consciousness that can be grown and activated. In Sanskrit, these are referred to as the chakras.

These contemplative states complete the objective of Patañjali's *aṣṭāṅga yoga.* They lead the contemplative up to the point of being able to enter the state of *samādhi* at will during meditative practice. However, in the Tibetan tradition the Sanskrit word *vipaśyanā* is generally used rather than the term *samādhi* due to the emphasis that the word *vipaśyanā* has on "vision" (the Sanskrit word *vipaśyanā* is derived from *vi* [super] and *paśyanā* [seeing]). Often *vipaśyanā* is translated as "in-sight" to connote that it is a state of special supersensible vision, a direct perception of the highest truths of reality that are found deep within one's consciousness. By contrast, the word *samādhi* is more frequently found to describe the means by which the insight flows. It is a subtle distinction, similar to the distinction between the words *vision* and *sight.* For purposes of this discussion the two words *samādhi* and *vipaśyanā* are used to describe the same aspect of consciousness as can be seen in figure 12.5.

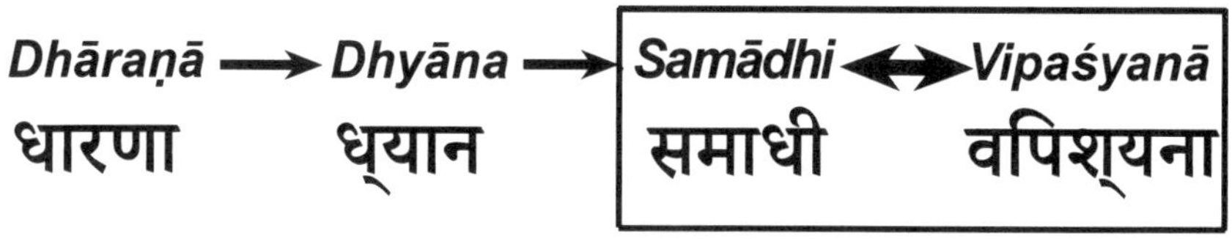

Fig. 12.5. The final stages of Patañjali's *aṣṭāṅga yoga.*

Beyond the acquisition of *samādhi* (*vipaśyanā*), the Tibetan teaching map goes much further than Patañjali's *Yoga Sūtras* by focusing upon the steps and stages of consciousness that can be experienced *beyond* the initial acquisition of the ability to enter *samādhi*. An analogy between psychonautics and space exploration (astronautics) might be that Patañjali's *Yoga Sūtras* take us through eight stages to escape the earth's gravity and get us up into orbit, while Düdjom Lingpa's *Vajra Essence* takes us out further into the solar system and the galaxies beyond, giving us access to the higher stages of consciousness that have been mapped during the thousand years of Tibetan contemplative practice since Patañjali first compiled the *Yoga Sūtras*.

Patañjali's teachings eventually moved north into Tibet, where a growing body of Tibetan contemplatives practiced and extended psychonautic explorations of the universe of consciousness for many intervening centuries. Centuries after Patañjali, a mature path for contemplatives that articulates stages of experience beyond those discussed by Patañjali in his *Yoga Sūtras* was also mapped out in the nineteenth century by the Tibetan Vajrayāna master Düdjom Lingpa. The following sections follow the "stages" of evolution of psychonauts/contemplatives as they progress beyond the acquisition of the state of *samādhi* as described in Patanjali's *aṣṭāṅga yoga*. These seven stages have been depicted previously on page 221 (fig. 12.1). They are:

- Yoga
- *Dhyāna* (*Śamatha*)
- *Samādhi* (*Vipaśyanā*)
- Generation (nourishment of chakras)
- Completion (activation of chakras)
- Tuning ("cutting through to pristine awareness")
- Joining ("crossing over")

The Ladder—Stage 2: *Śamatha (Dhyāna)*

Dhyāna is an easily identifiable state in which memory, cogitation, and the external senses have all been subdued and attenuated and the mind is able to enter a state in which it is able to abide in uninterrupted concentration upon the object of contemplation for an unbroken thread of time duration.* Stage 2 in figure 12.6 indicates that the contemplative has mastered the ability to enter the state of *dhyāna* and is able to reach a state of uninterrupted, undistracted space-time flow upon the object of concentration.

Düdjom Lingpa's Approach to *Śamatha*

In the *Vajra Essence*, Düdjom Lingpa stresses three sequential stages of contemplative effort to attain *śamatha*†:

1. Mindfulness of breathing (Patañjali's *prāṇāyāma*)
2. Taking the impure mind as the path
3. Awareness of awareness

At this stage is assumed that the contemplative has mastered all of the preliminary seven steps of *aṣṭāṅga yoga* and has gained experience and a beginner's skill at entering *dhyāna*. Patañjali's *prāṇāyāma* ensures that the contemplative practices focusing upon the process of breathing during the transition period while all other activities of the external sensory systems, as well as thoughts, and memories, are being attenuated as consciousness moves toward deeper levels of awareness.

The second practice that Düdjom Lingpa suggests is beneficial to achieving the *śamatha* stage is "taking the impure mind as the path." In this practice, one uses the activities of the mind itself as "the path." The word *śamatha* has been translated as "shining," "calm abiding," "mind calmness," or "meditative quiescence" and can be thought of as the entranceway or portal into the wider ocean of consciousness that then opens for navigation by psychonauts.

The third practice suggested by Düdjom Lingpa for the mastery

*The duration of time might be as short as three seconds for a beginner, ten seconds for an intermediate contemplative, but a full minute or more for an advanced psychonaut.

†The first of Düdjom Lingpa's steps includes Patañjali's first five limbs of *aṣṭāṅga yoga* that lead to *dhyāna*. What Düdjom Lingpa calls *śamatha* in his second step is Patañjali's *dhyāna*.

of *śamatha* is "awareness of awareness," the practice of observing the activities of the mind-brain and while so doing developing the skill to distinguish between movements of the mind and the stillness of pure awareness, so as to be able to immediately separate the two and then detach from and drop the mental activity just as it arises and before it can distract awareness and plunge it into activated mental activity. Düdjom Lingpa wrote that during this practice meditators "observe their thoughts 'over there' like an old herdsman on a wide-open plain watching his calves and sheep from afar."[3] One learns to separate and detach the observer from the observed, whereas by contrast in the everyday normal state of consciousness one distinguishes no separation. (Without training in *dhyāna* the observer tends to immediately latch on to the observation, shifts the focus upon this interruption, begins to analyze and think about it, and is immediately taken away from the former objective by becoming attached to the suddenly erupting cognitive movements of the mind.)

For example, one might simply assume "I am my anger," or "I am my thoughts," rather than realizing that "I" am in reality different from those thoughts and that anger. During this third practice leading to *śamatha* there is no overt suppression of mental activity (memory, thought, sensations); however, the observer learns the habit of detaching quickly and completely from such interrupting activities as they arise and to continue the effort to focus on the breath, on quiescence, and on the stillness of pure awareness.

Düdjom Lingpa points out that the goal is to eventually arrive at an awareness of the pure void, the "substrate consciousness," the *ālayavijñāna,* which can only be experienced once awareness has been *as fully detached as possible* from the normal cognitive activities of the brain-mind. This state has often been called simply "trance" in shamanic traditions and in modern approaches to meditation is often termed "mindfulness" in the early stages of practice.

In this third stage of *śamatha* or "awareness of awareness" the observing consciousness is no longer "looking out" through the external senses, or hopping around from thought to thought or memory to memory. Instead, the contemplative has reached a feedback state of being aware of pure "awareness" itself, without any other object of awareness interrupting the flow of consciousness as it builds up an intensity of concentration in a cyclic fashion. In his own essays, Teilhard de Chardin often characterized such a state with the term "co-reflexion," and it can also be seen as equivalent to Patanjali's state of *asamprajñāta samādhi,* "consciousness without an object" (also described at length in *The Philosophy of Consciousness without an Object,* a book by the twentieth-century mathematician-mystic Franklin Merrell-Wolff).

A Nine-Stage Guide to *Śamatha*

In the thousand years since Patañjali's time, the Tibetan approach to contemplative practice has distinguished and enumerated the following nine stages of meditation to act as guides or milestones that a student can use to evaluate progress in these observed stages that lead up to the culminating experience of pure *śamatha*. The distinction among these various stages reminds us that acquisition of the skill that is *śamatha* is generally one that is not mastered overnight, but that in practice, requires a consistent regular investment of time and effort. Being familiar with these various conditions can be a useful aid to the budding psychonaut in determining how far one has come and how far one has to go in mastering *śamatha* prior to developing the power of *samādhi* that will enable them to enter and explore the cosmic ocean of consciousness. In order of manifestation, the following table describes the stages that lead to the mastery of *śamatha*.

According to Düdjom Lingpa, the experience of consciousness in the state of *śamatha* is not only important for gaining the next stage, *samādhi* (*vipaśyanā*), but that it has major benefits to the individual in its own right, for it is during *śamatha* that consciousness is released to flow through the body unobstructed to irradiate the systems of the physical body while healing and upgrading various mind-brain centers. This flowing communication with the deepest levels of consciousness also occurs during the healing process, particularly when an individual is at rest or asleep. However, rather than simply trying to heal some injury to the body, the contemplative psychonaut is seeking to develop completely new functional abilities for conscious awareness by upgrading and then activating the various "organs of perception" (for example,

DÜDJOM LINGPA'S STAGES LEADING TO MASTERY OF *ŚAMATHA*

Experience	Purpose
Placement of the mind	Ability to focus upon object of meditation
Continuous placement	Longer periods of continuous focus
Repeated placement	Skill in returning to focus after interruptions
Close placement	Continuous focus on object during session
Taming	Attainment of periods of deep tranquility
Pacifying	Ability to attenuate interruptive distractions
Fully pacifying	Complete elimination of distraction
Single-pointing	Single-pointed focus with no fatigue
Balanced placement	Continuity of focus throughout entire period
Śamatha	Deep continuous contemplative quiescence that opens up to the experience of *samādhi*

the chakras). This is greatly facilitated by the neuroplasticity of the nervous system, the ability to reprogram neuronal systems to provide new functionality. As B. Alan Wallace says:

> Even when you emerge from meditation, this body-mind upgrade is yours to employ in your dealings with the world. . . . Here we're allowing the entire system of the subtle body-and-mind to balance and heal itself.[4]

The Ladder—Stage 3: *Vipaśyanā (Samādhi)*

While achieving peace and tranquility, tuning up the entire physiological system, improving health and healing injuries are all definitely facilitated by the practice of *śamatha,* the primary objective for developing *śamatha* is to attain entry into the state called *samādhi* or *vipaśyanā*. As we have dealt with Patañjali's approach to *samādhi* in some detail in the previous chapter, the emphasis here is on the Tibetan teachings that are based upon attainment of *samādhi,* the gateway to the higher stages of consciousness that can now be explored through use of this heightened mode of perception.

According to *Vajrayāna,* upon attaining the experience of *vipaśyanā* (the Tibetan equivalent of *samādhi*) one experiences directly the *ālayavijñāna,* translated variously as "source consciousness," "base consciousness," "storehouse consciousness," or "causal consciousness." It is perhaps the access or "in-sight" into this storehouse consciousness that influenced the Tibetans to focus upon the word *vipaśyanā.* This *ālayavijñāna* is the level of normally subliminal mental consciousness (out of which our transitory individual ego construct arises) that occurs uninterruptedly throughout one's life and that continues from life to life when and if the individual *puruṣa* reincarnates.

The *ālayavijñāna* is said to be the base-level or ground of consciousness for all human experiences. It acts as a base container for all ordinary human sensory and cognitive experiences in space and time. Within the *ālayavijñāna* are stored what are called seed patterns or *bijas,* tendencies that have been etched into this level of consciousness by prior experiences, somewhat as water flowing over a dry land etches a distinctively unique fractal flow pattern or channel in the soil. All traces of past actions may be found within the *ālayavijñāna* as cognitive "seeds" that are ready to ripen into future experience should triggers be encountered that direct the flow of energy-consciousness into that channel of habitual action/reaction and the flow is not immediately stopped through the practice of detachment (*pratyāhāra* or "letting go").

It should be noted that *dhyāna* and *samādhi* are so closely connected that one affects the other in a sort of feedback loop. The initial practice of *dhyāna* leads to the opening into the *samādhi* experience, and the state of *samādhi* is then conducive to maintaining the *dhyāna* experience. This cyclical process is found in many psychophysical processes and can be seen symbolically in the Taoist yin/yang symbol discussed in chapter 2. In the introduction to his translation of Düdjom Lingpa's *The Heart of Great Perfection,* B. Alan Wallace explains the importance of the integrated practice of *śamatha* and *vipaśyanā* as expressed in the Vajrayāna of Düdjom Lingpa:

> One major outcome of *śamatha* is experiential access to the substrate consciousness (*ālayavijñāna*), characterized by bliss, luminosity, and nonconceptuality. Through the achievement of *śamatha,* the body-mind is made supple and marvelously serviceable, preparing one to utilize the distilled clarity and stability of the mind to cultivate contemplative insight, which lies at the heart of the higher training in wisdom. With the union of *śamatha* and *vipaśyanā*, one is well prepared to achieve a radical, irreversible healing and awakening of the mind through gaining direct insight into the ultimate nature of reality. . . . The unified practice of *śamatha* and *vipaśyanā* as taught in our texts is an essential aspect of meditation in all Buddhist traditions.[5]

In the same discussion, Wallace refers to *śamatha* as "meditative quiescence," and to *vipaśyanā* as "contemplative insight."

The Ladder—Stage 4: Generation

Once the psychonaut/contemplative has acquired the ability to enter the state of *samādhi* (*vipaśyanā*) it is possible to further what is called "generation and completion" of various subsystems of psychical communication or centers of transception known as the chakra centers within the physical body. These centers act to some extent like "distributed brains" throughout the body. In many traditions of Indian yoga there are seven distinct chakra centers in the body, though in some traditions, particularly among Taoists in China, there are innumerable chakras, perhaps hundreds of distributed "centers" that can be cultivated and activated through contemplative focus within those centers. Physiologically it can be noted that the major centers such as the center in the brain behind the forehead (*Ājñā* chakra), the throat center (*Vishudha* chakra), the heart center (*Anāhata* chakra), the center of the abdomen (*Manipura* chakra), the genital region (*Mūlādhāra* chakra), and of course the crown region (cerebral cortex surface just below the skull) at the top of the head (*Sahasrāra* chakra) contain rich complex arrays of nerve plexi, blood capillaries, and endocrine (hormone secreting) tissues. Focusing awareness in these regions causes the capillaries within the region to dilate, providing additional blood flow with associated heat rise, nourishment, and cleansing of all the tissues in the limited region of awareness.

During *vipaśyanā* the contemplative makes an effort to sustain the focus of awareness one-pointedly upon an individual chakra region within the body (this is an example of a *sabija samādhi* practice, i.e., contemplation "with object"). This practice cultivates uplinks and downlinks between multiple dimensions to initiate a flow of energetic information exchange. This practice nourishes and tunes each chakra center to activate communication within the vastly wider cosmic bandwidths of consciousness than are normally available to the individual during normal waking activities.

For example, if I am able to lead a life that is (relatively) free of underlying causes that might generate underlying anxieties and concerns that might distract my awareness when I am trying to quiet my mental activity, and assuming my body is relaxed and free of distracting pain (through having practiced various *āsana* exercises), then I am able to spend an uninterrupted period practicing *prāṇāyāma* breathing exercises (which is stoking the body with oxygen and *prāṇā* vibrations). Assuming I am able to practice in a quiet and dark place where I am able to detach and withdraw my mind and external sensory systems (the yogic practice called *pratyāhāra*) to the point where the mind-body becomes sufficiently quiet, then I am able to initiate the sequence of *dhāraṇā-dhyāna-samādhi*. This then is the point of entry into "insight" which literally is being able to "look within" with laser-like focus of conscious awareness, focusing upon internal regions of nerve-plexi-rich endocrine organs that begin to resonate with higher frequency bands of conscious awareness. This initial practice of *samādhi* (also called *sabija samādhi,* or "with-seed-*samādhi*/*samādhi*-with-object) during which one is able to focus on a single chakra region, for example, and by sustained focus on (within) this physiological region, nourishes and develops it to the point where it "opens" (like a flower blooming), making it a powerful "psychic tool" or instrument that can be used to explore various unique bandwidth regions of consciousness.

The sound-syllables of a mantra, whether recited audibly or

internally, generate frequencies that tune in to the unique region of the transcendent frequency domain that the conscious energy of all beings who have previously chanted the mantra create. In other words, the mantra acts as a sort of telephone number that brings the consciousness of the practitioner into alignment with those who have previously recited these particular frequency syllables (or are even now reciting them). Each time one recites the mantra an increase in the strength of the connection grows. Consequently there are certain powerful mantras that have been recited by many thousands of adepts countlessly throughout the centuries.

The Ladder—Stage 5: Completion

Eventually the individual chakra regions begin to "open" (the analogy is the opening of a lotus blossom) and proceed to function as channels of communication linked to heightened levels of supersensory awareness. The entire third chapter of Patanjali's *Yoga Sūtras* is an attempt to describe various *siddhis* or "supersensory powers" that can be experienced when the various chakras are activated. While material scientists ignore or scoff at such claims, the various descriptions of *siddhis* (Sanskrit that can be translated as "accomplishments," "powers") compiled by Patañjali have in many cases been corroborated by the direct experiences of modern psychonauts when their consciousness has been fueled by entheogens. Various chakra regions of the human body seem to be able to tune in to unique domains, dimensions, or frequency bandwidths of consciousness, resulting in communication that does not depend on sound or human language but opens up more direct communication similar to the observed "empathic links" or emotive "touch" between pet owners and their pet, for example.

The chakra region of the heart is one such region that can be developed and activated to reach out and connect with the departed through emotional waves of empathy that are sensed as real and transcend space and time. That the physics of such links is possible via properties of sub-quantum relationships can be seen in the holoflux theory of consciousness that has been developed by the quantum physicist David Bohm and his colleague, the brain scientist Karl Pribram (discussed elsewhere in this book). With the completion of the growth stage of a particular chakra, the contemplative can begin to explore supersensible domains of consciousness by learning to tune the frequency band of energies being detected by the chakra.

The Ladder—Stage 6: Tuning

With the aid of various activated chakras that are able to detect and amplify new modes of supersensory perception, the psychonaut is able to "join to the universe" by tuning in to new frequency channels of awareness. The formerly isolated individual awareness suddenly has capabilities of becoming fully conscious of and in potential communication with many other "centers of consciousness," both those functioning within his or her own individual body, but also through contact with external domains of consciousness, both near and far, throughout the planet, the space-time cosmos, and transdimensionally. These new sensory modes that have been identified as *siddhis* by Patañjali have the ability to communicate with other conscious entities, including those local entities seen and reported by mystics and shamans of many cultures and variously termed angels, elves, ghosts, fairies, leprechauns, *rakshasas,* kami, demons, and such.

The various *siddhis* described in texts by Patañjali and Düdjom Lingpa can also be found mirrored in various phenomena explored as "psi phenomena" by scientists exploring the paranormal. These paranormal phenomena currently being explored include such things as telepathy, psychokinetics, and precognition, among others, many of which, reported during the Middle Ages, led to the death of individual psychonautic explorers through their being accused of witchcraft.

The Ladder—Stage 7: Joining

But at some point in the practice one turns from the *sabija* to the *nirbija* mode of *samadhi* focus. This is focus upon *śūnyatā* or the void, the space without objects, or conversely the "All" or the "No-thing." Obviously words are not well equipped to articulate these things. As Wallace puts it, the "highest stage" in Vajrayāna is called "crossing over." From my own understanding of quantum physics (Bohm's ontology in particular), it means crossing over from space-time to the transcendent nonspatial, nontemporal dimensions of the "implicate order." This implicate order is the repository of the *ākāśa* or in physics, the "frequency domain"—a sort of holographic repository of all information-vibration-frequencies that have ever been generated out in space-time domains. So the yogi (psychonaut) works to develop channels or links between the center of his or her perception and what is termed the implicate order ("the Shining Void" in Buddhist terminology). These connections bring a flow of wisdom, understanding, and other supportive energy phenomena from the transcendent back into the space-time world of the contemplative. For the contemplative it is akin to Prometheus bringing fire down from the mountain into the world of space-time.

Thus if all goes well with the practitioner's efforts within the earlier stages of practice, at some point in their silent meditation periods there will occur a direct "crossing over" from space-time to the transcendent as the psychonaut's center of consciousness "joins" with the transcendental Self in a state the Buddhists call the *dharmakāya*. Düdjom Lingpa writes about reaching "timeless awareness" in this quote from his *Vajra Essence*:

> Hold this to be the most excellent key point—to practice with intense and unflagging exertion until you attain supreme timeless awareness (*jñāna*), which is total omniscience.[6]

How does one describe such an experience? Unfortunately it is difficult and almost impossible to return from such an experience carrying any clear memory since the memory-generating function of the mind's normal activity must be suspended during such a union with the nonspatial, nontemporal dimensions of reality. As the philosopher Ludwig Wittgenstein wrote, "Whereof one cannot speak, thereof one must be silent."[7] On the other hand, for psychonauts who have progressed beyond simple intermittent "joining" moments and who are able to sustain the link between consciousness in the world of space-time and consciousness in the world of the transcendent (implicate order), there is available to the smaller self in space-time a channel that links it to the enormous *ākāśa* or holonomic frequency-patterned information stored within the implicate order. This is the source of teachings and pronouncements from many great mystic sages (including Jesus, Muhammad, Gautama Buddha and others throughout history). Having established the primary goals as taught in Tibetan Vajrayāna, we turn now to several primary psychonautic techniques of contemplative practice that have been found to be highly effective as developed over the centuries in Tibet.

13

Further Techniques of Tibetan Psychophysics

The core objective of this chapter is to develop not only a map of higher stages of consciousness but also the knowledge of practical efforts developed over the centuries in Tibet to cultivate psychoenergetic tools that have been found especially useful for the acquisition and exploration of "higher states" of consciousness. The Tibetan Vajrayāna is a thoroughly Buddhist-based teaching and thus presents its knowledge in the rich frameworks both of Buddhism and the earlier Bön culture that developed among the people of the Tibetan plateau. While there are innumerable psychophysical techniques found in Tibetan traditions, we will focus here on the following five: visualization, chakras, mantra, *nada yoga,* and ritual.

Tibetan Visualization Yoga

One of the characteristics of the Tibetan Vajrayāna is its extensive use of techniques of visualization, a practice that is widespread among all of the Tibetan sects and perhaps more pervasively explored there than among Indian Tantric traditions. Visualization is typically performed in private within a monastic meditation cell, a shrine room of a monastery, or an upper room in a private house. The purpose of the yoga of visualization is to use a known sensory system of the mind-brain to achieve higher states of consciousness. The contemplative visually focuses on the immediacy of a static image, striving to bring the entire image into maximum clarity and stability without distraction. While conscious energy is being focused and channeled on the object being visualized, other systems of the cognitive mind quiet down, attenuate, and fall into the state of quiescence that is requisite for breakthrough into higher channels of communicative awareness. At some point the mind-brain's quiescence allows the observer "to become the observed," and a shift occurs at which moment the contemplative identifies with the image under focus. Beginner contemplatives are given simple images to visualize such as the single *bīja* (seed) syllable, the Tibetan character equivalent of the Om symbol in India (fig. 13.1).

Fig. 13.1. Tibetan Om *bīja* symbol.

Once mastered, the student must commit to memory a visualization of the mantra that is ubiquitous in Tibet, "Om Mani Padme Hum" (fig. 13.4; discussed later in this chapter), after which the student proceeds to visually memorize line drawings and finally commit to memory the visualization of complex and colorful *thangka* paintings.

The cognitive "location" of the visualized image is also of importance. Most frequently the visualization for beginners is that of a small two-dimensional symbol in an interior space to the front of the visualizer. However, more advanced practices involve visualizing three-dimensional images sitting at the top of the contemplative's head or small images situated at the center of interior spaces corresponding to a chakra (such as the heart region, the throat, or the center of the cranium). Eventually the adept is given a *thangka* painting to visualize (fig. 13.2).

Ideally, the contemplative enters the state of *samprajñāta samādhi* (*samādhi* "with object") holding the focus of awareness on an internal (mental) visualization of a *thangka* painting.

Monks who paint *thankga* images are required to memorize the entire image, much as an opera singer is required to memorize an entire operatic score. After initiation and instruction the student practices visualization as often as possible, ranging from one to several hours in length daily. The *thangka* are often teaching tools, depicting important deities or lamas (monks) within the particular tradition of the contemplative. Once the visualization of the images has been mastered, the monk is encouraged to paint physical *thankga* of the image that can then be used in liturgical rites and by others. Highly advanced adepts are able to visualize extremely complex images. One of the most frequently visualized is the Wheel of Life (fig. 13.3, p. 246) which represents the cycle of existence of an incarnated being.

The Wheel of Life

The Wheel of Life is perhaps the oldest of all Buddhist teaching images and its visualization has been practiced by *thangka* painters, monks, and psychonauts for over two millennia. It is found prominently painted and displayed in the entranceway of the oldest Buddhist monasteries in Tibet.

The image in totality is a complete symbolic representation of Tibetan Buddhist psychology, mapping incarnated beings in the unending cycle of existence. The root of this map can be seen in the symbolic forces represented by the three animals shown in the center of the image. These are referred to as "the three poisons" and from them the whole cycle of existence is initialized, energized, and sustained. These three animals are a pig (representing ignorance), a snake (representing anger or aggression), and a bird (representing desire or attachment).

Under the influence of one or all of these three poisons an incarnated consciousness moves from one to another of the six stages of

Fig. 13.2. Monk painting a *thangka* in Tibet (1938).
Photograph by Ernst Krause, courtesy of the German Federal Archives.

Fig. 13.3. Tibetan *thangka* the Wheel of Life. From the nineteenth century.

life or realms of *saṃsāra** as shown separated by the spokes of a larger circular region in the diagram. The upper three regions indicate the three "higher realms" (god realm, demigod realm, and human realm) while the lower three regions depict the "lower realms" (animal realm, hungry ghost realm, and hell realm).

None of these realms is truly desirable, even the god realm, for they all continue to trap the incarnate soul within the endless revolving cycle of *saṃsāra* from which the object of contemplative efforts is to escape and become one with the one true Self (in Jungian terms) or the Buddhist Void (which is also "One-without-an-other," void of the little seemingly separate incarnated selves).

Dzongsar Jamyang Khyentse, a Bhutanese rinpoche, recently explained the value the human realm in the map of the six realms:

> If we need to judge the value of these six realms, the Buddhists would say the best realm is the human realm. Why is this the best realm? Because you have a choice. . . . The gods don't have a choice. Why? They're too happy. When you are too happy you have no choice. You become arrogant. The hell realm: no choice, too painful. The human realm: not too happy and also not too painful. When you are not so happy and not in so much pain, what does that mean? A step closer to the normality of mind, remember? When you are really, really excited and in ecstasy, there is no normality of mind. And when you are totally in pain, you don't experience normality of mind either. So someone in the human realm has the best chance of acquiring that normality of mind. And this is why in Buddhist prayers you will always read: ideally may we get out of this place, but if we can't do it within this life, may we be reborn in the human realm, not the others.[1]

This map of the six realms has often been taken to be a description of six different states into which an incarnate being will be

---

**Saṃsāra* is from the Sanskrit root *saṃsṛ* (संसृ), translated as "to go round," "revolve," "pass through a succession of states," "to go toward or obtain," "moving in a circuit."

reborn (i.e., re-incarnation into one of the various states of being in a virtually endless spinning of the wheel of *saṃsāra*). However, the map has perhaps even more significance when it conveys to the psychonaut the understanding that these six states *are continually experienced*, or at least latently possible and often emerging to the forefront of experience in the daily life of a human individual. As Dzongsar has expressed it:

> The word "born" or "reborn" means a lot. It does not necessarily mean that right now we are all in the human realm and we are not in the other five realms. Depending on what kind of *karma* we create, we will go to other realms. If the *karma* to be reborn or to experience the hell realm is the strongest, then you will change this form and then with another form you will experience a hellish kind of perception. According to Mahayana Buddhism the six realms are something that can happen during the course of a single day![2]

Yet all of these six "realms" are experienced within space-time. The objective of Tibetan Vajrayāna (and all Buddhist schools) is to move beyond the rat race that is eternally experienced while one is spinning round and round on the revolving wheel of life. The goal (for the Buddhist monk as well as the psychonaut in general) is to master the dynamics of consciousness while enmeshed in *saṃsāra* and to acquire the ability to move beyond (or outside of) time and space, to arrive at Düdjom Lingpa's fifth stage, "Joining" (or the direct crossing over or union with Bohm's implicate order).

Tibetan Chakra Meditation

As discussed in previous sections, there has long been a tradition among Tantric contemplatives of focusing conscious awareness upon specific regions or sensitive centers within the human body that are referred to as chakras. These centers have been found to be particularly responsive to contemplative stimulation and exploration. Numerous centers within the body can be felt to resonate in a clearly perceivable way when the focus of consciousness can be maintained within the specific region for an extended period of time. It has been widely recorded that the centers can be made to grow in sensitivity and "utility" with continued regular practice, as if the rays of consciousness falling upon the chakra nourish the center and results in growth, much as a living plant grows in response to the energy coming in from the rays of the sun. In fact, the analogy of the "opening" of a chakra to the unfolding of a lotus blossom is found in a wide range of traditional Buddhist and Hindu texts on contemplation. The term *chakra (cakra* in Sanskrit*)* can be found in numerous Vedic hymns dating back several millennia, where the meaning has been taken not precisely in the sense of psychic energy centers, but rather as *cakravartin* or a king who turns the wheel of his empire in all directions from a center, representing his influence and power. The contemplative philosopher M. P. Pandit has written extensively on chakras:

> There are in the being of man certain nodii which are so to say centres connecting him with other universal planes of existence; and when properly tapped they open up in one's being their respective planes and the powers that are characteristic of the principles governing those planes. Within the Indian Yogic system, these are called "chakras" or "Centers."[3]

A more Western, medical description of these areas was presented in 1926 before the Bombay Medical Union by Dr. V. G. Rele, who read a paper for those interested in "the science of Yoga" (discussed earlier in chapter 10). Rele presented a theoretical psychophysical explanation for some of the experiential changes in consciousness described by yogis as a result of Tantric practices and worked to relate nerve plexi to inner chakra centers (fig. 13.4, p. 250).

Being a medical doctor, Rele was able to identify correlations between the location of what he and others experientially determined to be concentrated regions of particular sensitivity during contemplation (chakra centers) with internal physiological structures, in particular regions of dense nerve and endocrine configurations. Every Tantric tradition uses chakra diagrams to guide practitioners. An Indian Tantric diagram from the nineteenth century is shown on page 251 in figure 13.5.

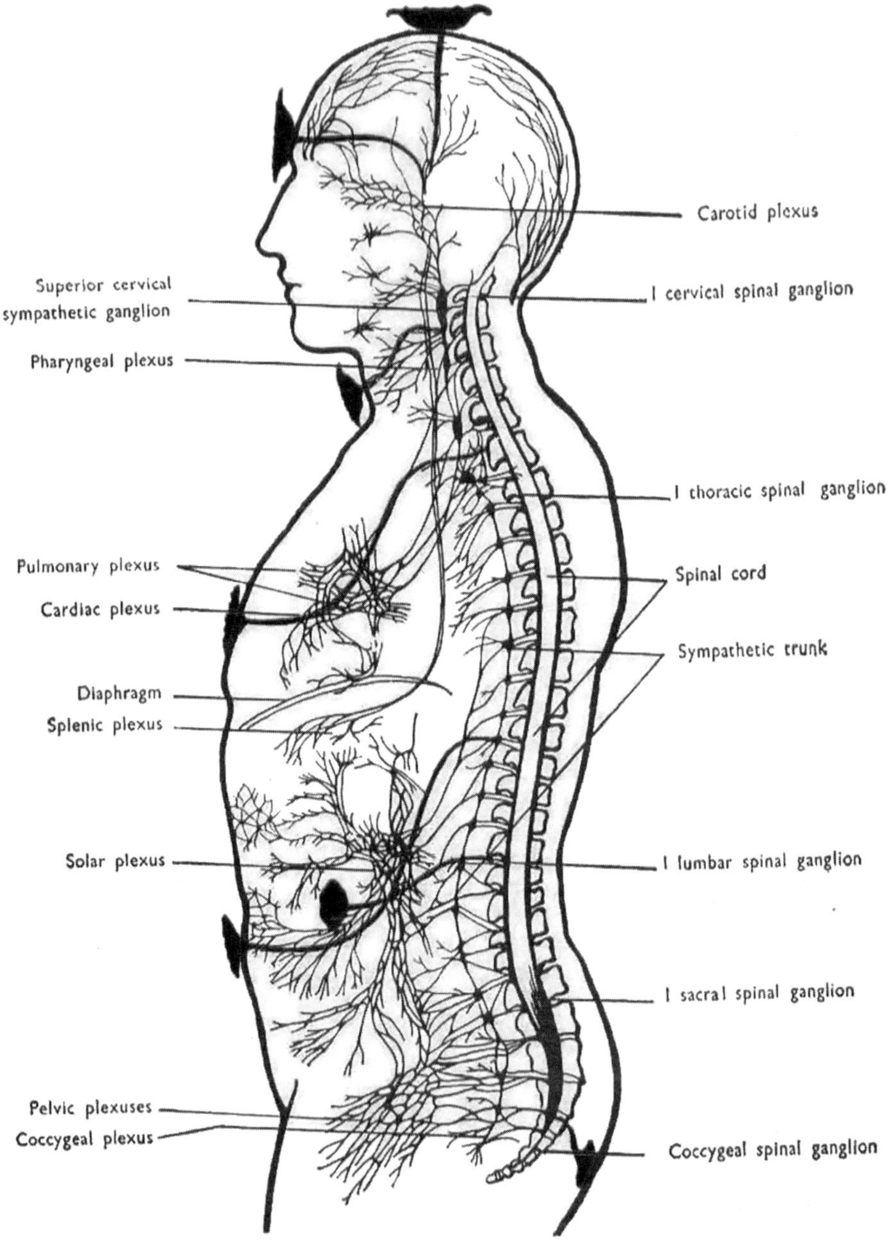

Fig. 13.4. Diagram of human chakra centers relative to nerve plexi. Adapted from C. W. Leadbeater, who first published the idea of the chakras for the West in *The Chakras,* 1927.

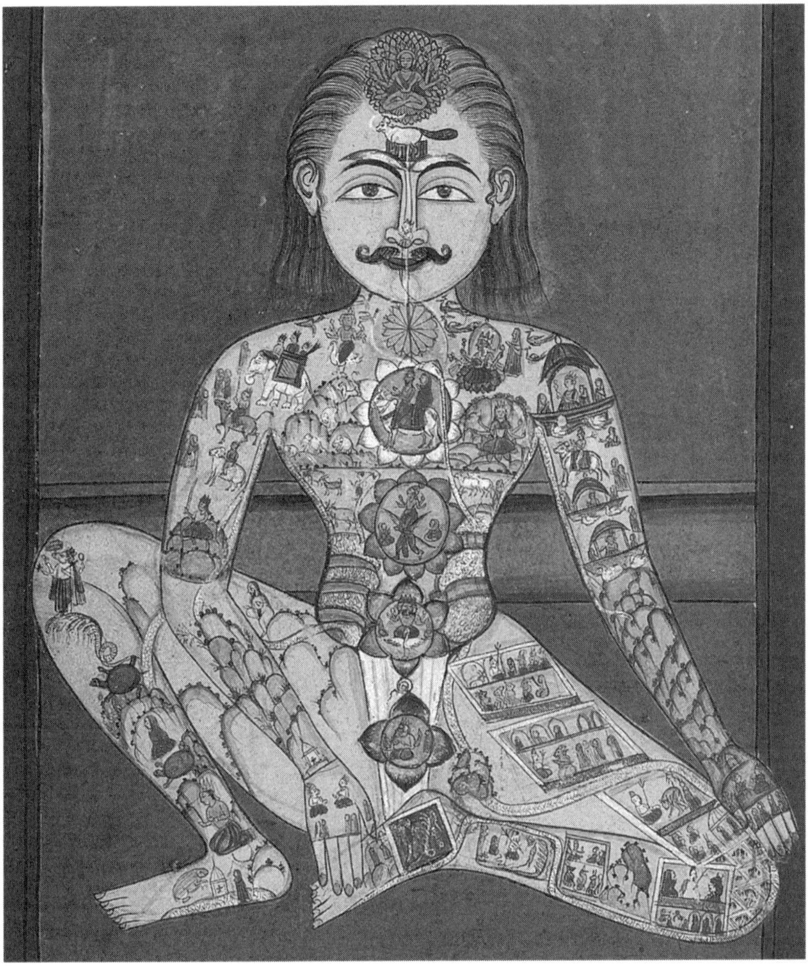

Fig. 13.5. Diagram of chakras and energy channels
from an 1899 manuscript
now in the British Museum.

As chakras can be experienced as a psychophysical matrix with a definite spatial location within the human body, diagrams of chakras are used as mnemonic tools to assist the practitioner recall the various locations within which to focus consciousness during periods of contemplative practice. The *Ājñā* chakra, for example, a center that can be seen in every chakra diagram, and located behind the forehead in the cranium, is here described by Rele:

> This *chakra* has two petals or branches and is situated between the eye-brows. Many Hindus place a dot of color on their forehead to indicate the opening of this chakra or *bija* as it is thought to indicate the awakening of intuition and higher intellect. It is the spot which is contemplated while undergoing the process of *prāṇāyāma*.[4]

The contemplative practice of focusing upon chakras has long been a major feature in Tibetan Vajrayāna, and numerous traditional *thangka* paintings act as visual aids to reveal a map of various chakra centers that have been discovered and developed by generations of psychonautic exploration. Modern medical science reveals the chakra centers to be especially rich centers of nerve plexi and also centers of major endocrine systems within the body. Figure 13.6 presents a Tibetan chakra diagram that is virtually identical in placement of the chakras when compared with the chakra map presented in the Indian chakra diagram of figure 13.5.

Tibetan Mantra Yoga

The Sanskrit word *mantra* is itself a combination of the word *man,* "the thinking mind" and *tra,* "crossing" or "traversing." These mantras, repetitions of short rhythmical phrases, have been found by sages in many cultures throughout the ages to be extremely effective as tools with which to bridge the mental activity of the brain, allowing awareness to pass beyond discursive thought into the vast oceans of "higher consciousness." This process entails a shift of focus, a relocating of one's center of gravity of awareness, inwardly, penetrating into ever smaller dimensions, below the verbal-activity levels into the nonverbal (preverbal) regions of consciousness. A scholarly definition of mantra can be found in volume IV of the *History of Ancient Indian Religion* (1975):

> A *mantra* may be conceived as a means of creating, conveying, concentrating thought, and of coming into touch or identifying oneself with the essence of the divinity which is present in the mantra.[5]

This description of mantra can be understood by other traditions as *prayer.* In Eastern Christianity, the widespread use of the "Jesus Prayer,"

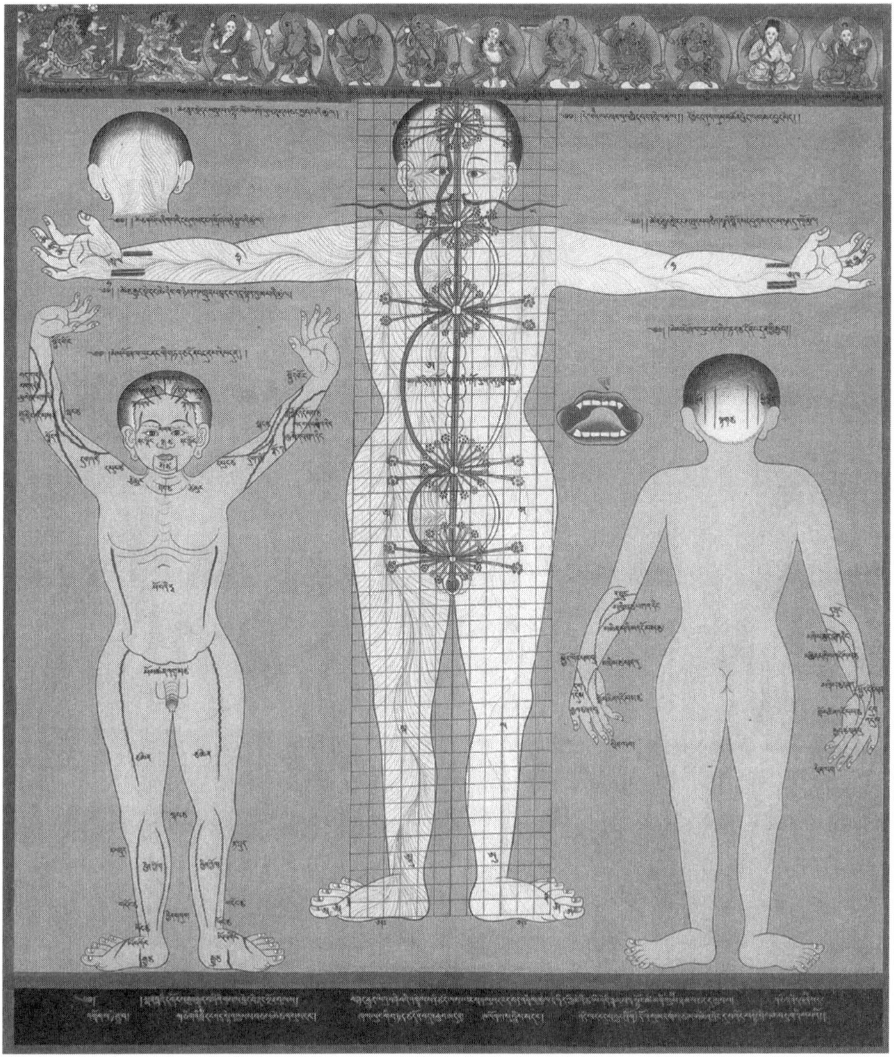

Fig. 13.6. Tibetan chakras diagram.

practiced by monks and hermits for centuries, falls under this definition, as does the Rosary (a series of "Our Father" and "Hail Mary" prayers) recited by Roman Catholics, or the Takbir "Allahu Akbar" ("God is Great") recited daily by Muslims. The importance of repetition of the mantra or prayer cannot be underestimated. With sufficient repetition, deep resonances build up in the vast web of reality that is everywhere connected.

The mantra in figure 13.7 is by far the most famous mantra recited by Buddhists throughout Tibet and can be found carved on innumerable stones and printed on countless prayer flags throughout the Himalayas. It is uttered continuously by all types of people, from monks to farm workers, and it sums up (and is a reminder of) a primary map in Tibetan Vajrayāna.

Fig. 13.7 Tibetan mantra technology.

Mantras are much more than words, even sacred words, though all prayer can be mantra. Even single words or sounds (*bīja* mantras), repeated over and over, will function as mantras when practiced with a continuous effort to focus awareness. The repetition does *not* have to be audible and is often a silent repetition heard only in the head or localized in one of the chakra areas of the human body. The audible resonance is consciousness itself, and internal repetition leads to contact with the transtemporal source of the vibrations located outside of space-time and within the frequency domain of consciousness, Bohm's implicate order. The repetition of mantra can be viewed as an effective gateway to supersensible modes of consciousness associated with Patañjali's *samādhi* or Düdjom Lingpa's *śamatha*.

Here the scientist and philosopher I. K. Taimni (who obtained his Ph.D. in chemistry from London University in 1928 and later became president of the Theosophical Society in Adyar) describes his understanding of mantra, based upon his own lifetime experience of regular mantra practice:

> The aim of all *mantra*, in short, is to purify and harmonize the vehicles of the seeker so that they become increasingly sensitive to the subtler layers of his own spiritual consciousness. As he comes into contact with these he becomes increasingly aware of that Reality of which his own consciousness is a partial expression.[6]

Rephrasing this statement in psychophysical terms we would say that the aim of mantra is to tune in to, or to resonate with, a particular bandwidth of energy frequencies, a spectrum of energy accessible to our own consciousness that can be contacted through mantric vibration resonating in a bandwidth of atemporal conscious energy.

Within this bandwidth or region of atemporal consciousness (which cannot even really be called a region as it is both nontemporal and nonspatial, outside of time and space), in what is called the frequency domain in the electromagnetic field theory of consciousness, can be found all of the vibrations that have ever been generated, interpenetrating in all of their complexities. This is called, in many Indian schools of thought, the *ākāśa* or *alayavijñana,* the "storehouse of all consciousness," and it is this domain that is "touched" by the contemplative yogi during sessions reaching *asamprajñata samādhi*, when the various separate cognitive systems of thought and perception have been attenuated and the deepest silence has been entered. It may also be seen as a means of tuning in to Teilhard de Chardin's noosphere (described in chapter 5).

It is ironic that in order to reach the state Patañjali calls *asamprajñāta samādhi* and to tune in to the Ākashic records one must have stopped one's memory formation activity. A contemporary computer analogy would be to put one's computer system into "sleep mode." One must learn to be able to suspend the brain's computational activity, and this includes suspension of both short-term and long-term memory creation. One of the best tools to accomplish this is the practice of mantra repetition (which of course could range from a single "meaningless" syllable to a Christian or Muslim prayer). The key here is the practice repeating the syllable, phrase, mantra, or prayer; through repetition the brain-mind will maintain a connection, even if tenuous at times, with something beyond the normal bounds of cognitive thinking in words and memories.

At some point in time during mantric repetition consciousness may be able to detach from the normal activities of the brain and the flow of time. The normal functions of the brain-mind have now been "silenced," attenuated, and deactivated. Hence the difficulty (once the computational brain has left sleep mode and resumes "thinking") of communicating the "experience" or of describing this state, and thus the resulting myriad metaphors and symbols throughout cultures and religions serving as substitutes for the authentic experience.

Nada Yoga Meditation

Nada is the Sanskrit word for "sound," and *nada yoga* means meditating on sound. This technique is an ancient one, described in the *Mahāsakuludāyi Sūtra* where the Buddha teaches the technique of "transcendental hearing" now referred to as *nada yoga*. It is widely practiced by practitioners of Tibetan Vajrayāna, and one of the most succinct descriptions of the technique was recently published by Dzogchen Ponlop Rinpoche, born in 1956 in Sikkim, a *tulku** of the Nyingma lineage:

> To detect the *nada* sound, turn your attention toward your hearing. If you listen carefully to the sounds around you, you're likely to hear a continuous, high-pitched inner sound like white noise in the background. It is a sound that is beginningless and endless. There's no need to theorize about this inner vibration in an effort to figure out exactly what it might be. Just turn your attention and focus upon it. If you are able to hear this inner sound, you can use the simple act of listening to it as a powerful form of meditation practice, in the same way one uses the breath as an object of awareness. Just bring your attention to focus upon the inner sound and allow it to fill the whole sphere of your awareness. The more precise and clear your focus is, the more vivid and sharp the sound becomes. Eventually, your experience of the sound deepens to the point that you experience its emptiness, which here is known as the *self-sound of the emptiness of dharmata*.[7]

---

*In Tibet, a *tulku* is regarded as a reincarnated custodian of a specific lineage of teachings. All of the Dali Lamas have been *tulkus*.

While not a well-known yogic practice, particularly in the West, a little search will reveal quite a few contemporary yogic practitioners who have "discovered" this yoga of the inner sounds. An example is the modern British symphonic composer, author, and mystic, Edward Salim Michael (1921–2006), who began practicing meditation in Manchester at an early age. Being a composer with a great love for music and drawn to sounds from any source, his contemplation often led him to focus his awareness on what appeared to him as a high-pitched mysterious sound "which he perceived in his ears and inside his head," though he had never heard of *nada yoga* until one summer as he was exploring Rajasthan.[8] One day in an alcove of a small temple in Jaipur his companion pointed out a wall painting showing a contemplative in lotus position with an inscription stating that the particular form of yoga conducted in this region of the temple was that of *nada yoga*. Some months later Salim was again reminded of *nada yoga* as he read a translation of a fifteenth century Sanskrit manual, the *Hatha Yoga Pradipīkā*. Nevertheless, though he spent the summer studying many types of yoga in India, he could not find anyone who practiced *nada yoga*. He soon noticed that the intensity of this interior sound seemed to rise and fall in proportion to the intensity of his concentration. The deeper his concentration, the louder and clearer the sound would become.

> The more he listened to the sound, the more he felt himself in an inexplicable state of inner security which bore no relation to the tangible world, a mysterious inner security in which he felt that death was an illusion. This mysterious inner security was independent of all problems that he might encounter in the tangible world, including illness. He decided to listen to it, without interruption, for one hour each day. As a result of his efforts, a moment finally arrived when he became strangely distant from himself, and he started viewing everything around him from another perspective altogether. He felt that his vision seemed to have inexplicably receded to the outside top part of the back of his head, from where he silently and impartially began to witness all that was taking place around him.[9]

One of my own early teachers, Dr. Rammurti Mishra, was a neurosurgeon who had been raised in a devout traditional Brahman family in which he mastered Sanskrit at an early age. In his classic translation of Patañjali's *Yoga Sūtras,* Dr. Mishra states that there is no distinction between *Īśvara** and *nādam* and states:

> The relationship between sunlight and sun is analogous to that between *nādam* and *Īśvara* . . . the universe is a concentrated form of *nādam*. Nādam is the subtle form of the universe. Manifestation of *nādam* is not the end of practice; it is only the beginning. By practice of meditation it should evolve into all forms of cosmic energy because all cosmic energy is a manifestation of *nādam*.[10]

The German Indologist and specialist in yoga, Georg Feuerstein (1947–2012) believed that *nādam* is associated with the heart chakra:

> When the heart center is activated, it is possible to hear the subtle inner sound called nāda, which is "unstruck" because it is not produced by any mechanical means and is not propelled through space but is a fundamental omnipresent vibration—the sound om. This idea has its parallel in the Gnostic notion of the "music of the spheres," first mentioned by Pythagoras.[11]

A passage found in the *Surangama Sūtra* is also highly revealing in a passage where the bodhisattva Mahasattva Akshobya rises and speaks directly to the Buddha as follows:

> I reflected upon these various things and marvelled at their great sameness without any difference save in the rate of vibration. I realized that the nature of these vibrations had neither any source for their coming nor destination for their going, and that all sentient beings, as numerous as the infinitesimal particles of dust in the vast spaces, were each in his own way topsy-turvy balanced vibrations,

---

**Īśvara* can be translated as God, Supreme Being, personal god, or highest Self.

> and that each and every one was obsessed with the illusion that he was a unique creation.[12]

Tibetan Tantric Liturgical Ritual

In all of the Buddhist Tantra sects the rites accompanying mystical practice, liturgical ceremonies, and initiations are among the most elaborate and colorful liturgical productions as can be found in any world religion. Many of the details have been borrowed from ancient Tibet's Bön religion.

With knowledge that Tantric practitioners have adopted "what works" based upon lifetimes and generations of direct experience, we can be assured that there is some psychonautic advantage to be attained through participating in worship of any liturgical kind. In his book *The Tantric Mysticism of Tibet,* after having lived and studied in Tibet for five years during the 1930s, John Blofeld describes his understanding of how ritual is integrated with contemplative practice in Tibet, and gives us a rational for liturgical traditions in every religion:

> The reasons for this unusual combination of mental practice and rites are manifold, but they can be summarized as falling into four categories:
>
> 1. The belief that meditation unsupported by devotion can lead to a kind of spiritual pride incompatible with the effort to negate the ego;
> 2. The Tantric insistence on involving body, speech and mind so that the adept will ultimately develop into what is called an Adamantine Being through subtle changes in his physical and mental constituents;
> 3. The conviction that sensuous, aesthetic and emotional impulses are a valuable source of spiritual energy;
> 4. The discovery that some of the deeper levels of consciousness unapproachable through conceptual thought can be reached directly by means of appropriate symbols.[13]

Padmasambhava's Integration of Mantra with Chakra Meditation

One of the more integrated practices is that of what is called the Vajra Guru Mantra, originally developed by the great Tantric contemplative Padmasambhava during the eighth century CE. This has become one of the primary contemplative mantras among Tibetan adepts of the Vajrayāna:

Oṃ Āḥ Hūṃ Vajra Guru Padma Siddhi Hūṃ

I was taught the use of this mantra by Chögyam Trungpa Rinpoche at his retreat, Tail of the Tiger, in 1972. Beginning with the seed syllable *Oṃ* in the center of the cranium, one moves the focus of awareness slowly downward with laser-like precision to each chakra in sequence as indicated in fig. 13.8 until *Padma* is recited in the locus of the *Mūlādhāra* chakra (between the perineum and the coccyx), at which point one moves the focus up to the *Ājñā* chakra region (often called the "third eye") behind the forehead while reciting the word *Siddhi,* and ending the sequence by focusing upon the *Sahasrāra* chakra ("the crown chakra") centered at the top of the skull (the fontanelle). The entire sequence can then be repeated. The contemplative keeps track by grasping the next bead on a string of 108 "prayer beads," called a *mālā.*

Over the centuries during which these chakra regions have been explored, a wealth of detail has been associated with each specific chakra, such as a characteristic color, a unique seed syllable (*bīja*), a unique *yantra* image, a particular *deva* (spiritual personality), and specific powers (*siddhis*) when fully activated. For example the heart chakra (*Anāhata*) is said to be red in color and is associated with love and compassion, while the throat chakra (*Vishuddhi*) is said to be blue in color and can be of particular importance for practicing dream yoga (it is said that if one focuses upon the throat chakra while falling asleep, one will experience lucid dreams). A detailed description of these chakras is beyond the scope of this book, but references to these various centers can be found in many cultures, though the wealth of details describing them seems to have been most highly developed among Tantric contemplatives in Tibet and India.

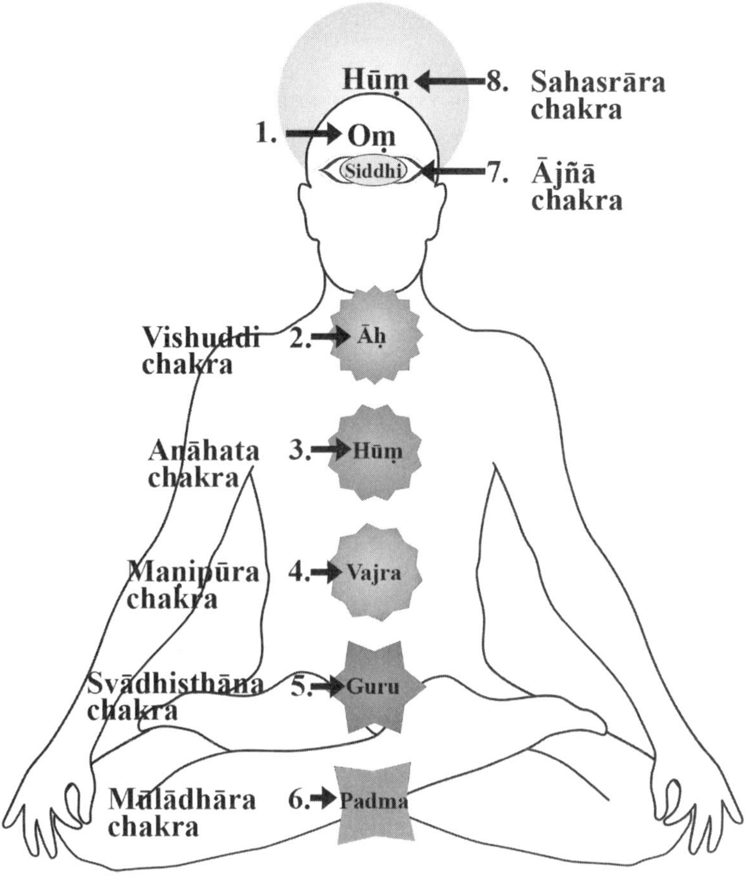

Fig. 13.8 Chakra sequencing of Padmasambhava's Vajra Guru Mantra.

The Vajra Guru Mantra practice ensures that a balance is developed among each of the seven psychic centers (chakras) within human psychophysiology. As has been mentioned previously, each chakra acts somewhat independently, almost as a separate brain center, interfacing with specific bodily functions within its area of specialization. It is fairly easy to see the effect in a person who does not have an integrated set of chakras that work together in a synergetic way for the good of the entire person. For example, an individual with an overdeveloped throat chakra (*Vishuddi*) may be a great orator but can often be seen to talk excessively. An individual with an overdeveloped *Svādhisthāna* chakra may be seen to obsess on culinary delights and overemphasize eating. A person with an overdeveloped lower chakra (*Mūlādhāra*) may obsess on sexual activities. The goal of chakra development is to cultivate a system of coordinated, integrated, communicating chakras, acting much as distributed servers in a highly integrated computer network. When an individual's chakra system is unevenly developed, various chakra centers may compete with one another, often fighting for control of the individual's attention and intentions. In such a situation the individual may occasionally exhibit activities that seem quite out of character. An example might be a highly regarded politician with great oratory skills and charisma who, through an overdeveloped *Mūlādhāra* chakra (the center of sexual activity), might have their consciousness "taken over" at times by this rogue chakra's impulsive need for expression that seems to be completely at odds with the individual's other centers. This can lead to shockingly out-of-character promiscuous sexual activities with great damage to reputation and career. Similarly, the commonly observed example of an individual obsessed by overeating, even though they wish they could stop, may be the expression of an overactive rogue *Svādhisthāna* chakra in the abdominal area. Thus it is of the greatest importance for an individual to make the effort to spend time cultivating each of the chakra centers in turn, and the Vajra Guru Mantra practice offers a methodology to include each of these major centers of psychophysical activity in sequence simply by reciting the mantra slowly while moving awareness sequentially to each center in a continuous contemplative loop.

Having reviewed traditional maps for the cultivation of consciousness as they have evolved within specific major cultural paths (Western, Indian, and Tibetan) we now present several additional perspectives and observations that may be of practical use for contemporary contemplative psychonauts.

PART FIVE

Practical Advice for Modern Psychonauts

14

Mapping the Psyche for Direct Exploration

This chapter offers a number of maps and models of consciousness that can be useful to anyone seriously interested in psychonautic exploration with or without entheogenic assistance. Having a number of different maps gives the traveler a wider range of alternate perspectives and thus a greater chance of being able to locate where they themselves might be in their progress, what they might be seeking, and to recognize various topographical relationships that might make the territory and goal more familiar.

The maps presented here are efforts to track psychonautical phenomena, consciousness sailing out into the oceans of higher, nonmaterial worlds. Accordingly, the information is a great simplification of the supporting data and theory that may be found in the original works in each of these approaches to mapping states and stages of consciousness.

These maps trace the basic geometry and psychophysics of consciousness. They are all quite distinct and yet they do not contradict one another. They are grounded in twenty-first-century science, even as they support the many traditional techniques described in Tantric texts that were written many centuries prior to our current technical knowledge of invisible ways and forces that configure the cosmos. The various maps should be of substantial use while navigating the dynamics of conscious energy in space-time and beyond, offering an essential guide for psychonauts navigating previously unexperienced regions that open up with the acquisition of supersensible perception.

Philosophers, metaphysicians, and mystics continue to look for some as yet undetected conscious energy field variously called chi, *prāṇā,* mana, orgone energy, holy spirit, morphogenetic fields, or animal magnetism. But our entire existence—the universe into which we are born, live, and die—is literally filled at every point with an omnipresent matrix of transforming electromagnetic energy that cannot be created or destroyed.

But what if this omni-transformable energy plasma field is not a dead thing? What if it is the very living stuff of consciousness? What if this field—the electromagnetic being they have been taking for granted as a lifeless, unaware physical "property"—is actually the living being of the universe itself, gleefully hiding in front of (and within) the scientist, philosopher, and the mystic?

HOFFMAN'S MAP: AGENTIAL REALISM

A commonly held realization is that every human being has multiple "minds." The multiple community of minds that operate within a single human being might be seen as subprograms woven together interactively in a highly networked computer operating system. This view, called "agential realism" or "conscious realism," has been studied in great detail by Donald Hoffman, a professor of cognitive science at the University of California, Irvine.[1] Hoffman developed a model in which conscious agents combine to create even more complex, higher level complex agents. He makes the following bold claim:

> Consciousness, not space-time and its objects, is fundamental reality and is properly described as *a network of conscious agents.*[2]

While Hoffman's statement might seem heretical to modern material scientists, it would be taken for granted by traditional Tantric practitioners in Tibet and India. Yet he foresees an eventual reconciliation between science and "spirituality":

> I also think that conscious realism can breach the wall between science and spirituality. This ideological barrier is a needless illusion,

> enforced by hoary misconceptions: that science requires a physicalist ontology that is anathema to spirituality, and that spirituality is impervious to the methods of science. I see ahead an uneasy truce and eventual rapprochement.[3]

Using Hoffman's approach we can see, at the top level of human cognitive activity, *two minds* operational as one self. Split-brain research supports this contention by noting that what is referred to as your mind is actually a blending of two distinct personalities, two architecturally separate conscious entities, likely inherited ("booted") initially from the unique holonomic plasma energy signatures of your mother and father, blended into one new configuration ("you") during the brief moments of procreative inception. Your left-hemispherical mind-avatar was seeded with a clone of your father's electromagnetic plasma holonomic "vibrations," while your right-hemispherical avatar was booted up with a clone of your mother's plasma vibrations.

From birth onward, your life experiences began to superimpose (additively merge) with those two personalities creating increasingly individuated energy patterns, uniquely modulated by your immediate family, community, society, and cultural environment and your uniquely selective, ever-changing interests in books, knowledge, and experiences.

Even so, the real *you* is not either of these two "mind" avatars. The real preexisting you is simply riding on the backs of your cognitive multimind, using them as interfaces to experience in a complex network of awareness. In most people the two avatars act as one, generally dominated by the distinct side matching the genetic physical gender of the individual. Thus, if you are born into a male body, your left-hemispherical agential agent or avatar becomes the dominant side of your nature and calls all of the shots. In a female body it is usually the right hemisphere that dominates. Of course, in transgender individuals this is not the case, as there seems to be a mismatch of mental gender with physical gender.

These two "computational mind systems" do not always agree with one another, and likely the incompatibility of the two in many human individuals is a root cause of psychological disorders. In some human individuals, when the two are highly compatible, and even, perhaps, synergetic, the two get along just fine, a "happy marriage" of two minds, and the person is said to be individuated, whole, healthy. In other individuals one hemispheric system dominates the other, often forcefully, becoming the root cause of various dysfunctional states such as schizophrenia and obsessive-compulsive disorders.

However, there is a third major component of human consciousness, a body-wide electromagnetic component, a magnetic plasma flux maintained within the coursing warm ionic bloodstream. According to quantum brain mechanics (QBM, discussed later in this chapter), this acts much like a single-distributed entity, somewhat like the internet, and a good analogy might be seen in the "Wi-Fi" and "Bluetooth" electromagnetic fields that transmit and receive high rates of information in typical contemporary networks of interactive devices and computers. During contemplative silence of the bi-hemispherical cerebral "laptop-minds," it is this electromagnetic consciousness that "comes forward" into the forefront of the contemplative's focal of awareness. The center of gravity of consciousness shifts out from within the attenuated electrical activities of the two electrical hemispheric "minds," and into a single higher-level magnetic flux system generated by the swift flow of the ionized bloodstream throughout the body. In the case of a psychonaut who has ingested an entheogen, the complex hydrocarbon psychotropic material releases unique energy spectra as it breaks down, decomposing slowly (or quickly) within the coursing bloodstream. These unique energy spectra interact with the baseline magnetic "self" flowing through the bloodstream via superposition, and the resulting new frequency spectra becomes a combination of the new substance's electromagnetic frequency pattern and the individual's normal pattern, thus driving the normal human consciousness into new regions of awareness. During one of my ayahuasca experiences I saw, visually, tiny distinct luminescent wire-frame nanobot entities emerging from some sort of wall of quantum black energy. I imagine that they were little nanobot "selves," for what else could they be if the cosmos is really one, a Universe, one story, one Being at the heart of reality?

Thus, we are not the "person" we think we are—we are much much more. In fact, we are the universe looking out from within a central consciousness and obtaining a particular, unique perspective of itself and its vast creation in time and space. Carl Jung called this "person" the

Self, while Indian philosopher/mystics called it Brahman, and of course many cultures simply termed this One being "God" in various local languages and dialects. But how does this map of consciousness relate to psychophysics and psychonautics? Hoffman tells us that an understanding of conscious realism allows us to ask the following question:

> Can we engineer our interface to open new portals into the realm of conscious agents? . . . I think so. I think that we can open new portals into consciousness, just as microscopes and telescopes open new vistas within our interface.[4]

This is precisely what generations of Tantric practitioners have claimed—that we can "engineer our interface" (though they would use different terms) to open our awareness to new dimensions of reality.

HEILE'S MAP: BI-MODAL CONSCIOUSNESS

Frank Heile's recent description of a bi-modal nature of consciousness is also relevant here. Heile, a physicist from Stanford University, puts forth a theory of two categorically different modes of consciousness operating in parallel (simultaneously) within a single human mind. Calling them the Symbolic Consciousness and the Primary Consciousness, Heile sees these two seemingly independent categories of awareness coexisting within one individual human-consciousness "whole."

The earliest modern humans fossils date from the Middle Paleolithic Age, approximately 200,000 years ago. In terms of the evolutionary arc of human consciousness over that time span, Heile's Primary Consciousness was the first to awaken, as it is the mode of consciousness that observes through the sensory systems and is able to store and to retrieve memories. Over numerous subsequent generations this primary mode of conscious awareness gradually evolved a completely new capability that we now call *logic,* the ability to process previously stored memories and compare them to current observations in order to discern similarities and patterns, and thus unleash the ability to plan and to predict future outcomes.

In contrast to the original Primary Consciousness of 200,000 years ago, Symbolic Consciousness only came into operation somewhere between "30 to 100 thousand years" ago,[5] and it is through use of this symbolic mode that human consciousness began to speak to itself and others using sound patterns that could be associated symbolically with externally observed objects, events, and activities. The symbolic mode of mind-consciousness gifted the evolving human with an internal and external "voice" now operational within the now-bifurcated mind of individual humans.

Heile's model can be used to understand Patañjali's model in the *Yoga Sūtras.* We can identify the *puruṣa* as equivalent to Primary Consciousness, and *citta* as equivalent to Symbolic Consciousness. Thus, Patañjali's phrase *citta-vṛtti* used in the very first (and perhaps most important) line of the *Yoga Sūtras*, might easily be translated as "the gyrations of Symbolic Consciousness," the fluctuations associated with logic and memory processing within the mind-brain complex.

This fluctuating symbolic consciousness (*citta-vṛtti*) is at the heart of cognition, encompassing all of the senses from touch to vision, the sense of "I-ness," and the ego. Among contemporary people this *citta-vṛtti* has come to dominate consciousness, and as a result communication with the *puruṣa* has largely been lost, except during sleep, intoxication, encounter with the sublime, contemplation, and other nonverbal modes of consciousness. Through the rise of Western culture's increasingly verbal and digital technology the Symbolic has prevailed, ballooned, and hijacked human attention away from Primary Consciousness. Thus, *citta-vṛtti* can generally be found dominant during waking states, primarily in the lingual area of the left cerebral hemisphere in modern *Homo sapiens.*

On the other hand, what Heile calls the "Primary Consciousness," Patañjali's *puruṣa*, is an ancient, wideband spectrum of energy, a matrix of flux that is always perceiving and parallel-processing in the very heart of the eternal present's "now."

Experience of *puruṣa* consciousness is the gateway to *kaivalya*, described in Patañjali's final *sūtra* (IV.34.), where *kaivalya* has been variously translated as "the power of pure consciousness settles in its own pure nature" (Satchidananda), "Enlightenment" (Shearer), and "the Power of Knowledge in its own Nature" (Vivekananda).[6]

Unfortunately, connection with this primary *puruṣa* consciousness has been almost completely lost by contemporary humans. Masked by the dominance of verbalized abstraction and the analytical language gyrations fueled by a hyperactive *citta-vṛtti* consciousness, the isolated thinking brain-mind has become the dominant mode of consciousness. Nevertheless, the practical application of Tantric psychophysics offers a way to reconnect this normally isolated consciousness with the wider ecologies of consciousness operational throughout the universe and beyond.

Another point of congruence supporting Heile's bicameral map of the human mind can be found at the heart of Jungian analytical psychology. While Patañjali's term *puruṣa* matches Heile's term "Primary Consciousness," both terms can be seen to be in full alignment with the central Jungian concept of the Self.

In *Man and His Symbols,* Marie Louise von Franz (1915–1998), one of Carl Jung's most famous students, describes the Self in her essay "The Process of Individuation" as follows:

> The Self can be defined as an inner guiding factor that is different from the conscious personality and that can be grasped only through the investigation of one's own dreams. These show it to be the regulating center that brings about a constant extension and maturing of the personality. But this larger, more nearly total aspect of the psyche appears first as merely an inborn possibility. It may emerge very slightly, or it may develop relatively completely during one's lifetime. How far it develops depends on whether or not the ego is willing to listen to the messages of the Self.[7]

Von Franz here speaks of communication between "the conscious personality" and "the Self," stating categorically that the conscious personality can connect with the Self "*only* through the investigation of one's own dreams" [emphasis added]. It is my belief that von Franz was incorrect in stating that the conscious personality can *only* connect with the Self through dreams. Contemplative practices lead to sufficient quiescence of the normal awakened state so as to allow the perception of the Self resonating with the self to arise within various cavities throughout the body and beyond (i.e., within nonspatial, nontemporal dimensions) when they are made objects of sustained contemplative concentration. It is my belief that this resonance experienced by contemplatives and variously termed "Nirvana," "God," the "Divine," or the "Absolute" is that same *Puruṣa* described in the *Yoga Sūtras* and in the *Sāṃkhya* philosophy.

Note that she also describes the Self as "this larger, more nearly total aspect of the psyche," and as that which sends "messages of the Self" to the conscious personality through dreams. If we equate this larger (cosmic) Self with Heile's Primary Consciousness, then the *Yoga Sūtras* is the instruction book for establishing a more lucid and intense perception of the Self than occurs during the state of dreaming. In *Sāṃkhya* philosophy this more lucid contact, the direct experience of *Puruṣa* by *puruṣa*, or Primary Consciousness with Symbolic Consciousness, is called the state of *samādhi*.

ELECTROPHYSIOLOGICAL MAP: HEART AND VENTRICULAR HORNS

It is thought that the human heart generates enough radiant energy to interact with Earth's geomagnetic field. Joseph Chilton Pearce (1926–2016) describes here the electromagnetic toroidal field (fig. 14.1, p. 272) generated by the human heart:

> All living forms produce an electrical field because in some sense everything has an electromagnetic element or basis, but a heart cell's electrical output is exceptional . . . electromagnetic energy arcs out from and curves back to the heart to form a torus . . . that extends as far as *twelve to fifteen feet* from the body. . . . The dipole of this heart torus extends through the length of our body, more or less, from the pelvic floor to the top of the skull.[8]

The heart has also been the focus of innumerable contemplative traditions for centuries. A widespread Christian devotion that arose first in Benedictine monasteries as early as the eleventh century CE is called "The Sacred Heart of Jesus" (Latin: *Sacratissimum Cor Iesu*). The heart

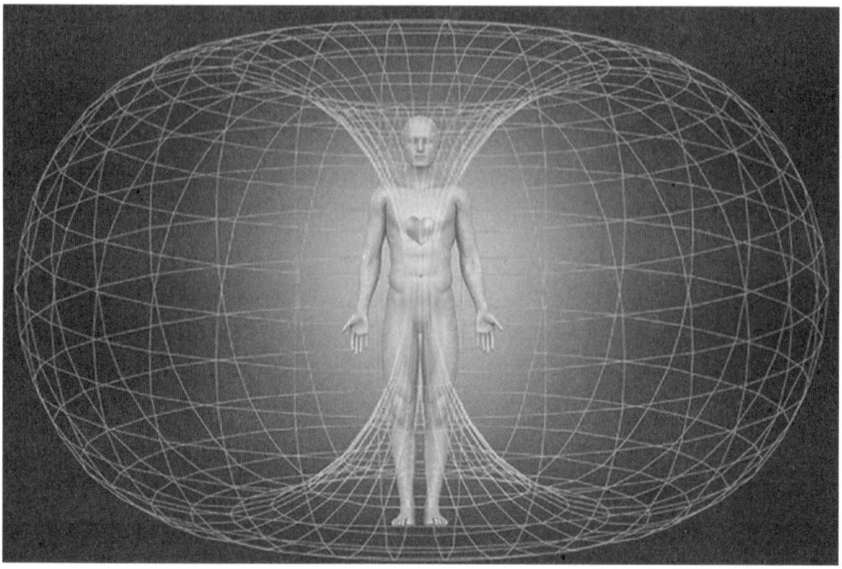

Fig. 14.1. Toroidal electromagnetic field generated by the heart. Image of toroidal heart field is reprinted with the permission of Rollin McCraty of Heartmath.

(*hridayam*) is often found in Vedic hymns thought to have been composed 4,500 years ago, where it is considered to be the location from where the "I" springs. Tantric traditions declared to be a major focal center of contemplation, the *Anāhata* ("unstruck") chakra. In Buddhism, the recitation of the *Heart Sūtra* (Sanskrit: *Prajñāpāramitāhṛdaya*) is known to be perhaps the most frequently used and recited text in the entire Mahāyāna Buddhist tradition.[9] If we assume that consciousness is an electromagnetic-field phenomenon, such widespread traditional attention to the heart is supported by what is now known in terms of modern electrophysiology:

> The electromagnetic fields produced by the heart are involved in energetic communication, which we also refer to as *cardio electromagnetic communication*. The heart is the most powerful source of electromagnetic energy in the human body, producing the largest rhythmic electromagnetic field of any of the body's organs. The heart's electrical field is about 60 times greater in amplitude than the electrical activity generated by the brain. This field, measured

in the form of an electrocardiogram (ECG), can be detected anywhere on the surface of the body. Furthermore, the magnetic field produced by the heart is more than 100 times greater in strength than the field generated by the brain.[10]

If there is a correlation between the psyche and electrophysiology, then the individual human psyche should, following the range of the electromagnetic toroidal energy field extending out from the human heart, also extend in some sense "twelve to fifteen feet" from the body. If our Primary Consciousness or *puruṣa* does have an energy component in the electromagnetic spectrum, then it must be affected, to some degree, by the electromagnetic environment of the earth due to the known fact that all electromagnetic fields interact through what is called resonance.

Many animals possess a "magnetic sense" and appear to be able to track the magnetic field of the earth, which is generated by the flow of molten material in the earth's core and the corresponding flow of ions in the atmosphere. Magnetoreception is an accepted phenomenon among a wide range of animals: birds, fruit flies, honeybees, turtles, lobsters, sharks, stingrays, whales, and even bacteria.[11] Even animals not normally known for their migration habits have been discovered to possess such a sense.

Recent publications from a German research group relate the discovery that cattle (and other herd animals, such as red and roe deer) tend to situate themselves on a magnetic north-south axis, as if involuntarily directed by the earth's magnetic field.[12] These surprising results were discovered when satellite images provided by Google Earth were used to analyze herding patterns and behavior. However, the built-in magnetic compass becomes confused and misaligned the closer the cattle get to high-voltage power lines, and the cattle then align with the power lines instead.[13]

Contemporary research in electrophysiology indicates that our human bodies may be more involved in sensing electromagnetic fields than has previously been acknowledged. Research at the California Institute of Technology has discovered traces of magnetite in the human brain and heart in about the same density as that found in migrating animals and has proven that onset of rapid eye movement in sleeping humans is shortened in the E-W orientation of sleepers compared to the N-S position.[14]

If consciousness itself has a spectral vibrating-energy frequency component, then is it not likely the human biosystem has evolved physiological modulators, transmitters, and receivers for this frequency component? It is common knowledge that some type of antenna is required both to transmit and to receive radio waves, and accordingly the image of an antenna is usually either that of a vertical metal antenna "whip" at the top end of a tall mast, or a long horizontal wire. Antennas designed for higher frequencies are dish-shaped, and at the highest microwave frequencies microwave cavity antennas are constructed to channel the waves in the desired direction. Microwave cavities are used to focus and channel signals in the microwave energy spectrum in a similar way as glass lenses focus visible light waves. During my senior year in electrical communication engineering we had to design resonant waveguide cavity "horn antennas" to amplify and modulate microwave signals.

The enormous horn antenna (fifty feet long and eighteen tons in weight) constructed at Bell Labs in Holmdel, New Jersey, can be seen in figure 14.2. The antenna was used to receive signals from one of the earliest communication satellites, Telstar, and in 1965 it received the signals that proved the existence of cosmic microwave background radiation. High-frequency microwave radiation is guided by a tapered waveguide horn, and the horn shields the antenna from any interference from spurious electrical noise outside of the antenna.

In another of my senior classes, taught by an M.D. who also had a Ph.D. in electrical engineering, we studied the electrophysiology of the nervous system. When I noticed the striking similarities between the shape of a waveguide horn antenna (fig. 14.2) in the advanced communication lab and the images of the ventricular cavities within the human cranial cavity (fig. 14.3), I mentioned this to my professor, pointing out the possibility that the ventricular horns in the brain might be functioning as a microwave horn antenna, focusing extremely high frequencies to help the brain "see" internal visual images with eyes closed (such as when dreaming). My professor assured me that it was common knowledge in medicine that the ventricular system *was only designed* to deal with thermal equilibrium of the brain and to act as a shock absorber, cushioning trauma to the skull.

Fig. 14.2. Horn antenna at Bell Laboratories.
Microwave horn antenna at Bell Laboratories in New Jersey.
Image from NASA.

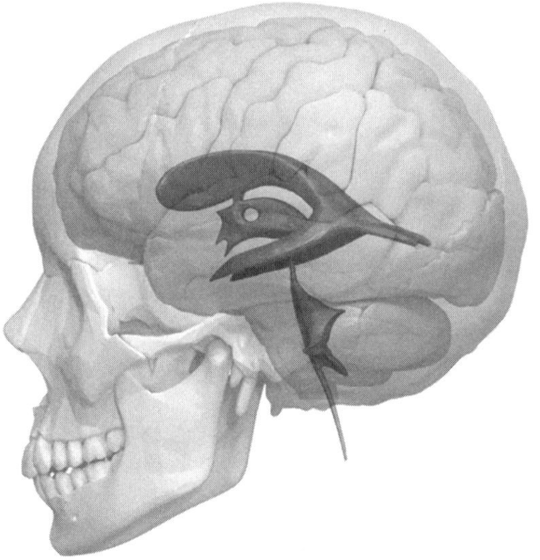

Fig. 14.3. Lateral view of the ventricular cavities.
Image by BodyParts3D by DBCLS.

However, the structures of these ventricular cavities are embryologically derived from the center of what is called a *neural tube* that is the first observed structure to develop in a newly formed embryo. In the developing vertebrate, this hollow tube is the first distinguishing prefiguration of the spinal cord and central nervous system.[15] In the mature human the ventricular cavities are filled with cerebrospinal fluid, an extremely clear, protein-free liquid created within the brain by special cells on the inner walls of the ventricular caverns. The horns or caverns of the two ventricles are separated only by a small opening between them, and the ventricular system is contiguous down the spinal column within the central neural tube of the spinal cord.

As noted by my professor, the currently accepted explanation of the role of the ventricular cavities and the clear cerebrospinal fluid within the cavities is as follows: although the system has some thermodynamic stabilizing properties, its function is primarily a hydraulic one that the body uses to cushion the brain during trauma; it simply "protects the brain tissue from injury when jolted or hit."[16] It should be noted that prior to the twentieth century the accepted physiological description of the functioning of nerve fibers within the nervous system was that nerves were a type of plumbing pipe vessel and that the nervous system and brain operated in fact as a hydraulic system, moving fluid according to Bernoulli's law in a similar way as the cardiovascular system. A better explanation for the nervous system awaited the understanding of electrophysiology in the twentieth century, as does yet, perhaps, a better explanation of the ventricular cavities and their clear cerebrospinal fluid. Figure 14.4 compares the lateral view with the anterior view of the ventricular cavities.

It is not unreasonable to imagine that modern physiologists are mistaken about the role and function of the ventricular cavity horns and the clear cerebrospinal fluid within, much as they were mistaken over the function and role of the nervous system in previous centuries.

If the psyche does indeed have an electromagnetic-frequency energy component, then the horn-shaped ventricular cavities within the cranial cavity indicate the possibility that nature might very well have already designed and implemented its own energy-frequency signal communication system.

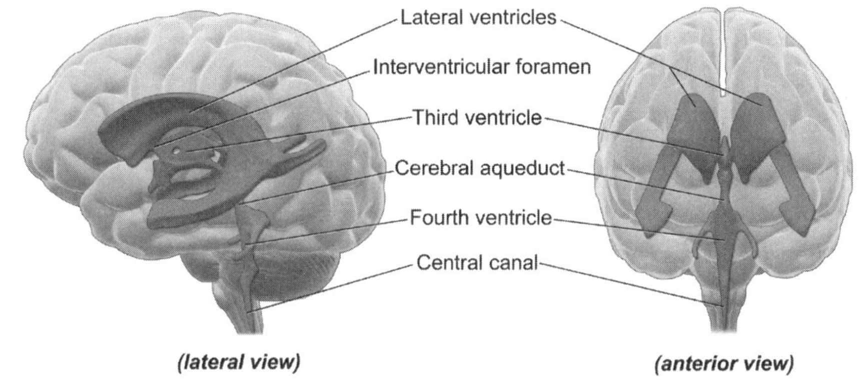

Fig. 14.4. Two views of the ventricular cavity of the brain.
Image by Bruce Blaus.

Is it not then likely that this communication system is being used unconsciously (or consciously) by humans in various processes of the psyche? Could this "cave" be where internal vision is projected during dreaming states?

TAOIST MAP: "ORIGINAL CAVITY OF SPIRIT"

Contemplative experiences throughout many cultures corroborate the existence of a potential gathering and localization of psychic energy within the central region of the cranium. However, few descriptions are as relevant to our discussion about the possibilities of finding aspects of psyche within the ventricular cavities as are exhibited in this following passage from a text on Taoist yoga:

Question: Will you please give me the exact position of the original cavity of spirit?

Answer: It is (in the centre of the brain behind) the spot between the eyes. Lao Tzu called it "the gateway to heaven and earth"; hence he urged people to concentrate on the centre in order to realize the oneness (of all things). In this center is a pearl of the size of a grain of rice, which is the centre between heaven and earth in the human

> body (i.e., the microcosm); it is the cavity of prenatal vitality. . . . He who knows this cavity can prepare the elixir of immortality.

Therefore, during the training both eyes should turn inward to the centre (between and behind them) in order to hold on to this One which should be held in the original cavity of spirit (tsu ch'iao) with neither strain nor relaxation; this is called "fixing spirit in its original cavity."[17] This original cavity of spirit is thought correspond to the ventricular cavity (fig. 14.5).

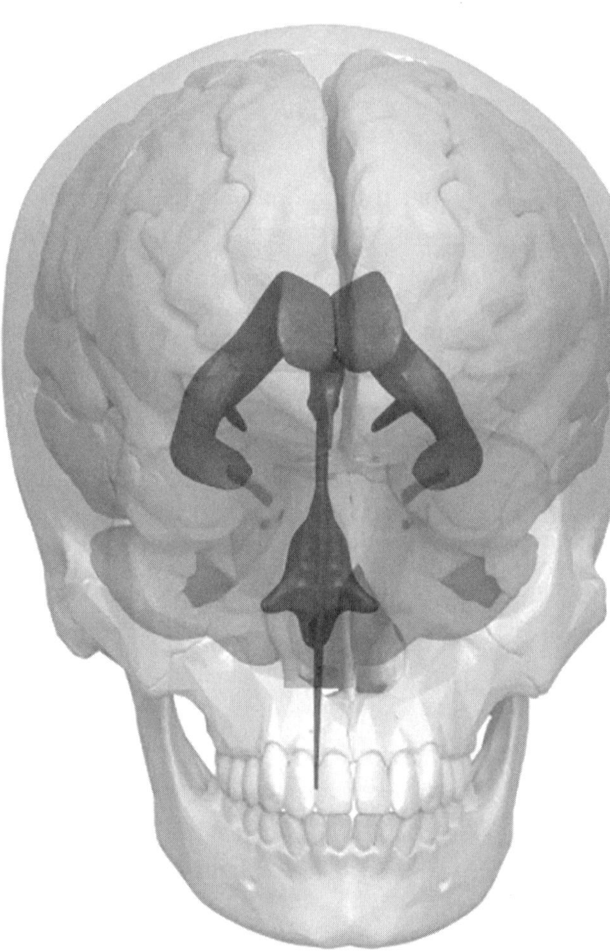

Fig. 14.5. Illustration from front, revealing horns of the ventricular cavity. Image by BodyParts3D by DBCLS.

PERSINGER'S MAP: GEOPSYCHE AND THE "GOD HELMET"

In a career largely focused upon efforts to harness modern electromagnetic technology to the exploration of human consciousness, the neurophysicist Michael Persinger (1945–2018) was one of the few scientists to have engineered electronic interfaces linking the electromagnetic fields of the brain in order to influence consciousness. Persinger, who published over five hundred technical articles in scientific journals and authored seven books, developed a magnetic stimulation device—popularly known as the "God Helmet"—to explore consciousness. A professor of psychology at Laurentian University for forty-seven years prior to his death in 2018, Persinger's primary area of research was exploring electromagnetic fields as they interact with biological organisms, and his primary focus was upon the human brain.

As director of Laurentian University's Neuroscience Department, Persinger tasked one of his department researchers, Stanley Koren (1943–2014), to develop a prototype "helmet" as a means of testing his own "bicameral mind" brain theory. Persinger's theory rested largely upon the interdisciplinary ideas of Julian Jaynes (1920–1977).

In 1976, Jaynes published *The Origin of Consciousness in the Breakdown of the Bicameral Mind,* in which he articulated the belief that the two hemispheres of the brain are fundamentally two separate "selves."[18] According to Jaynes, who found support for his idea through a great range of interdisciplinary material, prior to about 1000 CE human consciousness operated quite differently than it does in modern humans. The dominant left hemisphere received "suggestions" from the right hemisphere through auditory verbal hallucinations, and individuals in many instances assumed that the "voice" was that of God. Jaynes put forth evidence indicating that around 1800 CE a major shift began to occur in the functional operation of the human brain as it shifted from this bicameral mode to what we now refer to as "consciousness."

In modern times the left hemisphere of the brain generally dominates awareness and is experienced as the primary waking sense of self due in large part to increased integration of language and thought. While his theory was initially well received, particularly by the general public (the first edition of his book sold out quickly), neurophysical researchers found it difficult to assess the validity of his theory through use of clinical methods, and eventually the theory became a target of widespread criticism and was shelved. However, interest in the theory was revived during the late 1990s with the radical improvement in brain-imaging technologies, and new data seemed to confirm many of his early predictions.[19] Persinger called his own version of the Jaynes theory the "Vectorial Hemisphericity Hypothesis," proposing that the human sense of self has two components, one on each side of the brain.

After many years of research into the various ways that the electromagnetic field of the human brain interacted with the electromagnetic field of the planet, Persinger went much further, putting forth the theory that Earth has a dynamic *geopsyche* of its own that interacts with each individual human psychic field to form a global network, a theory that is congruent with the idea of the noosphere put forth in the work of Pierre Teilhard de Chardin.[20] Persinger here describes his view of the geopsyche:

> Our concept of a *geopsyche* essentially involves the interaction between large numbers of biological systems and the geomagnetic environment within which they are immersed. It contends that at certain critical numbers of biological units (of a species), an electrogeomagnetic matrix is formed with the capacity to be energized by the intense geophysical forces of nature. When energized, this matrix acquires the potential to display behaviours and patterns of its own. . . . We are hypothesizing another phenomenal pattern existing as an integral force and unifying unit at the level of a geopsyche.[21]

In Persinger's laboratory experiments the subject wore the helmet device within an anechoic (soundproof) chamber, constructed to act as a Faraday cage shielding the subject from spurious electromagnetic emissions and radiation other than Earth's magnetic field. Persinger himself, in summarizing the results from numerous experiments, stated that "At least 80% of participants experienced a presence beside themselves in the room, while others report less evocative experiences of another consciousness or sentient being."[22]

If true, these results would support the Jaynes theory of "the bicameral mind" as well as Persinger's hypothesis that external electromagnetic fields can be made to interact with the brain/mind systems (in some manner not currently understood).

THE QUANTUM BRAIN MECHANICS (QBM) MAP

Neuroscientists tacitly assume that consciousness can be associated only with the nervous system and the brain, but over a century ago Gustav Fechner, the founder of psychophysics, fought against this same assumption, which he called the "nerve issue." Fechner addresses this assumption with some amusing analogies:

> Since violins need strings to sound, then flutes also need strings; but since flutes have no strings, they cannot sound; candles and petroleum lamps need wicks in order to burn, so gas lamps also need wicks, but they have none; thus they cannot burn. Yet flutes sound without strings and gas lamps burn without wicks. . . . If fish and worms can breathe without having lungs, while mammals and birds can breathe only if they have lungs, why cannot plants without nerves experience perception, while animals can only perceive when they do have nerves?[23]

In recent years Japanese researchers in the field of quantum brain dynamics have concluded that consciousness is to be found not exclusively within the neuronal system of nerves and organs such as the brain, but within the entire distributed volume of blood plasma considered as one system of consciousness, a single entity, a major subsystem of your own collective mind of consciousness (one of your many distinct centers or frequency ranges of consciousness). Quantum activity (generated by flowing electrolytes of Na^+, Ca^{2+}, Mg^{2+}, HCO_3^-, Cl^-) within the blood plasma present a network of coherent electromagnetic-field energy radiating throughout the capillaries in the far infrared band.[24]

In 1995 several Japanese neurophysiologists published findings that are in accord with Fechner's view that living consciousness may exist in the bloodstream, not exclusively in the nerve tissue. In 1995, the Japanese neuroscientists Mari Jibu and Kunio Yasue described the creation and annihilation dynamics of units of concrescing consciousness, which they characterized as quanta of consciousness, and linked these quanta to the physical properties of water, stating that they are "energy quanta of the water rotational field extending to the whole assembly of brain cells, and photons, that is, energy quanta of the electromagnetic field."[25]

Jibu and Yasue go on to describe a theory in which the polarization of water molecules plays an exceptional part, and on the macro level produces a single resonant water "macromolecule" in bodies of living, water-based creatures. Within this nonlocal quantum field that is generated within the human circulatory system is embedded an electromagnetic field that, contiguous throughout the body, comprises a magnetic plasma within the bloodstream. That our circulating blood generates a plasma state should not be surprising; the first line in a recent textbook on plasma physics reads: "It has often been said that 99% of the matter in the universe is in the plasma state."[26]

Professors Jibu and Yasue go even further by describing quantum brain mechanics as explaining how biological life might be seen as manifesting in matter as a "single molecule in living matter," a single magnetic dipole in "the unity of water" of the human body:

> There are two basic fields in quantum brain dynamics (QBD): the water rotational field and the electromagnetic field. The two must be described simultaneously by quantum field theory because they interact with each other. . . . All H_2O molecules bound together in a QBD vacuum domain form a single, extensive molecule of water in a macroscopic domain. That is, water throughout the entire region of the cerebral cortex is thought to be composed of many macroscopic water molecules whose sizes are all comparable to the coherence length of the QBD vacuum, that is, about 50 microns. This remarkable feature of water in living matter might provide us with quantum field theoretical support for the idea that life is nothing but the unity of water as a single molecule in living matter.[27]

This observation from quantum brain dynamics (QBD) supports Steiner's model of an astral body of consciousness beyond the etheric body of the nervous system and brain. The supporting pattern can be seen in the QBD manifestation of a "single extensive molecule of water," dipolar in geometry like an antenna, generating a complex magnetic field through the circulation of the hot hydrogen ions of blood plasma.

DOMAINS AND RANGES OF HUMAN CONSCIOUSNESS

In comparing the maps we have examined in this book, it can be seen that Patañjali's *puruṣa* corresponds to what Heile calls "Primary" consciousness. This primary consciousness expresses itself in the toroidal electromagnetic energy field enveloping our bodies. It is possible to detect a radiant flux of this Primary Consciousness glowing within the ventricular cavities of the brain in the very center of the cranium, perceivable with the inner eye or "third eye" as described both in China and India:

> The pineal gland is a pine cone shaped endocrine gland that sits between the two hemispheres of the brain—a location which corresponds to what in Taoist practice is known as the "Crystal Palace." Lao Tzu called this little gland "the gateway to heaven and earth." In Hindu yoga, this same place is called the "Cave of Brahman," and corresponds to the *Ājñā Chakra*, or "third eye."[28]

Of this "Cave of Brahman," Swami Hariharananda Giri (1907–2002), a Bengali guru and teacher of Patañjali's yoga in the lineage of Paramahamsa Yogananda, wrote:

> The "Cave of Brahman" is an etheric chamber where Brahman, the creative essence of the universal spirit, manifests itself and radiates *pranic* life to the twenty-four gross body elements via the medulla, cerebellum and the spinal chord. The pituitary and pineal glands, at opposite ends of the cave, are the positive and negative poles of Self-knowledge.[29]

Such also could be the place of access to the Akashic record described by Alice Bailey in her commentaries (published in 1927) on the *Yoga Sūtras*:

> The *akashic* record is like an immense photographic film, registering all the desires and earth experiences of our planet. Those who perceive it will see pictured thereon the life experiences of every human being since time began, including:
>
> 1. The reactions to experience of the entire animal kingdom. The aggregation of the thought-forms of a karmic nature (based on desire) of every human unit throughout time.
> 2. The trained seer thus must learn to dissociate that which pertains to his own aura with that of the aura of the planet (which is in actuality the *akashic* record).[30]

In order for the "trained seer" to be able to tune in to and resonate with the noosphere or higher collective consciousness of the planet, one must be able to dissociate one's individual "aura" from that of the "aura of the planet" (i.e., Teilhard's noosphere, Jung's collective unconscious, David Bohm's implicate order, or Düdjom Lingpa's stage of "Joining").

Using mathematical tools from Fourier, we have been able to visualize the shapes and dynamics of these domains of consciousness as a manifestation of energy simultaneously swirling between two states, coexisting both in the temporal, spatial time domain (t_d) and in the nontemporal, nonspatial frequency domain (f_d).

A consciousness that extends not only throughout the time domain but has a component within the frequency domain goes far to explain the *siddhis* or "powers" described in the *Yoga Sūtras*, or the synchronistic phenomena observed by Jung and others, and provides a solid basis for Rupert Sheldrake's theory of morphic resonance,[31] which has as its central hypothesis that information can be transmitted instantaneously (or nearly so) among biological entities, whether pigeons, humans, or bacteria.

In the frequency domain all frequency spectral patterns coexist simultaneously as there is no temporal or spatial separation (space-time dimensions do not exist within the pure-frequency domain). Thus, all frequency (all information) immediately connects aperspectivally as there is no spatial or temporal separation, the entire frequency-information content is simultaneously superpositioned (or superimposed) as one field. While there is no spatial axis found in this frequency domain, there is also no time axis. Thus, many previously unexplained phenomena, including morphic resonance, telepathy, déjà vu, and others, may be understood as resonance processes within the frequency domain dynamically collapsing back into the space-time domain.

And yet the entire information-realm of the frequency domain is resonant with, and potentially omnipresent within, the space-time domain.

FINAL THOUGHTS: YOU ARE NOT YOUR MIND

To conclude this wide introduction to Tantric psychophysics, if I were to summarize the architecture of consciousness in one short sentence, it would be this:

> *You as a conscious entity are not simply your "mind"*
> *as conventional wisdom would have you believe,*
> *you are much, much more.*

While you do *have* a mind and you do often *use* your mind, your mind should be viewed more as a modern personal computer, not the essence of who you are. It should be taken as a useful instrument that has evolved to aid in survival by providing and interfacing with your sensory systems and mental-software tools for observing, remembering, and planning. Your computer-like brain-mind is complete with a talking, responding, personality component (much like "Siri," "Alexa," or "Hal,"), which all too often is mistakenly identified as "I" or "myself," but it is not your deepest, truest Self, that which was in existence at the very beginning of the growth of your first embryonic cells. This computer mind is a protein-generated avatar that is sustained and operated through complex electromagnetic force fields throughout your neocortex region and peripheral body, intimately interconnected and interfaced with your multiple external sensory-input systems (hearing, sight, smell, touch). The real *you* is much more than your mind; it is that which preexisted the growth of your mind. The absolute actual entity that is *you* is not only capable of traveling in consciousness far beyond the bounds of your physical meat-brain mind (as it does every night when you enter dreamtime), but according to innumerable sources throughout history, the real *you* will transcend the limitations of your brain-mind once your human body ceases to function.

The most important message of this book is that through practicing various contemplative exercises, many of which have been described here, you can transcend your computer-like meat-mind during your current adult life. While this is something that many monks and shamans throughout history have learned to do, you do not have to be a monk or a shaman in order to cultivate these innate capabilities of your body-mind-soul complex. The only requirement is that you have the intention to explore your awareness beyond everyday normal mental operations and that you take steps to begin practicing one or several of the numerous techniques that individuals throughout history have discovered as practical ways that can lead human consciousness to "liberation" from conventional, limited states of awareness. The good news is that you do not have to be highly educated, exceptionally intelligent, wealthy, good-looking, or lucky in order to make progress. All that is required is the sincere intention, the will to make progress, and regular efforts to practice such techniques (daily if practicable), whether they are entered into within the particular cultural context of your own religion or philosophy, or completely independent of any such group approach. No effort is wasted on this journey into the heart of consciousness!

15

My Personal Experience of Meditation and Contemplation

In contemporary culture the word *meditation,* following its traditional meaning, is invariably associated with practices that are embedded within a particular religion. Popular opinion holds that the practice of meditation can lead to a state of peace and tranquility or even to some rare mystical "enlightenment experiences" in which one feels to have expanded one's consciousness to include a sense of being "one with" or in "communion with" a higher Being, called variously God the Father, Allah, Ein Sof, Yahweh, Brahma, Buddha, Avalokiteshvara, Elohim, Heavenly Father, or in the Jungian sense, the larger Self. This chapter offers practical techniques of meditation, extracted from Indian, Tibetan, and Christian traditions, presented here for those interested in developing or enhancing their own specific approaches to their private practice. I will focus primarily upon my own story, my own somewhat unique daily practices, sharing my general approach to meditation and describing in some detail my own firsthand experiences. But to begin with, it may be useful for readers to understand the difference between the use of the word "meditation" and the word "contemplation."

In the Middle Ages, the prolific* religious writer Hugh of Saint Victor (1096–1141), in trying to put more structure into the monastic approaches to meditation, wrote that there are three possible activities

*The *Patrologia Latina,* widely used by scholars of the Middle Ages, is an enormous collection of Latin writings that contains forty-six works by Hugh of Saint Victor, and this is not his full collection.

or states of the soul (individual human consciousness): thinking, meditation, and contemplation.[1]

European monastics tended to emphasize meditation, the second of these three states of brain-mind, an approach which included a focus upon communal and individual recitation of prayer sequences as well as reading the Scriptures and spiritual texts very slowly with great focus of attention upon the meanings of words.* Hugh's third state of awareness, contemplation or *contemplatio,* described a practice of cognitive silence and divine listening that, as a portal to psychonautic exploration, was understood to be a more direct approach to the experience of God, as contrasted with meditation, the effort exercised within intermediate stages between normal everyday consciousness and the psychonautic oceans that one finds oneself entering within the higher stages of contemplation. Techniques† of meditation were understood as intermediary and leading up to the third state in which consciousness entered contemplation, which developed into the high art of what we would call psychonautics.

There are a wide range of techniques of prayer and meditation that have been developed within numerous cultural traditions. Previous chapters in this book have attempted to convey these techniques to the reader in plain language, while validating them with brief discussions of modern physics, physiology, quantum theory, and psychology. Yet perhaps the most important validation is that of direct experience. This chapter does not deal directly with psychophysics but describes my own specific experiences and practices that have evolved during my fifty years of introspective‡ exploration of the many Tantric techniques described earlier in this book.

First it should be noted that without thinking about it too much,

---

*This is a practice called *lectio divina,* primarily a technique used by monks and priests.

†Techniques of meditation are intermediate practices leading up to the breakthrough into contemplative stages, and include a wide range of physical, psychophysical, or purely cognitive practices (including but not limited to mindfulness, prayer, mantra, liturgy, TM, *hatha yoga,* and *t'ai chi ch'üan*).

‡I was eighteen when I first learned of the famous American psychologist William James (1842–1910) and his practice of "introspection," his approach to exploring and studying consciousness "firsthand."

over the years I have adopted "what works" into my daily contemplative meditation sessions. By no means am I suggesting that anyone interested in contemplative practice should copy my own sequence of practices. However, if it is true that every person's life and persona is the unique product of a particular era, family, society, and educational background, then it should be apparent that every person can and should discover "what works for them" by actually trying a range of different practices, even perhaps revisiting techniques they learned as children from within their own particular family, religion, and culture (such as prayers or other rituals).

The rest of this chapter will be rather informal as it will reflect my attempt to convey material that others might find of use in the development of one's own unique approach to an effective Tantric psychonautic contemplative practice. Much of the material will be of an autobiographical nature.

EARLY CONTEMPLATIVE EXPERIENCES

I first became serious in exploring contemplation when, shortly after graduating from an engineering program, I moved to New York City and become interested in *hatha yoga* practice. One late evening I was in the quiet windowless inner room of my fifth-floor walk-up in the Lower East Side of Manhattan doing my usual stretching exercises, trying to maintain a shoulder stand posture (*sarvāṅgāsana*) for ten minutes as part of my *hatha yoga* practice. Part of the exercise was to move into the pose, then to become as quiet as possible, practicing internal silence. This required making an effort to attenuate every thought that might arise, to detach from and not follow memories as they began to form, nor to allow any inner dialogue to resume streaming. The goal was to open up the bandwidth of awareness and to remain receptive, just listening. Suddenly, out of the silence, I heard a singular loud, high-pitched tone which seemed to be located somewhere within my cranium. I noticed that as I focused my awareness on the sound it seemed to coalesce into a point while substantially increasing in volume! I quickly feared I might be experiencing a brain aneurysm in progress. But as I soon discovered, by maintaining my focus, I was able to coax the sound into growing louder and more distinct, and my fears were transformed into awe at this audible tone coming from within. Even more strange was that accompanying the sound sensation was a sensation of "touch" detectible within this tiny region located somewhere within the upper right-hand quadrant of my brain.

Then things became even more strange. After noticing the initial "bright" sound, additional "points" of sound of distinctly different pitch began to rise into awareness *in other locations in my cranium*. I gently lowered myself from my shoulder-stand position and, ending my *hatha yoga* for the night, lay down under a blanket in the dark. For many hours that night I could not sleep, totally fascinated was I in focusing upon and listening to the sounds that would variously increase in volume according to the degree that I would be able to direct my attention toward them. I noticed, however, that as soon as I would begin consciously thinking "about them" or "thinking in words," letting my attention begin to stray, they would subside and contact would be lost. I quickly learned that by gently dropping my train of thought that seemed so insistent on thinking and classifying, I was able once more to enter the silence and the tiny sounds would suddenly peek out of the silence and increase in volume in what was clearly a feedback loop, a sort of reverberation responding to my search. The tones were quite pure, high-pitched, and I suppose most people would classify them as a "ringing in the ears." Several months later I discovered the term "tinnitus," which was defined by medical science as any perceived sound not brought in by the ear canal. Since perception of these sounds seemed to bother people, doctors decided that it must be a disease of the hearing system with an unknown (yet to be determined) source.

Nevertheless, by now being quite serious in my efforts to explore the phenomenon of "consciousness" by any means possible, I was completely fascinated by what was happening that night in my top-floor apartment. I found that by trying to ignore a particularly dominant bright sound and trying to focus on a fainter, more obscure sound ("further away from" or "behind" the first) the second sound would immediately grow louder in volume and become easier to focus upon using this inner focal-sense mechanism. Here was direct cause and effect, albeit in an internal domain of consciousness among some kind of living experiential fields of energy dynamics. All that night I lay awake in the dark, moving from sound to sound within my head, as each would rise and fall, almost as if each had an independent volition of its own. I experienced strong emotional oscillations between exaltation verging on disbelief, and terror that I might be damaging my neuronal centers, perhaps even encouraging (or experiencing) a brain-damaging hemorrhage.

As an electrical engineer, I had often listened to various single sinusoidal tones generated by equipment in laboratory sessions, yet this was not a single tone but a confluence of tones faintly making up a background of the perceived, sensed audio range, like those I had experienced in the forest at night at Hamilton's pool and taken to be peeper frogs. At specific points in space within my cranium, a tone would arise, from time to time, with an exponential sharpness high above the background level, to become a bright point, like a beacon, that, if I were able to sustain focus upon for a few moments, would become markedly louder with an accompanying intense tactile sensation.

During the course of what seemed a very long night my body grew hot and sweated profusely, soaking the sheets in what I assumed might be a fever caused by whatever was happening in my brain. I went through what seemed to be a long period of deep fear, suspecting that I had somehow damaged my nervous system. Yet, since that first night listening to the inner sounds, I have never experienced a headache or discomfort of any kind within my cranium.

Sometime in the early morning hours I fell asleep. When I awoke it was with great relief to find that my mind seemed to be back to normal, having returned to its familiar mode of verbalized thoughts, chatting away merrily once more. However, I now lived with these new memories and realization that something singularly strange had occurred, something I had never been prepared for and which I had never previously encountered in books or in life's experiences.

I continued to practice *hatha yoga* but spent increasingly long periods in silent meditation, finding that, now, I was able to fairly easily contact these resonant inner sounds. I began the practice of focusing upon them while falling asleep and found that when I would begin to awaken from a dream in the middle of the night I was able to quickly reenter the dream world by following these mysterious bright inner sounds.

My training in physics and electrical engineering led me to believe that these internal sounds were sine waves, not some sort of random noise. The tones also appeared to manifest in narrow spectrums centered about fundamental frequencies. For a time I conjectured that they might be mechanical resonances within the physical structures of my inner ear. At the time I worked as an engineer in a large building in lower Manhattan and began to experience, with great surprise, one of the high-pitched sounds flare up in my cranium whenever I approached certain electronic equipment, computer screens, or even certain vending machines. At such moments I found myself internally verbalizing, with some humor "incoming," a phrase widely heard in the media at that time from the front lines in Vietnam.

Over the next few weeks, I noticed that during my meditation sessions, if I concentrated awareness within different physical/spatial locations within my body, such as the heart or the throat, perceptually different sounds would arise in different locations and patterns, though the sounds were most clear and pronounced in the central region of my brain.

I soon concluded that the source of these perceived inner sounds must be of an electromagnetic nature, possibly the vibrations of a neuronal plexus within my nervous system resonating with electromagnetic modulations of our Earth's electromagnetic energy fields, or in the case of vending machines, the harmonic frequencies of some internal electrical radiation emanating from their circuitry and transformers.

In bookstores I began to browse through books on anatomical structures of the brain and the central nervous system. This was the age before the internet, but luckily I was living in New York City, and had access not only to the New York Public Library, but to many bookstores with medical sections. I was soon able to obtain excellent material with technical illustrations and x-ray photographs of internal physiological structures. I used these to visualize, with as much detail as possible, those internal areas, usually corresponding with the Indian chakra system, while meditating in the dark.

Over several years this process, concentrating and visualizing within areas of my body and focusing on the sound tones as they would arise, became a main source of meditative practice for me, and the inner sounds grew ever more richly complex and often markedly louder in volume, and began to produce distinct tactile sensations of flowing nature, unlike the sensations felt in the external senses of touch, vision, taste, and hearing.

On weekends I would also search for books for guidance in silent meditation, and in the process discovered Patañjali's *Yoga Sūtras.* My first copy was a translation with commentaries by Professor Ernest E. Wood (1883–1965)[2] I was thoroughly impressed that Wood had first been educated in the "hard" sciences of chemistry, physics, and geology, and only later had he become so thoroughly fascinated by yoga and meditation that he undertook to become a Sanskrit scholar. Wood's translations of the *Sūtras* seemed to me to be the perfect manual for the type of meditative exploration that had become my passion. After carefully studying Wood's translation for several months, I found a different translation of the *Yoga Sūtras* by a professor holding a Ph.D. in chemistry, I. K. Taimni (1898–1978).[3] To my surprise, many of the translations and commentaries differed markedly between the two books. This led me to attempt an understanding of each word in the context of my own experiences and practices.

COMMON ELEMENTS FOR BEGINNING PSYCHONAUTS

Several basic considerations for achieving the ability to enter the "inner silence" that is the beginning state of psychonautic exploration are as follows:

- Have a special, sacred space, a *temenos,* where you can "sit" and practice contemplation in relative silence free of distraction
- Hold a regular, preferably daily session with a minimum time goal (beginners often try for 10 minutes, experienced contemplatives can "sit" for 30 minutes, extremely advanced adepts can "sit" for multiple hours without interruption)
- Practice at the same time period of the day (early morning, sunset, or midnight)

Meditation Sitting on a Cushion (Zafu)

While one can certainly practice some forms of meditation while walking or lying down (though falling asleep can become a problem), most schools of meditation begin by suggesting the practitioner sit cross-legged close to the floor upon a stuffed cushion, called a *zafu* in Japanese. I have several zafu cushions of various color and fillings, but the key is to "sit" on a cushion daily, preferably at the same time period so that the body-mind-consciousness becomes used to the position and recognizes it and the associated activity that is expected (contemplative exercises, psychonautical exploration, indescribable journeys).

It is also suggested to put the zafu in the center of a wide flat cushion called a *zabuton* so your feet, ankles, and legs rest on a well-padded area, not on a cold hard floor. To meditate when traveling and in a hotel room, I sit upon two pillows from the bed upon a folded blanket.

The key is to sit on the cushion or pillows and teach yourself how to meditate simply *by trying to meditate.* As in many things in life, you learn most by direct experience. For example, when learning to ride a bicycle nobody can really teach you, but can only encourage you (especially when you fall down) as you *teach yourself* how to ride by reprogramming your mind-body of brain, muscles, and nerves. Although meditation is primarily a matter of learning through experience, here are a few additional tips that have worked well for me. Most spiritual progress results from *trying* various written or oral teachings, and in particular *not* just to try once or twice, but to give any particular technique a real chance to "grow." To begin to appreciate any new practice, as in learning to ride a bicycle, requires some actual repetition over at least several weeks. This gives the cognitive mind-brain the chance to learn, program, and thus create new relatively permanent skills within itself through neuroplasticity.

Find an area of about thirty-six inches along your floorboard that is clear of furniture. Or just use a clear area in the middle of the room. If you place the zabuton against the wall, leave about six inches of floor where you can place a candle or small lamp if you like. Place the zafu on the zabuton (or place the thicker pillows upon a folded blanket).

Use a timer. When I first began to practice meditation, I set a small timer for ten minutes. In 2020, I often use a free iPhone app called "Insight Timer," though there are many others currently available. The best times to meditate, according to many traditions, are during the four geophysical transitions: dawn, noon, sunset, and midnight. But I find I can enter the various contemplative stages at any time of the day as long as the room is quite dark and there is not much ambient noise. Years ago, I discovered that earplugs are useful to block out any random external noise, and they work quite well, once you get used to inserting them comfortably. They are also great if your companion snores!

Meditative Time Duration

For many months I found it quite difficult to suspend my thoughts in silence for the full ten minutes. Also, I would not practice every day; sometimes weeks would go by, but then I began discovering, or suspecting, various "benefits" of entering the silence. By just focusing within an area (chakra region) and sustaining that state of focus for at least thirty seconds, I would suddenly begin to sense a new, often unexpectedly perceivable sensation within those areas of my body.

Within a few months of beginning to practice, I set a goal to be able to practice for thirty minutes. To my surprise it took a few years before I was able to practice comfortably for up to thirty minutes, but then everyone will progress at a different rate. When we lived in the silent desert community of Abqaiq, Saudi Arabia, I managed to reach sixty-minute sessions now and then, but today I find thirty minutes is fine to "keep me charged," to allow me to connect with the deeper Self, and to practice psychonautic exploration. It is not the time *elapsed* that is most important but the *quality* of one's attention, one's sustained focus, during whatever time period has been set.

Warming Up the Chakras

The skill of supersensible perception initially grows fairly quickly if you are able to direct your attention on various internal regions of your physiology. It helps to be able to visualize these internal regions three-dimensionally, and to this end it is good to spend time looking through the internet or at drawings, sketches, and photographic images commonly found in a wide range of medical textbooks. Through earnest attempts to visualize and to tactically feel these internal physiological regions (the ventricular cavities visualized in the brain within the skull, the heart and its region, and the like) one will eventually begin to feel something new in these regions, a sense of immediate warming, some kind of activation or subtle vibration. In my own practice I have focused on eight of these regions that are known classically as the chakras, and in any one thirty-minute session (or at the beginning, a ten-minute session) I would usually pick only one center to focus upon/within. However, if I am practicing with a mantra, I usually use each syllable of the mantra to focus on a specific chakra briefly, before moving to the next syllable of the mantra and shift my focus to the next physiologically centered chakra.

The physiological basis of "warming up the chakras" can be understood in the same way as biofeedback can be used to make one's fingertips (or the tip of one's nose) warmer. When my son was twelve he entered a science-fair project exploring biofeedback. The objective of the project was to show how one could raise the temperature of a single fingertip by focusing awareness on the area for several minutes. We were both surprised at the results of his project during which we learned that during the first week of daily attempts to raise the fingertip temperature, no change was recorded. However, on about the tenth day my fingertip temperature rose by one and a half degrees Fahrenheit, and on the twelfth day my son's also increased by one degree. After a month of trying every day for about ten minutes, we were both able to increase our fingertip temperature by over two degrees and sometimes by three degrees. The explanation was that through practice (and neruoplasticity), the focus of efferent neurons within an area, say the center of the head, or the throat, or the heart, causes capillaries to expand in diameter which increases the capillary blood flow, increases the "heat" (infrared), and increases the rate of oxygenation and cleaning of the region of focus. This in turn seems to stimulate the afferent neuronal tracts with the effect that you begin to *feel* the region more distinctly as your awareness seems to flow into it and back in a sort of sensory feedback loop. I think, if nothing else, it is a really good way of taking care of internal systems, letting them warm up and relax and operate at a beneficial level.

Repetition of Prayer/Mantra

At times you might want to practice silent prayer or mantra. One way of looking at prayers and mantras is to see them as verbal tools that are used to keep verbal consciousness from wandering into regions of the mind that trigger new streams of thought, and thus distract from going into deeper levels of contemplative psychonautics. For example, the traditional Russian Orthodox practice (known as *hesychia*) is quite often taught as a focus of awareness within an area of the abdomen, a region that is similar to the Japanese *hara* region upon which martial artists focus. *Hesychasts* maintain this focus while repeating a Christian mantra known as the "Jesus Prayer." A contemporary practice among some Roman Catholic groups is to repeat the Aramaic word *maranatha* while maintaining focus within the heart region of the chest.*

Meditation Sequence

The sequence of my own meditation? I usually prepare by finding an interesting metaphysical, psychology, or philosophical book and then, sitting on the zafu (or two pillows in a hotel room), I read for a few minutes from a spiritual text (such as the Holy Bible, the Holy Qur'an, the Psalms, the Bhagavad Gita, the *Philokalia*) or from a book on contemplation or an essay by a monk and occasionally a poem. This acts as a transition from active, everyday cognitive thinking and allows my emotional being to move toward a more spiritual, psychonautic, silent state of awareness. After ten minutes or so of reading, I often smoke a small amount of cannabis (and light a bit of incense). I almost always also have a cup of tea or strong hot coffee within reach, which I occasionally sip, even during the contemplative session. Then I blow out the candle if one was lit. While thinking of people I love and have loved and care and have cared about, those who have died and those still alive, I say a few prayers for several minutes, often repeating ten times while counting on each finger in sequence. In many cultures this is done with

---

*John Main (1926–1982) was a Roman Catholic priest and monk who, during an early assignment to Kuala Lumpur prior to ordination as a priest, was taught the use of a mantra to reach meditative stillness. In 1972 Main returned to England where he began teaching the practice of using a Christian mantra at his monastery in West London.

some form of prayer beads such as the rosary used by Catholics, the "worry beads" used by Muslims, or the 108-bead *malas* used by Hindus and Buddhists. Some of the prayers I recite are Roman Catholic ("Our Father" and "Hail Mary" recited in English, though sometimes in Latin), others are Russian Orthodox or the few Sanskrit mantras I have memorized and work with, or even the single word *maranatha* such as is taught by several Catholic monks, which is Aramaic for "Come, Lord." The prayer period is just a period of transition from normal mental cognition and ideation to the "sitting consciousness" mode. It also brings a sense (and reality) of communion with all our ancestors (and contemporaries) who have ever recited the same sequence of words, whether prayer or mantra, with similar intentions. Frequency vibrations go out into the universe of space-time as well as into the frequency domain (the implicate order), where they call up and resonate with identical intentional vibration patterns. Like tuning in to a reliably good radio station, one's prayer or mantra allows one to join with the vibrant energy of every individual who has ever uttered the same word sequence (the same frequency patterns) either audibly or mentally. Such is the power of collective prayer and chanting (*kirtan* in India). Teilhard de Chardin might say that such prayer repetition leads us to establish a link with the noosphere* during contemplative sessions. We thus tune in to the collective harmonics of all who have gone before and all who are currently consciously alive and chanting or reciting the same words with similar intention, and we quickly begin to feel the power of this collective consciousness in which we are not alone but sustained by a vast community of brothers and sisters, mothers, fathers, and friends.

After five or ten minutes of internally reciting specific prayers or mantras, I select an area of focus (usually one of the traditional chakra regions in the body), while shifting my attention away from any distracting verbal cognitive thoughts or suggestions, and begin to sense the chakra itself in a deeply intentional, physical way. As my normal waking consciousness is located within my head behind my eyes, I usually begin silent meditation by working within the central region of my cranium, focusing on the very deep geometric center of my brain. After a minute or so of settling down,

*See my book *Exploring the Noosphere: Teilhard de Chardin.*

I shift to a focus within the heart region slightly to the left of the center of my chest. I make an effort to shift the center of gravity of awareness to a point in the exact center of my heart region, trying to establish my "sense of touch" there. Long ago I obtained several illustrated textbooks of human physiology, which I often study when trying to gain an interior sense of contact with a particular chakra region in that area of the body. Once focused within a single chakra region, I increase the effort to "let go," to refrain from "remembering" anything else other than sustaining my immediate concentration. I immediately banish any unbidden thoughts or short-term memories of recent activities, doing my best to detach from each distraction as quickly as possible as it begins to arise, in order to sustain a calm, direct, uninterrupted union with that region of physiological space.

Quieting the cognitive mind is surprisingly difficult in the beginning, but eventually one develops the skills and capabilities to "let go" of unbidden thoughts, to detach from them as they arise, no matter how tempting. You can think of it as saving brain "battery power." As less energy is used by the brain-mind to manipulate complex thoughts and retrieve and process memories, this energy seems to accumulate and increase the power behind the one-pointed focus. This can be of great advantage for creativity but the extra energy is also a danger to continued progress in meditation. As one gains skill in quieting the mind and mental "energy reserves" build up, so too does the pressure for newly generated creative ideas to emerge into full-blown thought. The danger here is that if one follows that tempting thought, then the forward progress of sustained meditation is broken, and mental activities, formerly in a state of suspension, suddenly spring into activity to analyze, support, enhance, and dialogue with the new thought, even activating memory storage activities in order to store the thought. It is as if you were traveling in a subway car with your goal being to remain on the train until you reach your faraway destination, but suddenly your subway car pulls into an intermediary station and you notice features that begin to capture your attention. You might become tempted to get off the train to explore this intermediate station, but you would be giving up the opportunity to persevere and remain on the train until you reach your original goal. A phrase from one of Patanjali's *sūtras* (discussed earlier) is apt here: *Abhyāsa-vairāgyābhyāṁ tan-nirodhaḥ*, which tells us that it is through "practice" and "detachment" that one makes progress on stilling the monkey-mind!

At some point in your session as you patiently watch with open attention, new dimensions will slowly unfold to your internal awareness as your sensitivity and skill of tuning into them increases with time and practice. You will begin to experience unusual sensations, sometimes hearing unusually pure sound frequencies, or the distinct sensation of *flow* of some liquid or plasma in various regions of your head, chest, or abdomen. Many of these same symptoms are experienced during the first thirty minutes or so after having ingested a powerful entheogen such as LSD or ayahuasca. You may begin to experience flashes of what feel (or sound) like electrical discharges, a high-pitched electrical crackling sound or sensation in your cranium, just beneath the bone of the skull.

And this is just the beginning!

I hope that my efforts here will encourage readers to undertake a practice of meditation and contemplation either as beginners or with renewed enthusiasm, as I know it will enrich your life and psyche in many ways. I believe your efforts, and all of our efforts, collectively, will work to heal yourself, our collective community of human beings on Earth, and the planet itself.

Notes

PREFACE: HOW I BECAME A PSYCHONAUT AND DISCOVERED TANTRA

1. Lilly, *Programming and Metaprogramming.*
2. Huxley, *Doors of Perception.*
3. Leary, Metzner, and Alpert, *Psychedelic Experience,* 1.

CHAPTER 1. TANTRA: AN INTEGRAL APPROACH TO ESOTERIC PRACTICES

1. Blofeld, *Tantric Mysticism of Tibet,* 42.
2. Fechner, *Elements of Psychophysics,* 27.
3. See Steiner's 1904 book, *Knowledge of the Higher Worlds.*
4. Chaudhuri, *Philosophy of Integralism,* 108.
5. Lilly, *Deep Self,* 100.
6. Lilly, *Mind of the Dolphin,* 78.
7. Lilly, *Mind of the Dolphin,* 101.
8. Lilly, *Mind of the Dolphin,* 266.
9. Lilly, *Mind of the Dolphin,* 268.

CHAPTER 2. WHAT TANTRA IS AND IS NOT

1. Flood, *Tantric Body,* 9.
2. M. Joye, "Philosophy, Practice, and History."
3. Blofeld, *Tantric Mysticism of Tibet,* 113.
4. Garrison, *Tantra of Sex,* 103.
5. *Encyclopedia Britannica Online,* s.v. "Hinduism: Tantric Ritual and Magical Practices."

CHAPTER 3. THE PSYCHOPHYSICS OF THE COSMOS

1. S. R. Joye, "Pribram-Bohm Holoflux Theory of Consciousness."
2. Bohm and Peat, *Science, Order, and Creativity,* 311–12.

3. S. R. Joye, "Pribram–Bohm Holoflux Theory of Consciousness."
4. Laszlo, *Science and the Reenchantment of the Cosmos,* 34–35.
5. Laszlo, *The Self-Actualizing Cosmos,* 44–45.
6. Laszlo, *Science and the Akashic Field,* 67.
7. Whicher, "Nirodha, Yoga Praxis, and the Transformation of the Mind," 67.
8. Whicher, "Nirodha, Yoga Praxis, and the Transformation of the Mind," 67.
9. Taimni, *Man, God and the Universe,* 203.
10. Bohm, *Wholeness and the Implicate Order.*
11. Laszlo, *The Self-Actualizing Cosmos,* 95.
12. Laszlo, *Science and the Reenchantment of the Cosmos,* 34.
13. Laszlo, *The Self-Actualizing Cosmos,* 13–15.
14. Smolin, *Time Reborn,* 123.
15. Laszlo, *Science and the Akashic Field,* 76.
16. Bailey, *Light of the Soul,* 78.
17. Laszlo, *The Self-Actualizing Cosmos,* 95.
18. Laszlo, *Science and the Reenchantment of the Cosmos,* 35.
19. Laszlo, *The Immortal Mind,* 113.
20. Laszlo, *The Immortal Mind.*
21. Schwartz, "Mind Rover: Exploration with Nonlocal Consciousness," 278.
22. Radin, "Journey to Idealism," 36.

CHAPTER 4. ON CHRISTIAN CONTEMPLATION: THAT THEY MAY ALL BE ONE

1. *New Oxford American Dictionary,* 3rd ed. (2010), s.v. "Contemplation."
2. Barnhart, "Christian Self-Understanding," 304.
3. Lilly, *Programming and Metaprogramming,* 27.
4. Lilly, *Deep Self,* 49.
5. Griffiths, *New Vision of Reality,* 252.
6. Griffiths, "Transcending Dualism," in *Vedanta and Christian Faith,* 92.
7. Griffiths, "Transcending Dualism," in *Vedanta and Christian Faith,* 85–89.
8. Panikkar, *Rhythm of Being,* 256.
9. *Atharvaveda-Samhita,* Saunaka recension, I,12.1c: "*Ekam ojas tredhā vicakrame.*" See Hariyappa, *Rigvedic Legends,* 73.
10. Assmann, *Of God and Gods,* 64.
11. Panikkar, *Rhythm of Being,* xviii.
12. Panikkar, *Rhythm of Being,* 256.
13. Barnhart, "Christian Self-Understanding," 292.
14. Barnhart, "Christian Self-Understanding," 296.

15. Barnhart, "Christian Self-Understanding," 305.
16. Barnhart, "Christian Self-Understanding," 306.
17. Barnhart, "Christian Self-Understanding," 303.

CHAPTER 5. PIERRE TEILHARD DE CHARDIN: NOOSPHERE

1. Teilhard, *Activation of Energy,* 383.
2. Teilhard, *Lettres Intimes,* 269.
3. Teilhard, *Heart of Matter,* 179–80.
4. Letter to Christophe Gaudefroy, 11 October 1936, *Lettres Inédites,* 110.
5. de Lubac, *Religion of Teilhard de Chardin*; Henri de Lubac, eventually Cardinal de Lubac, was a Jesuit friend and correspondent of Teilhard's for more than thirty years.
6. Teilhard, *Lettres Intimes,* 269.
7. Teilhard, *Phenomenon of Man,* xix; author's italics for emphasis.
8. Teilhard, *L'Oeuvre scientifique.*
9. Teilhard, *Divine Milieu,* 76–77.
10. Teilhard, "Heart of Matter," 17.
11. Cuénot, *Teilhard de Chardin,* 264–65.
12. Teilhard, "Heart of Matter," 21.
13. Teilhard, "Heart of Matter," 31.
14. King, *Spirit of Fire*, 233–34.
15. Teilhard, "Some Notes," 209.
16. Teilhard, "Some Notes," 83. Note that the Eocene Epoch lasted from 56 to 33.9 million years ago.
17. Teilhard, "Some Notes," 84.
18. Teilhard, *The Vision of the Past,* 78.
19. Morgan, *Emergent Evolution*, 82.
20. Haisch, *Purpose-Guided Universe*, 41.
21. Haisch, *Purpose-Guided Universe,* 44.
22. Leroy, "Teilhard de Chardin," 32.
23. Teilhard, *Letters from a Traveller,* 291.
24. Teilhard, *Human Phenomenon,* 2.
25. Teilhard, *Toward the Future,* 164. Essay referenced was written in 1948.
26. Teilhard, *The Future of Man,* 123. Lecture referenced was delivered in Peking in 1945.
27. Teilhard, *The Future of Man,* 122.
28. Teilhard, *Activation of Energy,* 231. Essay referenced was written in 1950.
29. King, *Pierre Teilhard de Chardin,* 17.

30. King, *Spirit of Fire,* 213.
31. King, *Spirit of Fire,* 213.
32. Teilhard, *Activation of Energy,* 393. Essay referenced was written in 1953.
33. Teilhard, *Activation of Energy,* 361–62.
34. Teilhard, *Activation of Energy,* 393.
35. Teilhard, *Activation of Energy.*
36. Teilhard, "The Spirit of the Earth," 34. Written in the Pacific, March 9, 1931.
37. Teilhard, *Activation of Energy,* 29. Essay referenced was written in 1941.
38. Bohm, *Wholeness and the Implicate Order.*
39. Teilhard, *Human Phenomenon,* 109.
40. Teilhard, *Activation of Energy,* 242.
41. Teilhard, *Activation of Energy,* 121, footnote 10. Essay referenced was written in 1944.
42. Teilhard, *Activation of Energy,* 120.
43. S. R. Joye, *Sub-Quantum Consciousness.*
44. Duffy, *Teilhard's Struggles,* 39.
45. Samson and Pitt, *Biosphere and Noosphere Reader,* 3.
46. Teilhard, *Heart of Matter,* 182. Essay referenced was written in 1918.
47. Teilhard, *Heart of Matter.*
48. King, *Spirit of Fire,* 84.
49. Speaight, *Life of Teilhard de Chardin,* 117.
50. Teilhard, as quoted in Cuénot, *Teilhard de Chardin,* 59.
51. King, *Spirit of Fire,* 84.
52. Bailes, *Science and Russian Culture*; the term *biosphere* had been in use since as early as 1900, popularized by the Austrian geologist Eduard Suess.
53. Vernadsky, *Biosphere,* 16.
54. Aczel, *Jesuit and the Skull,* 86.
55. Teilhard, *The Vision of the Past,* 61. Essay referenced was written in 1923.
56. Teilhard, *The Vision of the Past,* 62.
57. Teilhard, *The Vision of the Past,* 73–78.
58. Teilhard, *Activation of Energy,* 127.
59. Teilhard, as quoted in Cuénot, *Teilhard de Chardin,* 59.
60. Teilhard, *Activation of Energy,* 285. Essay referenced was written in 1951.
61. Teilhard, *Divine Milieu.*
62. Teilhard, *Divine Milieu,* 128–29.
63. Teilhard, *Divine Milieu,* 120.
64. Teilhard, *Christianity and Evolution,* 160.
65. Teilhard, *Divine Milieu,* 128.
66. Speaight, *Life of Teilhard de Chardin,* 135.

67. Allaby and Allaby, *Dictionary of Earth Science,* 72.
68. Malinski, *Chemistry of the Heart,* 61.
69. Radio Ukraine; Berg, *Broadcasting on the Short Waves,* 43.
70. Walker, *Three Mile Island,* 12.
71. McCraty, Deyhle, and Childre, "The Global Coherence Initiative," 75.
72. McCraty, Deyhle, and Childre, "The Global Coherence Initiative," 76.
73. Teilhard, "Sequel to the Problem," 231.
74. Teilhard, *Activation of Energy,* 402. Essay referenced was written in 1955.
75. Teilhard, *Activation of Energy,* 402.
76. de Terra, *Memories of Teilhard de Chardin,* 42.
77. Teilhard, *Activation of Energy,* 402.
78. Teilhard, *Activation of Energy,* 403.
79. Quoted in Robert J. Furey, *The Joy of Kindness* (Chestnut Ridge, N.Y.: Crossroad, 1993).

CHAPTER 6. RUDOLF STEINER: SUPERSENSIBLE PERCEPTION

1. Steiner, *Knowledge of the Higher Worlds,* 1.
2. Steiner, *Evolution of Consciousness,* 33.
3. Steiner, *What Is Anthroposophy?* 262.
4. Steiner, *What Is Anthroposophy?* 262–63.
5. Powell, *Etheric Double,* 4.
6. Powell, *Etheric Double,* 4.
7. Powell, *Etheric Double,* 4.
8. Sir John Woodroffe, *World As Power,* 109.
9. Bloom, *Republic of Plato,* 297.
10. Bloom, *Republic of Plato,* 297.
11. Bloom, *Republic of Plato,* 303.
12. William Blake, from "The Marriage of Heaven and Hell" in *William Blake: The Complete Poems,* edited by Alicia Ostriker. Lawrence, Kans.: Digireads, 2019. Page 108.
13. Steiner, *An Occult Physiology,* 42.
14. Steiner, *An Occult Physiology,*44–45.
15. Silburn, *Kundalini,* 51.
16. Silburn, *Kundalini,*51.
17. Silburn, *Kundalini,*52.
18. Teilhard, *Activation of Energy,* "Atomism of Spirit," 29.
19. Teilhard, footnote 10, *Activation of Energy,* 121.
20. Teilhard, *Activation of Energy,* 120.

21. Steiner, *How to Know Higher Worlds,* 35.
22. Steiner, *Evolution of Consciousness,* 30.

CHAPTER 7. G. I. GURDJIEFF: "REMEMBERING THE I"

1. Gurdjieff, *Beelzebub's Tales,* 38.
2. Pearce, *Biology of Transcendence,* 56.
3. Stuart, Takahashi, and Umezawa, "Mixed-System Brain Dynamics."
4. Jibu and Yasue, *Quantum Brain Dynamics,* 164.
5. As quoted in Wilber, *Holographic Paradigm,* 2.
6. Wilber, *Holographic Paradigm,* 34.
7. Bohm, *Wholeness and the Implicate Order,* 24.
8. Bohm, *Wholeness and the Implicate Order,* 149.

CHAPTER 8. PATAÑJALI: SAMĀDHI AND JÑĀNA YOGA

1. Bojonnes, "Tantra: The Next Wave in Yoga?" par. 21.
2. Whicher, *Integrity of the Yoga Darśana,* 42.
3. Feuerstein, *Philosophy of Classical Yoga,* 117.
4. McFadden, "Synchronous Firing," 23.
5. Pockett, *Nature of Consciousness,* 7.
6. Heile, "Time, Nonduality and Symbolic versus Primary Consciousness."
7. Bohm, *Wholeness and the Implicate Order,* 241.
8. S. R. Joye, *Sub-Quantum Consciousness,* 376.
9. Whicher, *Integrity of the Yoga Darśana,* 5.
10. Zambito, *Unadorned Thread of Yoga,* 10.
11. Bryant, *Yoga Sūtras of Patañjali,* xvii.
12. Gokhale, "Interplay," 109.
13. Whicher, *Integrity of the Yoga Darśana,* 44.
14. Whicher, *Integrity of the Yoga Darśana,* 6.
15. Whicher, *Integrity of the Yoga Darśana,* 204.
16. Bryant, *Yoga Sūtras of Patañjali,* 10.
17. Zambito, *Unadorned Thread of Yoga,* 12.
18. LeLoup, *Being Still,* 108.
19. Ward, *Desert Fathers,* 8.
20. Swami Satchidananda, *Yoga Sūtras of Patañjali,* 15.
21. Swami Satchidananda, *Yoga Sūtras of Patañjali,* 15.
22. Gonda, *History of Ancient Indian Religion,* 251.
23. See Merrell-Wolff, *The Philosophy of Consciousness without an Object.*
24. Eliade, *Yoga: Immortality and Freedom,* 69.

25. Whicher, *Integrity of the Yoga Darśana,* 45.
26. Bryant, *Yoga Sūtras of Patañjali,* 306.
27. Bryant, *Yoga Sūtras of Patañjali,* 306.
28. Gonda, *History of Ancient Indian Religion,* 259.
29. Feuerstein, *Yoga-Sūtra of Patañjali,* 125.
30. Swami Āranya, *Yoga Philosophy of Patañjali,* 350.
31. Zambito, *Unadorned Thread of Yoga,* 253.
32. Taimni, *Science of Yoga,* 431.
33. Kavanaugh, *Collected Works of St. John of the Cross,* 108.
34. Taimni, *Science of Yoga,* 443–44.
35. Heile, "Time, Nonduality and Symbolic versus Primary Consciousness," 5.
36. Heile, "Time, Nonduality and Symbolic versus Primary Consciousness," 10.
37. McFadden, "Conscious Electromagnetic Information," 23.
38. Kuo, *Network Analysis,* 1.
39. Wiener, *Cybernetics,* 202.
40. Wiener, *Cybernetics,* 202.
41. Wiener, *Cybernetics,* 200.
42. Le Cocq, *Radical Thinkers,* 108.

CHAPTER 9. SRI AUROBINDO: THE SUPERMIND

1. Sri Aurobindo, *Upanishads.*
2. Roy, *Sri Aurobindo Came to Me,* 49.
3. Heehs, *Lives of Sri Aurobindo,* 42.
4. Heehs, *Lives of Sri Aurobindo,* 15.
5. Heehs, *Lives of Sri Aurobindo,* 32.
6. Heehs, *Lives of Sri Aurobindo,* 18.
7. Heehs, *Lives of Sri Aurobindo,* 18.
8. Heehs, *Lives of Sri Aurobindo,* 24.
9. Heehs, *Lives of Sri Aurobindo,* 24.
10. Sri Aurobindo, *Tales of Prison Life,* 37.
11. Heehs, *Lives of Sri Aurobindo,* 441.
12. Sri Aurobindo, *Upanishads.*
13. Sri Aurobindo, *Upanishads,* 1.
14. Sri Aurobindo, *Upanishads,* 1.
15. Sri Aurobindo, *Upanishads,* 2.
16. Sri Aurobindo, *Upanishads,* 2.
17. Sri Aurobindo, *Upanishads,* 4.
18. Sri Aurobindo, *Upanishads,* 3.

19. Sri Aurobindo, *Upanishads,* 3.
20. Sri Aurobindo, *Upanishads,* 5.
21. Sri Aurobindo, *Upanishads,* 5.
22. Sri Aurobindo, *Upanishads,* 5.
23. Sri Aurobindo, *Upanishads,* 44.
24. Sri Aurobindo, *Upanishads,* 5.
25. Sri Aurobindo, *Upanishads,* 6.
26. Sri Aurobindo, *Upanishads,* 6.
27. Sri Aurobindo, *Upanishads,* 7.
28. Sri Aurobindo, *Upanishads,* 7.
29. Sri Aurobindo, *Upanishads,* 7.
30. Sri Aurobindo, *Upanishads,* 9.
31. Sri Aurobindo, *Upanishads,* 9.
32. Sri Aurobindo, *Upanishads,* 10.
33. Sri Aurobindo, *Upanishads,* 10.
34. Sri Aurobindo, *Upanishads,* 10.
35. Sri Aurobindo, *Upanishads,* 11.
36. Sri Aurobindo, *Upanishads,* 11.
37. Sri Aurobindo, *Upanishads,* 11, (italics added).
38. Sri Aurobindo, *Upanishads,* 12.
39. Sri Aurobindo, *Upanishads,* 12.
40. Sri Aurobindo, *Upanishads,* 12–13.
41. Sri Aurobindo, *Upanishads,* 13.
42. Sri Aurobindo, *Upanishads,* 13.
43. Sri Aurobindo, *Upanishads,* 11.
44. Sri Aurobindo, *Upanishads,* 14.
45. Sri Aurobindo, *The Synthesis of Yoga,* 392.
46. Sri Aurobindo, *Upanishads,* 14.
47. Sri Aurobindo, *Life Divine,* 623.
48. Sri Aurobindo, *Upanishads,* 15.
49. Merrell-Wolf, *Consciousness without an Object.*
50. Eliot, *The Four Quartets*, 17.
51. Sri Aurobindo, *Upanishads,* 16.
52. Sri Aurobindo, *Upanishads,* 22.
53. Sri Aurobindo, *Upanishads,* 24.
54. Sri Aurobindo, *Upanishads,* 26.
55. Sri Aurobindo, *Upanishads,* 28.
56. Sri Aurobindo, *Upanishads,* 31.
57. Sri Aurobindo, *Upanishads,* 45.

58. Sri Aurobindo, *Upanishads,* 39.
59. Sri Aurobindo, *Upanishads,* 42.
60. Sri Aurobindo, *Upanishads,* 47.
61. Bailey, *Study of Hinduism,* 139.
62. Sri Aurobindo, *Upanishads,* 48.
63. Joye, "Pribram-Bohm Holoflux Theory of Consciousness," 196.
64. Joye, "Pribram-Bohm Holoflux Theory of Consciousness," 271.
65. Bohm, *Wholeness and the Implicate Order,* 172.
66. Fox, *Coming of the Cosmic Christ,* 34.
67. Sri Aurobindo, *Life Divine,* 244.
68. Sri Aurobindo, *Synthesis of Yoga,* 827.
69. Fox, *Coming of the Cosmic Christ,* 37.
70. Joye, *Little Book of the Holy Trinity,* 24.

CHAPTER 10. FURTHER TECHNIQUES OF HINDU PSYCHOPHYSICS

1. Pandit, *Studies in the Tantras and the Veda,* 6–7.
2. Gonda, *History of Ancient Indian Religion,* 251.
3. Taimni, *Gayatri,* 24.
4. Khanna, *Yantra,* 11.
5. Khanna, *Yantra,* 110.
6. Pandit, *Lights on the Tantra,* 15.
7. Rele, *Mysterious Kundalini,* 29.
8. Rele, *Mysterious Kundalini,* 29.
9. Rele, *Mysterious Kundalini,* 50.
10. Rele, *Mysterious Kundalini,* 34.
11. Rele, *Mysterious Kundalini,* 37.
12. Woodroffe, foreword, ix.
13. Woodroffe, foreword, ix.
14. Woodroffe, foreword, xxi.
15. Rele, *Mysterious Kundalini,* 2.
16. Rele, *Mysterious Kundalini,* 5.
17. Rele, *Mysterious Kundalini,* 12.
18. Rele, *Mysterious Kundalini,* 15.
19. Rele, *Mysterious Kundalini,* 17.
20. Rele, *Mysterious Kundalini,* 22.
21. Rele, *Mysterious Kundalini,* 25.
22. Rele, *Mysterious Kundalini,* 25.

23. Rele, *Mysterious Kundalini,* 27.
24. Rele, *Mysterious Kundalini,* 56.
25. Rele, *Mysterious Kundalini,* 79.
26. Rele, *Mysterious Kundalini,* 83.
27. Rele, *Mysterious Kundalini,* 84.
28. Dyczkowski, *Doctrine of Vibration,* 8.
29. Mukharji, introduction, 18.
30. Anderson, "Do Vibrations Help Us Smell?"
31. Yirka, "New Study," par. 1.
32. Pockett, *Nature of Consciousness,* 7.
33. Swami Lokeswarananda, *Taittiriya Upanishad,* 78.
34. Taimni, *Self-Culture,* 21.
35. Jinarajadasa, *Hidden Work of Nature,* 108.
36. Dyczkowski, *Journey in the World,* 91.

CHAPTER 11. FOUNDATIONS OF TIBETAN TANTRIC PSYCHOPHYSICS

1. Bagchi, "Evolution of the Tantras," 219.

CHAPTER 12. THE TEACHINGS OF DÜDJOM LINGPA: TIBETAN VAJRAYĀNA

1. Wallace, *Fathoming the Mind,* 1.
2. Vig, "Yoga Market by Type."
3. Düdjom Lingpa, *Heart of the Great Perfection,* 145.
4. Wallace, *Fathoming the Mind,* 8–9.
5. Wallace, introduction," 18.
6. Düdjom Lingpa, *Heart of the Great Perfection,* 142.
7. Wittgenstein, *Tractatus Logico-Philosophicus,* 1922.

CHAPTER 13. FURTHER TECHNIQUES OF TIBETAN PSYCHOPHYSICS

1. Dzongsar, "The Wheel of Life," 3.
2. Dzongsar, "The Wheel of Life," 2.
3. Pandit, *Lights on the Tantra,* 15.
4. Rele, *Mysterious Kundalini,* 29.
5. Gonda, *History of Ancient Indian Religion,* 259.
6. I. K. Taimni, *Gayatri,* 24.
7. Dzogchen Ponlop Rinpoche, *Mind Beyond Death,* 190.

8. Michael, *The Price of a Remarkable Destiny,* 254.
9. Michael, *The Price of a Remarkable Destiny,* 254.
10. Mishra, *The Textbook of Yoga Psychology,* 142.
11. Feuerstein, *Tantra: The Path of Ecstasy,* 156.
12. Singh, *Naam or Word,* 77.
13. Blofeld, *The Tantric Mysticism of Tibet,* 131.

CHAPTER 14. MAPPING THE PSYCHE FOR DIRECT EXPLORATION

1. Hoffman, *Case against Reality,* 78.
2. Hoffman, *Case against Reality,* 198.
3. Hoffman, *Case against Reality* 199.
4. Hoffman, *Case against Reality* 199.
5. Heile, "Time, Nonduality, and Symbolic versus Primary Consciousness," slide 10.
6. Zambito, *Unadorned Thread of Yoga,* 413.
7. Franz, "Process of Individuation," 163.
8. Pearce, *Biology of Transcendence,* 57.
9. Pine, *Heart Sutra,* 11.
10. HeartMath Institute, "Energetic Communication," par. 2.
11. Wikipedia, s.v. "Magnetoception."
12. Sabine Begall et al., "Magnetic Alignment in Grazing and Resting Cattle and Deer." *PNAS* 105, no. 36 (September 2008): 13451–55.
13. Wiltschko and Wiltschko, "Magnetoreception in Birds and Other Animals," 675.
14. Ruhenstroth-Bauer, "Influence of the Earth's Magnetic Field," 335.
15. Romanes, *Cunningham's Textbook of Anatomy,* 51.
16. Romanes, *Cunningham's Textbook of Anatomy,* 21.
17. Lu K'uan Yu, *Taoist Yoga,* 4–5.
18. Jaynes, *Origin of Consciousness.*
19. Sher, "Neuroimaging."
20. Teilhard de Chardin, *Man's Place in Nature,* 186.
201. Persinger, *Space-Time Transients and Unusual Events,* 49.
22. Persinger and Booth, "Discrete Shifts," 281.
23. Fechner, *Religion of a Scientist,* 309.
24. Jibu and Yasue, *Quantum Brain Dynamics,* 72.
25. Jibu and Yasue, *Quantum Brain Dynamics,* 164.
26. Chen, *Introduction to Plasma Physics,* 1.

27. Jibu and Yasue, *Quantum Brain Dynamics,* 83.
28. Reninger, "Amazing Pineal Gland."
29. Hariharananda, *Kriya Yoga,* 108.
30. A. Bailey, *Light of the Soul,* 275.
31. Sheldrake, *Morphic Resonance*, 14.

CHAPTER 15. MY PERSONAL EXPERIENCE OF MEDITATION AND CONTEMPLATION

1. Cunningham and Egan. *Christian Spirituality,* 88.
2. Wood and Brunton, *Practical Yoga, Ancient and Modern.*
3. Taimni, *The Science of Yoga.*

Bibliography

Aczel, Amir D. *The Jesuit and the Skull: Teilhard de Chardin, Evolution, and the Search for Peking Man*. New York: Riverhead Books, 2007.

Adelman, George, ed. *Encyclopedia of Neuroscience*. vol. 1. Boston: Birkhäuser Boston, 1987.

Allaby, Michael, and Ailisa Allaby, eds. *A Dictionary of Earth Sciences*. 2nd ed. New York: Oxford University, 1999.

Anderson, Mark. "Do Vibrations Help Us Smell?" *Scientific American,* April 1, 2013.

Assmann, Jan. *Of God and Gods: Egypt, Israel, and the Rise of Monotheism*. Madison: University of Wisconsin Press, 2008.

Aurobindo, Sri. *Hymns to the Mystic Fire*. Pondicherry: Sri Aurobindo Ashram, 1972.

———. *The Life Divine*. *Arya* (1914–1920). Pondicherry: Sri Aurobindo Ashram Trust, 1990.

———. *Sri Aurobindo on the Tantra*. 3rd ed. Pondicherry: Dipti, 1972.

———. *The Synthesis of Yoga*. Pondicherry: Sri Aurobindo International University Centre, 1955.

———. *Tales of Prison Life*. Pondicherry: Sri Aurobindo Ashram, 1997.

———. *The Upanishads: Texts, Translations and Commentaries*. Pondicherry: Sri Aurobindo Ashram, 1972.

Bagchi, P. C. "Evolution of the Tantras." In *The Cultural Heritage of India,* vol. IV, edited by Haridas Bhattacharyya. Calcutta: The Ramakrishna Mission Institute of Culture, 1937.

Bailes, K. E. *Science and Russian Culture in an Age of Revolutions: V.I. Venadsky and His Scientific School, 1863–1945*. Bloomington: Indiana University Press, 1990.

Bailey, Alice A. *Light of the Soul: A Paraphrase of the Yoga Sūtras of Patañjali*. New York: Lucis Publishing, 1927.

Bailey, Gregory. *The Study of Hinduism*. Columbia: The University of South Carolina Press, 2003.

Barbour, Ian. *When Science Meets Religion*. San Francisco: Harper, 2000.

Barnhart, Bruno. "Christian Self-Understanding in the Light of the East." In *Purity of Heart and Contemplation: A Monastic Dialogue Between Christian and Asian Traditions*, edited by Bruno Barnhart and Joseph Wong, 291–308. New York: Camaldolese Hermits of America, 2001.

Berg, Jerome S. *Broadcasting on the Short Waves, 1945 to Today*. London: McFarland & Company, 2008.

Blake, William. *William Blake: The Complete Poems*, edited by Alicia Ostriker. Lawrence, Kans.: Digireads, 2019.

Blofeld, John. *Tantric Mysticism of Tibet: A Practical Guide to the Theory, Purpose, and Techniques of Tantric Meditation*. Boston: E. P. Dutton, 1970.

Bloom, Allan. *The Republic of Plato: Translated with Notes and an Interpretive Essay*. 2nd ed. New York: Harper Collins, 1968.

Bohm, David. *Wholeness and the Implicate Order*. London: Routledge, 1980.

———. "Hidden Variables and the Implicate Order." In *Quantum Implications: Essays in Honour of David Bohm*, edited by B. J. Hiley and F. David Peat, 33–45. London: Routledge, 1987.

Bohm, David, and Basil J. Hiley. *The Undivided Universe: An Ontological Interpretation of Quantum Theory*. London: Routledge, 1993.

Bohm, David, and F. David Peat. *Science, Order, and Creativity*. London: Routledge, 1987.

Bojonnes, Ramesh. "Tantra: The Next Wave in Yoga?" *Embodied Philosophy*, August 27, 2017.

Bryant, Edwin F. *The Yoga Sūtras of Patañjali: A New Edition, Translation, and Commentary with Insights from Traditional Commentators*. New York: North Point Press, 2009.

Chaudhuri, H. *Philosophy of Integralism*. Pondicherry: Sri Aurobindo Pathamandir, 1954.

Chen, Frances F. *Introduction to Plasma Physics and Controlled Fusion*. vol 1, *Plasma Physics*. 2nd ed. New York: Springer, 2006.

Cuénot, Claude. *Teilhard de Chardin: A Biographical Study*. London: Burnes & Oates, 1965.

Cunningham, Lawrence S., and Keith J. Egan. *Christian Spirituality: Themes from the Tradition*. Mahwah, N.J.: Paulist Press, 1996.

de Lubac, Henri. *The Religion of Teilhard de Chardin*. Translated by René Hague. New York: Desclée, 1967.

de Terra, Helmut. *Memories of Teilhard de Chardin*. New York: Harper & Row, 1964.

Düdjom Lingpa. *Heart of the Great Perfection*. Vol. I of *Düdjom Lingpa's Visions of the Great Perfection.* 3 vols. Foreword by Sogyal Rinpoche. Translated by B. Alan Wallace. Somerville, Mass.: Wisdom Publications, 2015.

Duffy, Kathleen. *Teilhard's Struggles: Embracing the Work of Evolution.* Maryknoll, N.Y.: Orbis Books.

Dyczkowski, Mark S. G. *A Journey in the World of the Tantras.* India: Indica Books, 2004.

Dzogchen Ponlop Rinpoche, *Mind beyond Death.* Ithaca, N.Y.: Snow Lion, 2008.

Dzongsar Jamyang Khyentse Rinpoche. "The Wheel of Life." *Gentle Voice: A Newsletter of Siddhartha's Intent,* April 2005.

Eliade, Mircea. *Yoga: Immortality and Freedom.* Princeton: Princeton University Press, 1954.

Eliot, Thomas Stearns. *Four Quartets.* New York: Harcourt Brace, 1943.

Fechner, Gustav. *Elements of Psychophysics.* Translated by Helmut E. Adler. New York: Holt, Rinehart, and Winston, 1966.

———. *Religion of a Scientist: Selections from Gustav Theodor Fechner.* Edited by W. Lowrie. New York: Pantheon, 1946.

Feuerstein, Georg. *The Philosophy of Classical Yoga.* Manchester: Manchester University Press, 1980.

———. *Tantra: The Path of Ecstasy.* Boston: Shambhala Publications, 1998.

———. *The Yoga-Sūtras of Patañjali: A New Translation and Commentary.* Vermont: Inner Traditions, 1989.

Feynman, Richard, Robert Leighton, and Matthew Sands. *The Feynman Lectures on Physics.* vol. 1. Boston: Addison-Wesley, 1964.

Flood, Gavin. *The Tantric Body: The Secret Tradition of Hindu Religions.* London: I. B. Tauris, 2006.

Fox, Matthew. *The Coming of the Cosmic Christ.* New York: Harper One, 1988.

Franz, M.-L. "The Process of Individuation." In *Man and His Symbols,* edited by C. G. Jung and M.-L. Franz, 158–229. New York: Random House, 1964.

Garrison, Omar. *Tantra: The Yoga of Sex.* Hong Kong: Causeway Books, 1964.

Glazewski, Andrew. *Harmony of the Universe: The Science behind Healing, Prayer, and Spiritual Development.* UK: White Crow Books, 2014.

Gokhale, Pradeep P. "Interplay of *Sāṅkhya* and Buddhist Ideas in the Yoga of Patañjali," in *Journal of Buddhist Studies* 12 (Sri Lanka and Hong Kong) (2014–15): 107–22

Gonda, J. *History of Ancient Indian Religion.* Vol. 4, *Selected Studies.* Leiden: E. J. Brill, 1975.

Griffiths, Bede. *A New Vision of Reality: Western Science, Eastern Mysticism, and Christian Faith.* Springfield, Ill.: Templegate Publishing, 1990.

———. *Vedanta and Christian Faith*. 2nd ed. Middletown, Calif.: Dawn Horse Press, 1991.

Gurdjieff, G. I. *Beelzebub's Tales to His Grandson or An Objectively Impartial Criticism of the Life of Man*. New York: Harcourt, 1950.

Haisch, Bernard. *The Purpose-Guided Universe: Believing in Einstein, Darwin, and God*. Wayne, N.J.: Career, 2010.

Hariharānanda, P. *Kriya Yoga: The Scientific Process of Soul Culture and the Essence of All Religion*. Delhi: Motilal Banarsidass, 2006.

Hariyappa, H. L. *Rigvedic Legends through the Ages*. Bombay: Mysore University, 1953.

HeartMath Institute. "Energetic Communication." Chapter 6 of *Science of the Heart: Exploring the Role of the Heart in Human Performance*. HeartMath Institute.

Heehs, Peter. *The Lives of Sri Aurobindo*. New York: Columbia University Press, 2008.

Heile, Frank. "Time, Nonduality and Symbolic versus Primary Consciousness." Lecture presented at the Science and Nonduality Conference, San Rafael, California, October 2011.

Hoffman, Donald. *The Case against Reality: Why Evolution Hid the Truth from Our Eyes*. New York: W. W. Norton, 2019.

Huxley, Aldous. *The Doors of Perception*. New York: Harper & Brothers, 1954.

Jaynes, Julian. *The Origin of Consciousness in the Breakdown of the Bicameral Mind*. Boston: Houghton Mifflin, 1990.

Jibu, Mari, and Kunio Yasue. *Quantum Brain Dynamics and Consciousness*. Philadelphia: John Benjamins, 1995.

Jinarajadasa, C. *The Hidden Work of Nature*. Whitefish, Mont.: Kessinger Publishing, 2010.

Jones, Roger S. *Physics for the Rest of Us: Ten Basic Ideas of Twentieth-Century Physics that Everyone Should Know . . . and How They Have Shaped Our Culture and Consciousness*. New York: Barnes and Noble, 1999.

Joye, Michael R. "The Philosophy, Practice, and History of Tantra in India." Master's thesis, California Institute of Asian Studies, 1978. ProQuest (1311340).

Joye, Shelli R. *Developing Supersensible Perception: Knowledge of the Higher Worlds through Entheogens, Prayer, and Nondual Awareness*. Rochester, Vt.: Inner Traditions, 2019.

———. *The Electromagnetic Brain: EM Theories on the Nature of Consciousness*. Rochester, Vt.: Inner Traditions, 2020.

———. *The Little Book of Consciousness: Holonomic Brain Theory and the Implicate Order.* Viola, Calif.: The Viola Institute, 2017.

———. *The Little Book of the Holy Trinity: A New Approach to Christianity, Indian Philosophy, and Quantum Physics.* Viola, Calif.: The Viola Institute, 2017.

———. "The Pribram-Bohm Holoflux Theory of Consciousness: An Integral Interpretation of the Theories of Karl Pribram, David Bohm, and Pierre Teilhard de Chardin." PhD diss., California Institute of Integral Studies, 2016. ProQuest (10117892).

———. "The Pribram–Bohm Hypothesis." *Consciousness: Ideas and Research for the Twenty-First Century* 3, no. 3 (2016): article 1.

———. *Sri Aurobindo: Quantum Physics and Consciousness.* Viola, Calif.: The Viola Institute, 2018.

———. *Sub-Quantum Consciousness: A Geometry of Consciousness Based Upon the Work of Karl Pribram, David Bohm, and Pierre Teilhard De Chardin.* Viola, Calif.: The Viola Institute, 2019.

———. *Teilhard's Hyperphysics: Energy and the Noosphere.* Viola, Calif.: The Viola Institute, 2020.

———. *Tuning the Mind: The Geometries of Consciousness.* Viola, Calif.: The Viola Institute, 2017.

Jung, C. G. "The Structure and Dynamics of the Psyche," in *The Collected Works of C.G. Jung*, vol. 8, and "The Archetypes and the Collective Unconscious," in *The Collected Works of C.G. Jung*, vol. 9. Translated by R. F. C. Hull. Princeton: Princeton University Press, 1960.

Jung, C. G., and M.-L. Franz, eds. *Man and His Symbols.* New York: Random House, 1964.

Kavanaugh, K., trans. *Collected Works of St. John of the Cross.* Washington, DC: Institute of Carmelite Studies, 1991.

Khanna, Madhu. *Yantra: The Tantric Symbol of Cosmic Unity.* London: Thames & Hudson, 1979.

King, Ursula. *Pierre Teilhard de Chardin: Writings Selected with an Introduction by Ursula King.* New York: Orbis Books, 1999.

———. *Spirit of Fire: The Life and Vision of Teilhard de Chardin.* New York: Orbis Books, 1996.

Kyczkowski, Mark S. G. *The Doctrine of Vibration: An Analysis of the Doctrines and Practices of Kashmir Shaivism.* Albany: State University of New York Press, 1987.

Kuo, F. *Network Analysis and Synthesis.* New Jersey: Bell Telephone Labs, Inc., 1962.

Le Cocq, Rhoda P. *The Radical Thinkers: Heidegger and Sri Aurobindo.* Pondicherry: Sri Aurobindo Ashram Press, 1969.

Laszlo, Ervin. *Science and the Reenchantment of the Cosmos: The Rise of the Integral Vision of Reality.* Rochester, Vt.: Inner Traditions, 2006.

———. *Science and the Akashic Field: An Integral Theory of Everything.* Rochester, Vt.: Inner Traditions, 2007.

———. *The Immortal Mind: Science and the Continuity of Consciousness beyond the Brain.* Rochester, Vt.: Inner Traditions, 2014.

———. *The Self-Actualizing Cosmos: The Akasha Revolution in Science and Human Consciousness.* Rochester, Vt.: Inner Traditions, 2014.

Leary, Timothy, Ralph Metzner, and Richard Alpert. *The Psychedelic Experience: A Manual Based Upon the Tibetan Book of the Dead.* New York: University Books, 1964.

LeLoup, Jean-Yves. *Being Still: Reflections on an Ancient Mystical Tradition.* Translated and edited by M. S. Laird. Mahwah, N.J.: Paulist Press, 2003.

Leroy, Pierre. "Teilhard de Chardin: The Man." Introduction to *The Divine Milieu,* by Teilhard de Chardin, 13–42. New York: Harper & Row, 1960.

Lindorff, D. *Pauli and Jung: The Meeting of Two Great* Minds. Wheaton, Ill.: Quest Books, 2004.

Lilly, John. *The Deep Self: Consciousness Exploration in the Isolation Tank.* New York: Simon & Schuster, 1977.

———. *The Mind of the Dolphin: A Nonhuman Intelligence.* New York: Doubleday, 1967.

———. *Programming and Metaprogramming in the Human Biocomputer: Theory and Experiments.* New York: The Julian Press, 1972.

Lu K'uan Yu. *Taoist Yoga: Alchemy & Immortality.* Boston: Weiser Books, 1973.

Malinski, Tadeusz. *Chemistry of the Heart.* Athens: Ohio University Biochemistry Research Laboratory, 1960.

McCraty, Rollin, Annette Deyhle, and Doc Childre. "The Global Coherence Initiative: Creating a Coherent Planetary Standing Wave." *Global Advances in Health and Medicine* 1, no. 1 (2012): 64–77.

McFadden, Johnjoe. "The Conscious Electromagnetic Information (CEMI) Field Theory: The Hard Problem Made Easy." In *Journal of Consciousness Studies* 9, no. 8 (2002): 45–60.

———. "Synchronous Firing and Its Influence on the Brain's Electromagnetic Field: Evidence for an Electromagnetic Field Theory of Consciousness," *Journal of Consciousness Studies* 9, no. 4 (2002): 23.

McKenna, Terence. *True Hallucinations: Being an Account of the Author's Extraordinary Adventures in the Devil's Paradise.* New York: HarperCollins, 1993.

Merrell-Wolff, Franklin. *The Philosophy of Consciousness without an Object*. New York: Julian Press, 1973.

Michael, Edward Salim. *The Price of a Remarkable Destiny: The Life and Spiritual Journey of Edward Salim Michael*. Livermore, Calif.: Michele Michael, 2015.

Mishra, Rammurti. *The Textbook of Yoga Psychology: A New Translation and Interpretation of Patanjali's Yoga Sūtras for Meaningful Application in All Modern Psychologic Disciplines*. New York: Julian Press, 1971.

Morgan, Conway Lloyd. *Emergent Evolution: Gifford Lectures, 1921–22*. New York: Simon & Schuster, 1978.

Mukharji, P. B. "Introduction." In Swami Pratyagatmananda Saraswati, *Japasutram: The Science of Creative Sound*. Madras: Ganesh & Co., 1971.

Nagel, Thomas. 1974. "What Is It Like to be a Bat?" *Philosophical Review* 83:435–51.

Netter, F. H. *The CIBA Collection of Medical Illustrations, Vol. I: The Nervous System*. Summit, N.J.: CIBA, 1972.

Panikkar, Raimon. *The Rhythm of Being*. The Gifford Lectures. New York: Orbis Books, 2010.

Pandit, M. P. *Lights on the Tantra*. Madras: Ganesh & Co., 1957.

———. *Studies in the Tantras and the Veda*. Madras: Ganesh & Co., 1973.

Parker, R. C. "The Use of Entheogens in the Vajrayāna Tradition: A Brief Summary of Preliminary Findings Together with a Partial Bibliography." Vajrayāna.faithweb.com, 2007.

Pearce, J. C. *The Biology of Transcendence*. Rochester, Vt.: Park Street Press, 2002.

Penrose, Sir Roger. *The Emperor's New Mind: Concerning Computers, Minds and the Laws of Physics*. Oxford: Oxford University Press, 1989.

Persinger, Michael. *Space-Time Transients and Unusual Events*. Chicago: Nelson-Hall, 1977.

Persinger, M., and J. N. Booth. "Discrete Shifts within the Theta Band between the Frontal and Parietal Regions of the Right Hemisphere and the Experience of a Sensed Presence." *Journal of Neuropsychiatry* 21, no. 3 (2005): 279–83.

Pine, R. *The Heart Sutra*. Berkeley, Calif.: Counterpoint, 2004.

Pockett, Susan. *The Nature of Consciousness: A Hypothesis*. Lincoln, Neb.: Writers Press, 2000.

Powell, A. E. *The Etheric Double*. Madras: The Theosophical Publishing House, 1925.

Radin, Dean. "Journey to Idealism." In *Is Consciousness Primary?* Battle Ground, Wash.: The Academy for the Advancement of Postmaterialist Sciences, 2020.

Rele, Vasant. *The Mysterious Kundalini: The Physical Basis of the 'Kundalini Yoga.'* Bombay: D. B. Taraporevala Sons & Co., 1927.

Reninger, Elizabeth. "The Amazing Pineal Gland." About.com, March 27, 2008. Page no longer accessible.

Romanes, G. J., ed. *Cunningham's Textbook of Anatomy.* 10th ed. London: Oxford Press, 1964.

Roy, Dilip Kumar. *Sri Aurobindo Came to Me.* Pondicherry: Sri Aurobindo Ashram Trust, 1952.

Ruhenstroth-Bauer, G. "Influence of the Earth's Magnetic Field on Resting and Activated EEG Mapping in Normal Subjects." *International Journal of Neuroscience* 73, no. 3–4 (June 1993): 331–49.

Samson, Paul R., and David Pitt, eds. *The Biosphere and Noosphere Reader: Global Environment, Society and Change.* New York: Routledge, 1999.

Schwartz, Stephan. "Mind Rover: Exploration with Nonlocal Consciousness." In *Is Consciousness Primary?* Battle Ground, Wash.: The Academy for the Advancement of Postmaterialist Sciences, 2020.

Shannon, C. E. "A Mathematical Theory of Communication." *Bell System Technical Journal*, no. 27 (July 1948): 623–56.

Sheldrake, Rupert. *Morphic Resonance: The Hypothesis of Formative Causation.* London: Blond & Briggs, 1981.

Sher, Leo. "Neuroimaging, Auditory Hallucinations, and the Bicameral Mind." *Journal of Psychiatry & Neuroscience* 25, no. 3 (2000): 239–40.

Silburn, Lilian. *Kundalini: Energy of the Depths.* Albany: State University of New York Press, 1988.

Singh, Kirpal. *Naam or Word.* Franklin, N.H.: Sat Sandesh Books, 1972.

Smolin, Lee. *Time Reborn.* London: Penguin Books, 2013.

Speaight, Robert. *The Life of Teilhard de Chardin.* New York: Harper & Row, 1967.

Stapledon, Olaf. *Last and First Men* and *Star Maker.* New York: Dover, 1968.

Stapp, H. P. *The Mindful Universe: Quantum Mechanics and The Participating Observer.* New York: Springer, 2007.

Steiner, Rudolf. *The Evolution of Consciousness as Revealed through Initiation-Knowledge: Thirteen Lectures Given at Penmaenmawr, North Wales 19th to 31st August, 1923.* Translated by V. E. W. and C. D., 2nd ed. Great Britain: Rudolph Steiner Press, 1966.

———. *How to Know Higher Worlds: A Modern Path of Initiation.* Translated by Christopher Bamford. Hudson, N.Y.: Anthroposophic Press, 1994.

———. *Knowledge of the Higher Worlds and Its Attainment.* Translated by George Metaxa, 3rd ed. Hudson, N.Y.: Anthroposophic Press, 1947.

———. *An Occult Physiology: Eight Lectures by Rudolf Steiner, Given in Prague, 20th to 28th March, 1911.* 2nd ed. London: Rudolf Steiner Publishing, 1951.
———. *An Outline of Esoteric Science.* Translated by Catherine E. Creeger. Hudson, N.Y.: Anthroposophic Press, 1997. First published in 1909.
———. *What Is Anthroposophy? Three Perspectives on Self-Knowledge.* Edited by Christopher Bamford. Hudson, N.Y.: Anthroposophic Press, 2002.
Stuart, C. I. J. M., Y. Takahashi, and H. Umezawa. "Mixed-System Brain Dynamics: Neural Memory As a Macroscopic Ordered State." *Foundations of Physics* 9, no. 3–4 (1979): 301–27.
Susskind, Leonard. *The Black Hole War: My Battle with Stephen Hawking to Make the World Safe for Quantum Mechanics.* New York: Little, Brown and Company, 2008.
Swami Hariharānanda Āranya. *Yoga Philosophy of Patañjali.* Translated by P. N. Mukerji. Albany: State University of New York Press, 1983.
Swami Lokeswarananda. *Taittiriya Upanishad: Translated and with Notes Based On Sankara's Commentary.* Calcultta: Ramakrishna Mission Institute of Culture, 2010.
Swami Satchidananda, trans. *The Yoga Sūtras of Patañjali.* Yogaville, Va.: Integral Yoga Publications, 1990.
Taimni, I. K. *Gayatri: The Daily Religious Practice of the Hindus.* Wheaton, Ill: Quest Books, 1989.
———. *Man, God and the Universe.* Madras, India: The Theosophical Society, 1969.
———. *The Science of Yoga.* Madras, India: The Theosophical Publishing House, 1961.
———. *Self-Culture: The Problem of Self-Discovery and Self-Realization in the Light of Occultism.* Madras, India: The Theosophical Publishing House, 1945.
Teilhard de Chardin, Pierre. *Activation of Energy.* Translated by René Hague. London: William Collins Sons, 1976.
———. *Christianity and Evolution: Reflections on Science and Religion.* Translated by René Hague. London: William Collins Sons, 1971.
———. 1960. *The Divine Milieu.* New York: Harper & Row.
———. *The Future of Man.* Translated by Norman Denny. New York: Harper & Row, 1959.
———. *The Heart of Matter.* Translated by René Hague. New York: Harcourt Brace Jovanovich, 1978.
———. *The Human Phenomenon.* Translated and edited by Sarah Appleton-Weber. Portland, Oreg.: Sussex Academic, 2003.

———. *Letters from a Traveller.* New York: Harper & Row, 1962.

———. *Lettres Intimes de Teilhard de Chardin a Auguste Valensin, Bruno de Solages, et Henri de Lubac 1919–1955.* Paris: Aubier Montaigne, 1972.

———. *Man's Place in Nature: The Human Zoological Group.* Translated by René Hague. New York: Harper & Row, 1956.

———. *The Phenomenon of Man.* Translated by Bernard Wall. New York: Harper & Row, 1959.

———. *Pierre Teilhard de Chardin: L'Oeuvre scientifique.* Edited by Nicole and Karl Schmitz-Moormann. 10 vols. Munich: Walter-Verlag, 1971.

———. "The Spirit of the Earth." In *Human Energy,* translated by J. M. Cohen, 93–112. New York: Harcourt Brace Jovanovitch, 1969.

———. *Toward the Future.* Translated by René Hague. London: William Collins Sons, 1975.

———. *The Vision of the Past.* Translated by J. M. Cohen. New York: Harper & Row, 1966.

———. *Toward the Future.* Translated by René Hague. London: William Collins Sons, 1975.

Tiller, William. *Science and Human Transformation.* Berkeley, Calif.: Pavior, 1997.

Vernadsky, Vladimir I. *The Biosphere.* Translated by D. B. Langmuir. New York: Springer-Verlag, 1998.

Vig, Himanshu, and Roshan Deshmukh. "Yoga Market by Type: Global Opportunity Analysis and Industry Forecast, 2021–2027." Allied Market Research website, September 2020.

Walker, J. Samuel. *Three Mile Island: A Nuclear Crisis in Historical Perspective.* Berkeley, Calif.: University of California Press, 2004.

Wallace, B. Alan. *Fathoming the Mind: Inquiry and Insight in Düdjom Lingpa's Vajra Essence.* Somerville, Mass.: Widsom Publications, 2018.

———. Introduction to *Heart of the Great Perfection,* by Düdjom Lingpa, translated by A. B. Wallace, 1–26. Somerville, Mass.: Wisdom Publications, 2015.

Ward, Benedicta, ed. *The Desert Fathers: Sayings of the Early Christian Monks.* London: Penguin Books, 2003.

Whicher, Ian. *The Integrity of the Yoga Darśana: A Reconsideration of Classical Yoga.* Albany: State University of New York Press, 1998.

———. "Nirodha, Yoga Praxis, and the Transformation of the Mind." *Journal of Indian Philosophy* 25, (1997): 1–67.

Wiener, Norbert. *Cybernetics: Or Control and Communication in the Animal and the Machine.* Cambridge: MIT Press, 1948.

Wilber, Ken, ed. *The Holographic Paradigm and Other Paradoxes.* Boulder: Shambhala, 1982.

Wiltschko, Wolfgang, and Roswitha Wiltschko. "Magnetic Orientation and Magnetoreception in Birds and Other Animals." *Journal of Comparative Physiology A* 191, no. 8 (2005): 675–93.

Wood, Ernest, and Paul Brunton. *Practical Yoga, Ancient and Modern: Being a New, Independent Translation of Patanjali's Yoga Aphorisms, Interpreted in the Light of Ancient and Modern Psychological Knowledge and Practical Experience.* Chatsworth, Calif.: Wilshire Book Co., 1976.

Woodroffe, Sir John. Foreword to *The Mysterious Kundalini: The Physical Basis of the 'Kundalini Yoga,'* by Vasant Rele, ix–xi. Bombay: D. B. Taraporevala Sons & Co., 1927.

———. *The Serpent Power: Being the Ṣaṭ-cakra-nirūpana and Pādukā-pañcaka.* Reprint ed. New York, Dover, 1974.

———. *The World As Power.* 3rd ed. Madras: Ganesh & Co., 1966.

Yirka, Bob. "New Study Strengthens Olfactory Vibration-Sensing Theory." *Phys.org,* January 29, 2013.

Zambito, Salvatore. *The Unadorned Thread of Yoga: The Yoga Sūtra of Patañjali in English—A Compilation of English Translations of the Yoga Sūtra of Patañjali.* Poulsbo, Wash.: The Yoga Sūtras Institute Press, 1992.

INDEX

Page numbers in *italics* refer to illustrations.